Moral CAPITALISM

Moral CAPITALISM

Reconciling
PRIVATE INTEREST
with the
PUBLIC GOOD

STEPHEN YOUNG

BK

Berrett–Koehler Publishers, Inc.
a BK Business book

Berrett-Koehler Publishers, Inc.
1333 Broadway, Suite 1000
Oakland, CA 94612-1921
Tel: (510) 817-2277   Fax: (510) 817-2278   www.bkconnection.com

ORDERING INFORMATION

Quantity sales. Special discounts are available on quantity purchases by corporations, associations, and others. For details, contact the "Special Sales Department" at the Berrett-Koehler address above.

Individual sales. Berrett-Koehler publications are available through most bookstores. They can also be ordered direct from Berrett-Koehler: Tel: (800) 929-2929; Fax: (802) 864-7626; www.bkconnection.com

Orders for college textbook/course adoption use. Please contact Berrett-Koehler: Tel: (800) 929-2929; Fax: (802) 864-7626.

Orders by U.S. trade bookstores and wholesalers. Please contact Ingram Publisher Services, Tel: (800) 509-4887; Fax (800) 838-1149; E-mail: customer.service@ingrampublisherservices.com; or visit www.ingrampublisherservices.com/Ordering for details about electronic ordering.

Production Management: Textbook Writers Associates

Berrett-Koehler and the BK logo are registered trademarks of Berrett-Koehler Publishers, Inc.

Printed in the United States of America

Berrett-Koehler books are printed on long-lasting acid-free paper. When it is available, we choose paper that has been manufactured by environmentally responsible processes. These may include using trees grown in sustainable forests, incorporating recycled paper, minimizing chlorine in bleaching, or recycling the energy produced at the paper mill.

Library of Congress Cataloging-in-Publication Data

Young, Stephen, 1945-
    Moral capitalism: reconciling private interest with the public good / by Stephen Young.
       p. cm.
    Includes bibliographical references and index.
    ISBN: 1-57675-257-7
    ISBN 13: 978-1-57675-257-9
1. Capitalism-Moral and ethical aspects. I. Title.
HB501.Y67 2003
174—dc 21   2003052077

First Edition
20   19   18   17   16   10 9 8 7 6 5 4 3 2

CONTENTS

GIVING PEOPLE MENTAL CONSTRUCTS like the Caux Round Table (CRT) Principles for Business to apply in their calculations of how best to gain business advantage will impact their behavior. Teaching of norms, while no guarantee that students will apply their lessons well, nonetheless is where we must start in building a moral community.

Great teachers like Jesus Christ, Confucius and the Gautama Buddha gave us stories and principles by which we could, in their minds, so order our daily lives that we would become more worthy and find greater happiness. The end of their teachings was that we would apply in our own lives—by means of our own mental and emotional abilities—ideas and understandings that we have learned from them.

Such idealists and teachers of morality, however, are often dismissed by self-proclaimed realists or "practical people" as being excessively naïve in that their aspirations for humanity go beyond the apparent scope of the possible. We may note that sin is still with us, even among his followers, though Jesus preached against it.

Nowhere is this skepticism more vibrant than in business. Ideals and morality are often spoken of as virtual antimatter to the behaviors allegedly needed to maximize profits. Allegedly, Brute Capitalism is the way to go, so that any admonitions contrary to its teachings are dismissed as drivel. So the CRT has a problem: publishing principles does little to get them implemented.

The CRT understands that morality works in the business corporation though hierarchy, moving from vague but lofty ideals down through principles and standards, to objectives and then to action. Consider the following chart illustrating the flow-throw of ideals into accomplishments:

This chart represents the value-action system of Moral Capitalism. It stands in contrast to the Enron Chart of Chapter 3, which illustrates the more brutish version of market capitalism.

At the highest level of the Moral Capitalism Chart directing our principles, our standards, our management benchmarks and our decisions, we find our best ideals, our highest aspirations, our vision of the common good. Setting these values and ideals in place for a corporation or a business is the responsibility of its owners, its board of directors and its top managers.

These governing ideals could be taken from religion, but they don't have to be found only there. People responsible for an enterprise could agree among themselves on a common goal, arriving at that end from different religious starting points. In just such a fashion did the CRT Principles for Business themselves arise from a blending of Roman Catholic teachings and American Protestant and secular traditions of stewardship with Japanese Buddhist and Shinto perspectives.

At the next level below our ideals, the socially responsible business should place a set of principles, like the CRT Principles for Business, or the nine principles of the United Nations' Global Compact.

Flowing down towards more objectivity and specificity, we next find standards and guidelines such as the self-assessment and implementation management process invented by the CRT and called "ARCTURUS".

At the level of stakeholder engagement, a company seeking to meet its proper responsibilities under a Moral Capitalism would apply to its decision making the considerations listed for each of the six stakeholder groups in Section 3 of the CRT Principles for Business. These specific stakeholder considerations are discussed in Chapters 7 through 12 following.

Then we come down to the most challenging level of all: the level of walking-the-talk—actual rubber-meets-the-road, shoulder-to-the-wheel, management performance. At this level, the devil is truly in the details. Judgment and intellectual effort are required to square-up the details with the company's standards, principles and ideals.

ACKNOWLEDGMENTS

A book such as this, which hopes to cover intellectual ground from ancient philosophers both Eastern and Western through theories of political jurisprudence and economics to practical business realities, has many authors. I especially want to acknowledge the following who contributed in specialways to my ability to write this book.

From my college years at Harvard, I am especially indebted to Professors David Riesman (a mentor until his death), Samuel Beer for his course Social Science II, and Samuel P. Huntington for advising my senior thesis. Also, Barrington Moore, who taught me Marxist analysis, and Evon Vogt, who accepted me for the Chiapas internship in social anthropology in 1965 and put me to the study of Tzotzil Maya.

At the Harvard Law School, Victor Brudney opened my eyes to the inner dynamic of capitalism—corporate finance—and Harold Berman showed me how law is given context by religion.

For learning to look at the First World from a Third World perspective, I am grateful to the late Chep Sanchez, Presidente of the Municipio, who brought me into the process of judicial decision making as a Mayol, or police deputy during my months in Zinancantan, Chiapas; to Nai Promee Srisanakrua and his family, who warmly introduced me to Ban Chiang, Thailand, in 1965; and to numerous village elders in Vinh Long, Vietnam.

For understanding how to rise above cultural relativity and to enter the cultural world of the Vietnamese, I am in special debt to my father-in-law, Mr. Pham Do Binh, and to Prof. Nguyen Ngoc Huy, whose wisdom and humanity were unsurpassed in his generation.

Lewis M. "Skipper" Purnell of the US Foreign Service and Dr. Walter Slote of New York City taught me how to see social psychology as the cauldron into which is poured politics, economics, culture, religion, life, and out of which come our destinies.

For an introduction to the Caux Round Table, I must thank Michael Olson, whose dedication to principled leadership is most worthy of rememberance. Winston R. Wallin and George J. Vojta have given me the opportunity to serve the vision of that organization under their guidance and instruction as successive Caux Round Table Chairmen. Jean-Loup Dherse of France, John Dalla Costa of Canada, and Prof. Kenneth Goodpaster of the University of St. Thomas gave shape to my thinking on business ethics.

And for the truth that service brings both honor and assurance of a life well-lived, I thank my great grandmother, Mina Lamb of Calais, Maine, my grandparents, George M. Morris and his wife Miriam Hubbard Morris, my grandmother Marion Hunt Young, my father, Kenneth Todd Young, Jr., and my mother, Patricia Morris Young.

For suggesting that this book be attempted all credit goes to Fred Senn of Minneapolis. My colleagues at the Caux Round Table—Maarten de Pous, Lorri Kopschike, Dean Maines, Ronald Lattin, Minoru Inaoka—and all those who read the manuscript to improve it—have my most grateful thanks for their support.

I offer this work to all these and more in partial payment of the debt of life.

Stephen Young
St. Paul, MN
October 2003

CHAPTER 1

IS MORAL CAPITALISM POSSIBLE?

The mind of the superior man is conversant with righteousness; the mind of the mean man is conversant with gain.

—Confucius, The Analects, Bk. IV, Chpt XVI

As there is a degree of depravity in mankind which requires a certain degree of circumspection and distrust, so there are other qualities in human nature which justify a certain portion of esteem and confidence.

—Federalist No. 55, Friday, February 15, 1788

THIS BOOK AFFIRMS that moral capitalism is possible. First, in Chapters 1 through 5, it justifies faith in moral capitalism; then, in chapters 6 through 12, it provides a practical guide for those who want to achieve moral capitalism in their business pursuits and professional undertakings. Finally, in a concluding chapter, it discusses how, in these times, we can cultivate leadership sufficient to build a moral capitalism.

Seeking market profit through business and the professions is honorable and worthy. Based on the ideas and principles set forth in these chapters, I believe that each of us can indeed go to work every day for any business, great or small, feeling genuinely happy and proud of our career commitment.

For those more removed from careers in business, this book affirms a vision of social justice: that moral capitalism is the most appropriate means by which our modern, global human civilization can empower people and enrich their lives materially and spiritually.

The understanding of human potential that I present in this chapter is not just mine. I have endeavored to link its main features to the thoughts and writings of great minds from different cultures throughout the centuries. In 1994, business leaders from Japan, Europe, and the United States met as a round table discussion group in the little Swiss mountain hamlet of Caux and proposed certain principles for moral capitalist decision making. These Principles are known as the Caux Round Table Principles for Business.

For several years now I have come to know these Principles well through my work as the global executive director of the Caux Round Table organization. I have seen them affirmed by experienced and successful business leaders in many cultures. The Caux Round Table Principles are a concentrate of moral, ethical, philosophical, and jurisprudential wisdom from many traditions. We have explored how they reflect teachings from Chinese moral philosophy, Islam, Hinduism, African Spirituality, Judaism, Roman Catholic social teachings, Protestant insights, Japanese Shinto, Mahayana and Theravada Buddhism, and the ethical traditions of native Meso-American peoples.

Importantly, however, the Caux Round Table Principles also draw wisdom from successful business accomplishment. Written by senior business leaders, these Principles combine social virtue and self-interest into one way of doing business. In this book, I present my view as to how the Caux Round Table Principles for Business justify and structure a moral capitalism for the world.

THE MOST PROFITABLE BUSINESS COMBINES VIRTUE AND INTEREST

A successful business maximizes the present value of future earnings. The first requirement, therefore, of business success is sustainable profits. One-time winnings, in business as in casinos, are disappointing. We expect more from our investments than that.

To sustain our profits over time, we need to replenish the capital we invest in the business. That capital comes in five different forms: social capital, reputational capital or "goodwill," finance capital, physical capital, and human capital. These forms of capital are the essential factors of production. We must pay for them out of the earnings of the business. A business that neglects to pay for its capital will soon lose access to capital. Then it will quickly lose its profitability. Failure results when capital flows are insufficiently nourished.

Social capital is provided by society; it is the quality of laws, the cultural and social institutions, the roads, ports, airports and telecommunications, the educational achievements, the health and value environments that encourage or discourage successful enterprise.

Reputational capital adds value to a business by attracting and keeping customers, employees, investors, and suppliers. Finance capital is the classic form of capital: access to money. Physical capital is land, plant, and equipment. And human capital embraces the quality, creativity, loyalty, and productivity of employees.

When a business contributes to social capital, it is acting responsibly and ethically. When a business invests in its reputation, it better serves the needs of consumers and meets the expectations of society. When a business invests in its human capital, it provides better lives and working conditions for its employees.

In preserving its access to these necessary forms of capital by paying a return on capital from earnings, a business acts from self-interest but promotes social well-being at the same time. The selfish pursuit of the "bottom line," therefore, leads a responsible business to satisfy the needs of others. The consequences arising from self-interest when a business seeks to maximize sustainable profits is selfish from one perspective but simultaneously moral from another.

Figure 1.1 illustrates the cycle of a successful, self-sustaining business. In one half of the cycle, five forms of capital inputs are converted by the business into a good or service for sale to a customer for a profit. Then, along the bottom, Figure 1.1 illustrates the other half of the business success cycle—the reverse flow of profits paid out as a return on all forms of business capital.

The successful business stays in business; it repeatedly cycles capital through the production of goods and services to please customers and make an attractive profit for itself. It maintains the adequacy of its capital inputs just as it continually attracts customers willing to buy its product or service. Michael Porter advises, "Gaining competitive advantage requires that a firm's value chain is managed as a system rather than a collection of separate parts."[1]

The wise steward of enterprise makes a profit in ways that preserve access to all forms of capital. The enterprise is not self-contained and self-sufficient but, rather, is importantly dependent on inputs controlled by others. It must please others in order to prosper. That service is a moral activity, subordinating self to what is beyond the self.

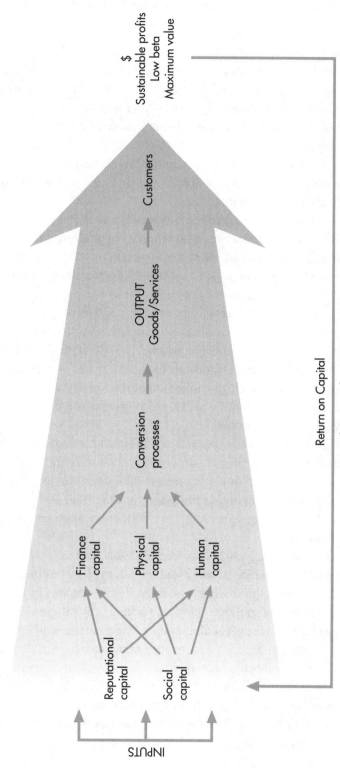

Corporate Stewardship (Value Governance)

Sustainable profits
Low beta
Maximum value
$

Customers

OUTPUT
Goods/Services

Conversion processes

Finance capital

Physical capital

Human capital

Reputational capital

Social capital

INPUTS

Return on Capital

(preserve adequacy of capital inputs)

4

In his books *Built to Last* and *Good to Great*, business researcher Jim Collins discovered in successful companies what he called the "genius of And."[2] This was an ability to embrace both extremes on a dimension, such as purpose *and* profit, continuity *and* change, freedom *and* responsibility. Suboptimal performance resulted when companies felt forced to choose one goal over the other. These companies fell victim to the "tyranny of the Or." Collins' findings support the insight that capitalism can indeed avoid choosing self-interest over virtue.

One dollar invested in Collins' good to great companies in 1965 had compounded stock returns of $471 by 2000. On the other hand, that same dollar invested in his group of direct comparison companies earned a cumulated return of only $93 during those thirty-five years.

Professors John P. Kotter and James L. Heskett of Harvard Business School found that companies with embedded cultures of respect for customers and employees as well as for stockholders outperformed companies without such a culture by a huge margin during an eleven-year period. The more successful companies grew their stock prices by 901 percent versus 74 percent for the less successful companies. Net incomes grew by 756 percent in the successful companies but only 1 percent in the others.[3]

In April 2003, London's Institute for Business Ethics published a study of United Kingdom companies showing that those companies with corporate codes of ethical conduct achieved profit-turnover ratios 18 percent higher than comparable companies without a similar explicit commitment to conduct business ethically. Companies with ethical codes also generated significantly more economic value added (EVA) and market value added (MVA) and exhibited less volatile price-earnings ratios for their shares.[4]

BUSINESS MORALITY: "SELF-INTEREST CONSIDERED UPON THE WHOLE"

Distinct from academia, politics, and bureaucracy, business enterprise calls for constant action and decision making. Every decision, every action, comes with risk of loss or even failure. Judgment must be applied in each instance to consider alternatives in order to, hopefully, minimize risk.

In Figure 1.1, each component function of a sustainable business—the capital employed, the conversion of capital into a product, the product, and the sale to customers—requires decision making. Just consider what must be attended to in a successful business: how to acquire cash, where to have a factory or office, who to employ, what to produce, how to produce it, how to market and advertise, what price to place on the product or service, how to deal with customer needs and concerns, etc. Every course in an MBA program and every business book offered for sale address these and similar decisions that have to be made in business.

By what criteria can we say that these business decisions are moral?

I answer: "By the extent to which business decisions take into account the needs and concerns of others."[5]

We are in business to serve ourselves and our needs, yes, to be sure. But reflection on our circumstances brings wisdom that we are not self-sufficient. We prosper through our interaction with others. One would easily conclude that, therefore, our prosperity is most secure where others wish and seek to help us be prosperous.

Our needs and preferences intersect from time to time with the needs and preferences of others. The more we take into account the needs of others when seeking to meet our own needs, the larger the overlap between our self-interest and our virtue. By taking into account only our own needs, we shrink the zone of overlap until we make ourselves morally irrelevant to others. When the zone is very small, we most often turn to means of manipulation, fraud, and coercion to impose our needs on others. We then act immorally and unethically.

That frame of mind which makes for a larger zone of overlap between our needs and the needs of others has often been called "enlightened self-interest." I prefer to use the term suggested by the philosopher Thomas Reid, the Scotsman who succeeded Adam Smith in holding the chair of moral philosophy at the University of Glascow in 1766. Reid referred to the zone of overlap as our "self-interest considered upon the whole."[6]

When virtue speaks to us, its voice may be too soft for us to hear. But where virtue is supported by the claims of interest, our resolve grows stronger to achieve what both virtue and interest jointly propose. The juncture of both motivations is crucial for virtuous conduct to prevail for most of us.

When we find a vocation, we fall on such a happy coincidence of virtue and interest. We benefit materially from our work, finding satisfaction in those self-interested accomplishments. And, simultaneously, we perceive our efforts to be in support of higher purposes as well, giving us rare and valuable levels of satisfaction and self-appreciation. We have found a becoming "fit" between ourselves and moral meaning.

When one is called to a task, work is transformed from something mean that we begrudge into that which nourishes us with life-giving energy and even delight. We are better to ourselves and to others when we fall into a vocation. Then, we prosper fully; everything is more real and more sustaining. We are happy; we have found our right way.

The possibility is reflected in the now trite comparison of three artisans. When asked what they are doing, one mason replies, "I am cutting stone." The second says, "I am building a wall." But the third says, "I am building a cathedral for the glory of God." The first two men have jobs; the third has found a vocation. For him, virtue and interest have fused into one calling.[7]

We have learned under principles of quantum physics not to see reality as separated "things" walled off from one another by boundaries. Subatomic activity arises from the interaction of fluid potentials, not from hard particles bouncing into each other. Whatever there is is both matter and energy. Whether it is one or the other depends on how we humans conceptualize it. Reality can look like matter and yet act like energy. As these subatomic chameleons interact with one another in our bubble chambers, they appear temporarily in our scientific instruments as up to 12 different particles.[8] But are they really 12 different Newtonian and Cartesian "things"?

As Margaret J. Wheatley writes: "There is no need to decide between two things, pretending they are separate. What is critical is the relationship created between two or more elements."[9] Similarly, at the level of the human, both virtue and self-interest can inhere in the same action. Which human potential prevails—either virtue as a check on self-interest or self-interest as a deviation from virtue—depends on the actors, the energy fields surrounding them, and the issues of the moment. To say that an action is either pure virtue or crass self-interest reflects intellectual poverty, conceptualizing only the two polar extremes, while ignoring the zone of overlap where self-interest is "considered upon the whole."

Looking at the effects of time gives another perspective on the overlap of self-interest and virtue. Decisions made for our short-term advantage often bring negative long-term consequences that can far outweigh in their effects any advantages we have initially gained. Thus, in business, the results of fraud are short-term profit but, once discovery of our deceit occurs, our fraud brings about long-term and possibly permanent corruption of our ability to get what we want from others. Whenever we focus on the short term, we tend to minimize our goals, falling victim to the tyranny of the "Or" and forgetting the genius of the "And."

CAN WE OVERLOOK BIBLICAL TEACHINGS AND SERVE BOTH GOD AND MAMMON?

The Christian tradition teaches us to choose between God and Mammon and to lay up our treasures in Heaven and not to seek them among earthly things. The Christian Gospel of Matthew explicitly assigns all earthly powers and attractions to the dominion of Satan, a dominion rejected by Jesus on the grounds that "Man does not live by bread alone."[10]

Wise prophets over the ages in many cultures have urged people to turn away from the things of this world. To become divine, the flesh must be mortified. Must we, however, choose only between God and Mammon? Can we not live with the pressures of markets and under the influence of money and still set before ourselves every day certain reasonable expectations of behaving justly in the eyes of the best angels of our nature?

The Caux Round Table Principles for Business call on a tradition of moral character in seeking to live by a third way—one in this world but guided by higher aspirations. I have learned from reading philosophers such as Hegel that moral visions arise from the human mind. They are not natural in the sense that rain and snow and gravity are natural. They find their role in life though the application of human will and in human actions. Without human action, there's no morality that we can see, touch, or feel. A moral capitalism, therefore, asks that, in their business affairs, people use willpower to check and balance abusive internal forces such as greed and temptation; that they strive to expand the zone of overlap between virtue and self-interest.

Indeed, we can seek profits for ourselves in the markets of capitalism without becoming mean or avaricious. Leaders of the Caux Round Table such as Frederik Philips of the Philips Company in The Netherlands; Ryuzaburo Kaku, CEO of Canon; and Winston Wallin, CEO of Medtronic, have done so. Both Mencius in ancient China and Adam Smith in eighteenth-century Scotland argued that we have within us a powerful moral sense, which, if attended to, can lift us above our potential for being only base and mean.

The prominent contemporary German philosopher and sociologist Jurgen Habermas has noted that we live aware of a realm of "normativity," which is conceptual and linguistic, but in a realm of "facticity," which is more tangible, objective, specific, and determinative of our physical conditions. Through the medium of action, however, we can impose normativity on the facticity around us.[11] A moral capitalism, therefore, would have us do as Habermas suggests: impose norms on our behaviors in seeking profits.

Capitalism is of this material world; it provides us with the means to live; it empowers us within the known world of sense and human reason. If it is to be measured by a strict standard of holiness, by religious normativity alone, then there can never be a moral capitalism.

Since it belongs exclusively to this world of sorrow and sin, this existential realm of facticity, moral capitalism cannot require our spiritual perfection, only that we seek always to do better than heed our base inclinations. Moral capitalism, nevertheless, asks much of our potential for humanity. It asks that we activate something of the divine within our world of facts and death, that we guide our passions by our chosen virtues. Moral capitalism seeks to infuse the teachings of philosophy and the wisdom of religion into the search for profit.

Can we do this? Can you do this?

If so, moral capitalism is possible; if not, its strictures are only a kind of misleading vanity, the rhetoric of a secular piety.

Plato and Aristotle were in agreement that the life of aspiration was one where some personal capacity of willpower governed the passions. People, Aristotle thought, could work their way to happiness through the forming of ethical habits. Jesus Christ preached parables to encourage his audiences to put aside selfish pursuits, the better to enter the Kingdom of Heaven. In India, the Gautama Buddha provided a complex theology of seeking escape from desire, sensation, and striving. The Koran revealed to Mohammad instructs many times that people will enter Heaven only if they have faith and do good works of benefit to others. The goals set by Allah, therefore, are not those of selfish cravings or the abusive prerogatives that come with possession of earthly power.

Confucius drew a dichotomy between those who had mastered their base instincts and those who had not. Those possessing mastery, he called "lordly" or "superior" persons. Those still in thrall to their selves he called "small" or "mean" persons. He made the following distinctions between these two categories of people:

"The superior man does not even for the space of a single meal, act contrary to virtue."[12]

"The master said is virtue a thing remote? I wish to be virtuous and lo! virtue is at hand."[13]

Today, we need not be as restrictive in our categories as Confucius was. There are doubtless intermediate steps between the conflicting extremes. The propensities for both good and evil are truly mixed within most of us.

In China, not long after Confucius drew attention to his faith in the constructive impact of moral capacity, another Chinese, Fan Li, assembled twelve axioms for success in business. Fan Li was also known as Tao Zhu Gong, so his axioms have come down to us as the "Business Principles of Mr. Tao."[14] Tao Zhu Gong evidently believed that living by principles can make a difference in your life. His principles have been followed by Chinese business families for centuries.

Under the new science of quantum physics and chaos theory, order and form in the universe are not created by complex controls and commands. Our reality, rather, results from the active presence of a few guiding principles or formulas repeating back on themselves through the operation of individual freedom for highly autonomous decision makers within the overall system.[15]

Every person has some capacity for acting ethically. Both Mencius and Adam Smith vividly argued that humans are a distinct species due to a capacity for moral awareness.

All of us possess the capacity—weak or strong, proven or untested—to align our behaviors with our will and our better understanding. We act not always from raw instinct, unguided and unpredictable. We have interests we seek to further, ideals we value, emotions that move us, and self-concepts and personalities that govern our interactions with others. We also have what the ancient Chinese called a "calculating mind." We look into the future as best we can and take action today to achieve specific results later. Our minds may be clouded by emotions or poor judgment, but the psychological and moral machinery of following some specially chosen course always remains in place within us.

Starting the engine of morality and bringing it to full throttle are the tasks of parenthood and socialization. People must learn to be good; they are not born good, only with the seeds of goodness in them. Buddhists refer to that capacity as the Buddha mind within us, resting until awakened. Taoists claim that washing the mind free of thoughts brings us to the point of appreciation of truth, the Tao, and suddenly therefore to an ability to act correctly. Jesus said, "The Kingdom of Heaven is all around you, yet you see it not."[16]

Contrary to advice to conform to moral principle is the reasoning of Sigmund Freud. In his little tract *Civilization and Its Discontents*, Freud argued that building moral society, or "civilization" in his terms, required repression of instincts and passions.[17] In his mind, this systematic repression led to neurosis in the individual, which as a result turned Freud away from efforts to instill rigorous moral faculties in the young.

Yet people can't live without the moral dimension. First, we are not emotionally self-sufficient, but are social, born both into society and for it. We have needs for love, esteem, and consideration, which only others of our species can supply.[18] Morality reflects the regard for others that arises in a social setting. Ethics is the course of conduct that makes room for others in our decision making.

Second, we have an unquiet consciousness of reality. We feel fear looking out on an often unforgiving cosmos that gives us little evidence of our importance to it. Where we find genuine and lasting psychological rest and inner comfort is not in material things.

FINDING THE PERSONS WHO WILL BUILD MORAL CAPITALISM

Others have noted the proclivity of people to act from a range of morally worthy motivations. For example, the Harvard psychologist Lawrence Kohlberg provided a well-known set of stages of moral development.[19] Individuals in stage 1 sought avoidance of punishment and deference to power. Stage 2, higher in moral capacity, was action calculated to satisfy one's own needs and occasionally the needs of others. In stage 3, good behavior is that which pleases or helps others and conforms to social stereotypes. In stage 4 we seek to do our duty and obey legal norms, maintaining the social order for its own sake. In stage 5 we assert our rights as society gives them to us, using contract to obtain binding obligations. Then, finally, in stage 6, right is defined by the decision of conscience in accord with self-chosen ethical principles appealing to logical comprehensiveness, universality, and consistency.

In Kohlberg's typology, stage 6 would have our self-interest consider a vast range of needs and concerns embracing a very large number of other people. Perfectly moral capitalism would require us to use only Kohlberg's stage 6 reasoning in business decision making.

Robert J. Spitzer, Jesuit and Doctor of Philosophy, now president of Gonzaga University, gives us a similar hierarchy of starting points for moral undertakings. He believes that there are four main desires or drivers in the human personality. At the lowest moral level is immediate gratification, that is, actions taken to maximize our pleasure and minimize our pain. Second is ego achievement, that is, promotion of self and gaining advantage over others. Third is to do good beyond the self, invoking principles such as justice, love, and community. Here, intrinsic goodness is an end in itself, and leadership of others becomes possible. Fourth, and highest, is participating in giving and receiving ultimate meaning, goodness itself, and living with ideals and love.[20]

If moral capitalism will need people willing and able to seek out moral considerations—the higher levels of consideration noted by Kohlberg and Spitzer—and apply them in their lives, where will such people be found?

Figure 1.2 roughly illustrates how ethics work in individual lives. It needs to be understood before we can invoke moral power to drive the dynamics of capitalism.

Figure 1.2 represents the dynamics of human action as seen by moral philosophers. At the top of the pyramid is a realm of abstract thought and understanding, what Habermas called the realm of normativity. This realm is beyond nature and exists only in human consciousness.

At the bottom of the pyramid is the realm of action, what Habermas called the realm of facticity. The objective of morality is to impose on the level of action goals and ideals drawn down from the realm of abstract normativity. The force that draws goals and ideals out of inner awareness and imposes them on the life world is human willpower and decision making.

At the highest level of abstraction, which I believe is consistent with the teachings of Buddhism, Taoism, Adam Smith, and Mencius and with Jesus Christ's references to an invisible Kingdom of Heaven that is all around us, lies an awareness of life and existence that we find very hard to put into words. It is what Smith and Mencius called the "moral sense"; it is most easily approached through prayer and meditation; we have possession of it when we find a "Zen mind."

At a lesser level of abstraction, at a level of spoken thoughts and written conceptions, we find religious understandings. These are guiding visions

The Moral Individual

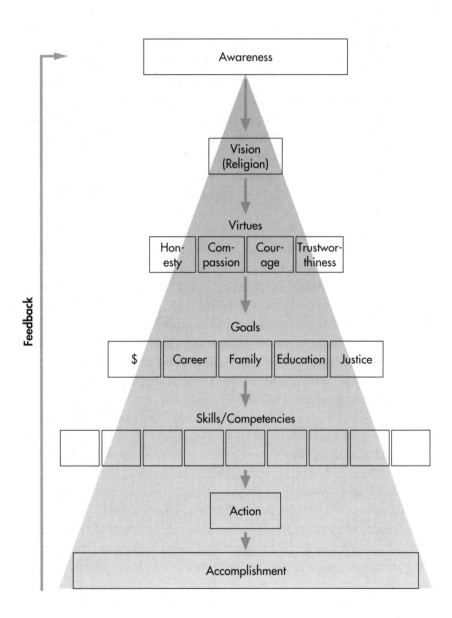

to us of how the world works and what our purpose in life is to be. We come to these beliefs through reflection, education, reading, discourse, and listening to the insights of others.

Dropping down to the next level, we begin to engage the world. We define our identity by bringing certain virtues into our behavior. Practice and the formation of habits inculcates virtues into our lives so that we live them out spontaneously, without questioning our actions or our motivations. At this level we find Spitzer's fourth and most admirable set of good motivations. In the Confucian paradigm, here is where a person would be either "masterful" or "mean."

At this level we are often conflicted in our decision making. Pressures from others to conform to their values and desires, the psychic weight of a superego or a moral code implanted by parents or social tradition, and the conflict between virtues and immediate advantage strain the alignment of our character with our religious insights and beliefs. Developing powers of reflective self-control, finding mentors, and building good habits are tools to help us manage these conflicting pressures.

Next, dropping down to the level of setting goals and of calculating what is in our best interest, the possession of courage and practical wisdom and the finding of mentors and coaches are very helpful. Finding that equilibrium between the extremes of pure virtue and raw self-interest that is called "self-interest considered upon the whole" is relevant here.

Kohlberg's stages of reasoning have their application at this level of response to life's opportunities. Do we set as goals narrow and self-serving concerns described in his stage 1? Or, do we set our course to implement higher notions of universal justice and good?

The American psychologist Abraham Maslow offered a now widely accepted way of thinking about our personal goals. He made a distinction between the value set of individuals focused on meeting their basic needs and the value set of more secure and high-minded persons.[21]

Persons who, in Maslow's framework, act from the more basic set of needs accentuate "D" or "deficiency" values. Their goal is to make up for felt or perceived deficiencies. Their value set subjects them to fears of self-betrayal, to living by fear, and to anxiety, despair, boredom, inability to enjoy, intrinsic guilt and shame, emptiness, and lack of identity.[22] These people are always grasping for power with which to reassure themselves that they are "somebody." The person whose goals seek to remedy deficiencies is likely to look on others as a means-object, a source of money, food, security, or such. Seeking only to overcome deficiencies inhibits full awareness of mutuality and of reciprocity in social settings.

A capitalism dominated by people seeking to overcome deficiencies would be most unpleasant. It would likely fit Thomas Hobbes' famous definition of humanity living outside of conventional social norms, where life would be "solitary, poor, nasty, brutish and short."[23]

The goals of high-minded persons (who possess what Maslow calls "B" or "being" values) include "justice, completeness, oughtness, fulfillment—telos and finis, fairness, structure, order, honesty, essentiality, beauty (perfection, rightness, completeness), goodness, effortlessness, truth, honesty, self-sufficiency (not-needing-other-than-itself-in-order-to-be itself)."[24]

Maslow asserted that persons seeking these "B" goals tend toward serenity, joy in living, calmness, acting with responsibility, and having confidence in their ability to handle stresses, anxieties, and problems.[25] Presumably, people influenced by Maslow's "B" values when making decisions in the midst of market pressures would be more likely than not to leave room in their calculations for long-term consequences, for win-win relationships, and for acting with honor and integrity. Their word would be their bond. They would refrain from brutish actions.

Once we have settled on appropriate goals, to achieve them we pull together related skills and develop the personal competencies that others require from us. Education, training, and gaining experience are the means we all have to accomplish this task. But, here we need to be aware of our distinctive talents and abilities and not force ourselves to acquire competencies too much at variance with our natural genius. Assessments such as the Myers-Briggs inventory of personality styles are very revealing and helpful in guiding us towards work in which we can succeed and better align ourselves with our highest aspirations.

Once we have set goals and have put ourselves in a position to reach them, we take action and build a record of accomplishment. When our accomplishments conform to our highest aspirations, we have found our vocation.

Since it is not impossible for people to act from "self-interest considered upon the whole," we should demand such conduct from more and more people in business. The quality of ideals that a person, or a society, or a corporate culture, places at the apex of a value hierarchy, then, has not-to-be-overlooked implications for the quality of life to be lived by that person, society, or corporation.

Understanding how people can and do bring morality into their decision making illuminates an answer to the question of whether moral capitalism is a realistic possibility. The short, affirmative answer lies in training
and developing people with the capacity for moral decision making. The
more such people set the rules for capitalism, the more capitalism will
become.

CHOOSING THE MORAL WAY

Morality is a very personal decision to will what is right. Acting ethically
is a test of leadership and is an act of culture. Moral capitalism is nothing
other than a decision-making culture created and sustained by individuals acting from principle, regardless of their position in a formal bureaucratic hierarchy.

With reflection, prayer, meditation, and conversation, and by using our
intuition to obtain inspiration and wisdom, each of us can deepen our
awareness of what life is and can more and more clearly formulate our vision
of who we are, of where we are, and of where we need to go. The capacity
for cultural leadership, our moral sense, is right at hand, just as Confucius
advised and Adam Smith took for granted. Each of us can be a leader for
moral capitalism.

But it is wrong, in my mind, to require of any person that he or she
live a life of saintly perfection. We are, after all, only human. Adam and Eve,
relates the biblical story of Genesis, were banished from the Garden of
Eden not only because they ate the fruit of the tree of knowledge forbid-
den them but also because they might also eat of the tree of life and become
like the divine immortals. Icarus flew too close to the sun, melting the wax
of his man-made wings and falling to his death. Christian story and Greek
myth both point to a single truth: the proper scope of human ambition is
this-worldly. To do more is to risk idolatry, where we humans replace God
with an illusion of human perfection.

To demand that we live in the world according to the strict commands
of virtue alone points us awry. That way a certain form of madness lies.
The experience of earthly theocracies has not been encouraging: consider
the realities of Savanarola in Florence, Calvin in Geneva, Robespierre in
France, Lenin in Russia, the Ayatollahs in Iran, and Pol Pot in Cambodia.

Attempts to govern through pure virtue have lead to many deaths and much suffering.

We need only ask for the presence of mind—and the underlying character sustaining such a mind—to manage the tension implicit in the overlap of virtue and self-interest, the zone of "self-interest considered upon the whole."

GLOBALIZATION: INTENSIFYING THE CULTURE OF SELFISHNESS AND GREED

Yet, for many of us, the especially seductive Siren call of our passions and desires drowns out the appeal of other-regarding values.[26] Not everyone who hears the Sunday sermons will be saved on Judgment Day. Modern capitalism, by accelerating wealth creation and the provision of middle-class consumer comforts, poses a special challenge to moral leadership. The culture fostered by globalization undermines our individual and our collective capacity to choose "self-interest considered upon the whole."

The creation of a global culture of "teenagerism," propelled by consumer wealth, has commodified greed.[27] Thanks to the vast increases in productive forces, human identity now very easily, and more than ever before, grounds itself in possessions, not in ideals.

The "teenager" is a modern phenomenon following the emergence of a special kind of middle-class family. Before the 1950's, humanity never knew true "teenagers" in the sense of James "Rebel Without a Cause" Dean, Elvis Presley, The Beatles, and, now, Britney Spears.

Most sadly, through the enticements of globalization, the American culture of the free-spirited, free-spending, free-of-responsibility teenager is taking over the world, one youth at a time. The cult is now worldwide, with MTV promoting rap culture in South Korea and young Thai girls dressed as Britney, exposing to the public dainty and well-formed belly buttons just as she does.

In another spreading form of juvenile cheekiness, European roadways and fences are often decorated with graffiti inspired first by angry young African American men down and out in New York City putting their rather elegant "tags" on subway cars.

Everywhere, parental authority is on the defensive. The holdouts are tightly knit religious communities like the Mormons and fundamentalist circles in Islam, Protestant Christianity, and Judaism, which isolate themselves from the trends of modern times.

The teenager is more than a child but less than an adult, spending money on tentative self-definition through clothes, shoes, music, and other accoutrements. Teenagers are in escape from responsibility, seeking to postpone adulthood as long as possible. They build for themselves a culture of followership, where the restraints of moral leadership trigger fear and loathing.

And, since its birth in the 1950s, "teenagerism" is drawing to its ranks older and older Americans. As the baby boomers age into their fifties, their earlier cultural proclivities as teenagers remain active, seeking cultural space and economic resources with which to subdue opposition from adult responsibilities. They use their careers, in business or elsewhere, not to help others but to serve their identity deficiencies.

Although greed has been responsible for abuse of economic power over the centuries, the moral failures of Enron and WorldCom and the other recent abuses of capitalism in the dot.com and telecommunications investment bubbles grew apace in the post-1950s American culture of decadence and self-absorption, the culture that incubated Ken Lay, Jeffrey Skilling, Andy Fastow, and Bernie Ebbers, as well as the investors they charmed with visions of never-ending profits.

If possessions largely define the personal self for our times, then there can never be too much money in our wallets or too many lines of credit at our immediate disposal. Our individual value pyramids are then easily subordinated to the Golden Calf of conspicuous consumption. By prosperity are we firmly pulled away from God toward Mammon. This cultural trend may make it harder for people in business to choose higher values and enlightened self-interest over immediate gratification of sensual desires.

CONCLUSION

The challenge of a moral capitalism, then, is to tip the balance of wealth creation toward humanity's more noble possibilities and away from the dynamics of more brutish behavior. Chapter 2 begins a discussion of how values set in motion different kinds of capitalism.

CHAPTER 2

THE MANY VARIETIES OF CAPITALISM

It was God who created the heavens and the earth. He has sent down water from the sky with which He brings forth fruits for your sustenance. He has subdued the ships which by His leave sail the ocean in your service. He has subdued the rivers for your benefit, and subdued for you the sun and the moon, which steadfastly pursue their courses. And he has subdued for you the night and the day. Of everything you have asked for he has given you some. If you reckon up God's favors, you could not count them.

—The Holy Koran, Surah Abraham, 14:30

The Great Tao is universal like a flood.
How can it be turned to the right or to the left?
All creatures depend on it,
And it denies nothing to anyone.
It does its work,
But it makes no claims for itself.

—Tao Te Ching, No. 34

NATIONAL ECONOMIES MARCH to the beats of different drummers. Doing business in Japan differs from doing business in China. Corporate laws and forms of corporate finance are different in the United States than in Germany, France, and most of the European Union nations. Values, therefore, do make a difference to business. National economies like those of the Chinese and the Japanese, with deep and intense cultural foundations, construct patterns of business practice and legal regulation consistent with core principles of their national cultures.

Michael Porter, after close examination of reasons for different degrees of national success in global competition, pointed to the impact of each nation's differing ability to mobilize various capital inputs in support of business achievement.[1] Porter emphasizes that "some of the most important aspects" of national competitive advantage are "attitudes towards authority," "norms of interpersonal interaction," "attitudes of workers towards management and vice-versa," "social norms of individualistic or group behavior," and "professional standards."[2]

CHINESE BUSINESS VALUES

For example, the core principle of great importance to many Chinese is the preservation of order and harmony. This value is called *tai he*. It reflects a fear of uncontrolled individualism out of a belief that individuals, if left to pursue their self-interest, would promptly subvert social order in favor of a raucous anarchy.

We can read of this fear in the writings of Mo Di, who lived right after Confucius, and in many other Chinese moral philosophers, such as Xun Zi. The ancient Chinese believed that the cosmic forces of yin and yang can be balanced and manipulated by the state to produce order and harmony in society. From this perspective, Confucian propriety and filial piety are expressions of yang forces of discipline. Law, a yin force, is also needed from time to time to keep people in their place when yang forces are insufficiently powerful.

Figure 2.1 presents the traditional Chinese approach to business enterprise.

Figure 2.1 displays how the value of order and harmony works itself down into actual business outcomes through a level of principles, then through the application of standards to implement the principles vis-à-vis six groups of stakeholders in the business. At the level of business decision making, stakeholders are treated in culturally specific ways.

Doing business in China or Taiwan has its own rules and expectations, as set forth in Figure 2.1. Thus, for generations the Chinese have fashioned systems of market production within a framework of regulated competition. The successful economic development of Singapore has followed a variant of this value flowchart where intolerance of corruption is

Traditional Chinese Business Value

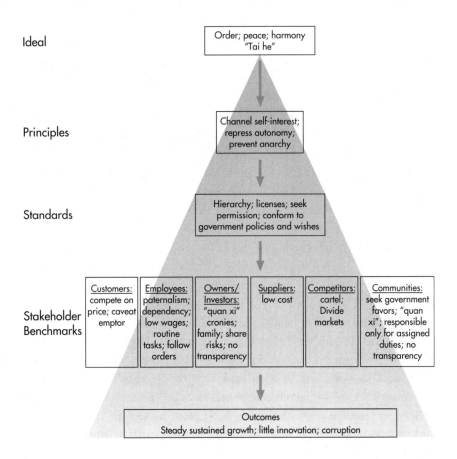

	Ideal	Order; peace; harmony "Tai he"

Ideal

Principles

Standards

Stakeholder Benchmarks

Order; peace; harmony
"Tai he"

Channel self-interest;
repress autonomy;
prevent anarchy

Hierarchy; licenses; seek
permission; conform to
government policies and wishes

| Customers: compete on price; caveat emptor | Employees: paternalism; dependency; low wages; routine tasks; follow orders | Owners/ Investors: "quan xi" cronies; family; share risks; no transparency | Suppliers: low cost | Competitors: cartel; Divide markets | Communities: seek government favors; "quan xi"; responsible only for assigned duties; no transparency |

Outcomes
Steady sustained growth; little innovation; corruption

built into the definition of order and harmony at the highest level of value choice.

To speak at a highly conceptual level of cultural preference, the Chinese traditionally value order and harmony, what they call the state of *tai he*. Under the cosmology legitimating the Chinese Imperial order, the duty of the emperor was to be the font of *tai he* and to share it with all under his suzerainty.

Confucius, who died in 479 B.C., offered a way to find *tai he*; if everyone followed the duties of their station, there would be order in the land.

A famous text in the Confucian tradition, *The Doctrine of the Mean,* advises, "Let the states of equilibrium and harmony exist in perfection, and a happy order will prevail throughout heaven and earth, and all things will be nourished and flourish."[3]

Mo Di, born in 372 B.C., followed Confucius with a different and far more draconian recommendation. He observed that the overwhelming majority of people fall short of possessing Confucian virtue, and therefore needed to be kept in place by rewards and punishments. Mo Di warned, "In the beginning of human life, when there was yet no law and government, the custom was 'everybody according to his own sense of righteousness.' Accordingly, each man had his own idea, two men had two ideas, and ten men had ten different ideas of righteousness—the more people the more different notions. And everybody approved of his own view and disapproved the views of others, and so arose mutual disapproval among men. As a result, father and son and elder and younger brothers became enemies and were estranged from each other, since they were unable to reach any agreement. Everybody worked for the disadvantage of the others with water, fire and poison. Surplus energy was not spent for mutual aid; surplus goods were allowed to rot without sharing. ... The disorder in the world could be compared to that among birds and beasts. Yet all this disorder was due to the want of a ruler."[4]

Mo Di's thinking was far more recently reiterated by Deng Hsiao Ping in 1989 when he ordered military repression of the demonstrations for democracy and liberty in Tien An Men Square, ironically named for the Gate of Heavenly Peace leading into the Imperial Palace compound. Deng warned his colleagues over the implications of the student protestors: "Imagine for a moment what could happen if China falls into turmoil. If it happens now, it'd be far worse than the Cultural Revolution. ... Once civil war got started, blood would flow like a river, and where would human rights be? In a civil war, each power would dominate a locality, production would fall, communications would be cut off, and refugees would flow out of China not in millions, but in hundreds of millions. ... So China mustn't make a mess of itself."[5]

To remedy what he saw as a deficiency in human nature, Mo Di recommended that everyone have a superior. The individual would take orders from his or her father, the father from the village chief, the village chief from the district chief, the district chief from the provincial governor, the provincial governor from the prime minister, the prime minister from the emperor, and the emperor from Heaven. There would be peace among humankind, but no autonomy for individualism. China's current leaders still prefer that everyone should have a superior, with the politburo of the Communist party as the superior of all superiors.

Other Chinese thinkers from other influential schools such as the Legalists, and the Yin/Yang school of policy advisors followed Mo Di's lead. These thinkers, too, called for intervention by government to manipulate the interests, fears, and desires of people to make them behave. If rewards would produce the right conduct, offer rewards; if fear of punishment would be more reliable, then government should use harsh punishments.[6]

Circumstances were named *shih*. The objective of government was to so arrange the *shih* that people had no choice but to be orderly. Even market forces were put to public use, as the following story relates:

Once, the Duke of Qi complained to his minister Guan Zhong that he loved to wear purple clothes but the cost of purple cloth was prohibitive. Guan Zhong replied, "Leave it to me. The next time someone wearing purple clothes comes near Your Highness, hold your nose." Apparently, the source of the purple dye left an odor in the cloth. The Duke did as instructed and soon no one wore purple garments. Purple cloth was dumped in the markets and its price plummeted. Guan Zhong bought it all for a song and presented the cloth to his delighted lord.

So for the Chinese to manage a market economy with a view toward achieving a state of *tai he*, they need to manage the *shih* of market forces and prevent selfishness from breaking down the hierarchy of power. This need for management becomes their principle for economic management.

To implement the principle, they set for their standards a hierarchy of decision making; the need to obtain licenses, from government or from trade associations; and conformity to government policies and wishes. Businesses that do not go along with these standards of practice are closed down or crippled one way or another. Businesses that accept these conditions are rewarded with secure markets and access to capital.

Within their market sphere, Chinese companies compete on price rather than quality, with the buyer accepting the risk of poor quality and shoddy performance. Employees are treated paternalistically as indentured servants bound to a communal endeavor. Owners and investors must be known and trusted; usually they are introduced by intermediaries within a patronage network; who you know is more important than what you bring to the table; there is no transparency of information to share, and different sets of accounts may be kept to be shown to different constituencies; supplies are bought at lowest cost; where possible, customers are divided up among competitors to establish cartel market control and permit some degree of monopoly pricing; government regulation is purchased through crony relationships and favoritism to maintain stable market shares. Companies assume responsibility only for what they are instructed to do; they have little concern for community needs.

JAPANESE BUSINESS VALUES

Since the industrialization of Japan in the second half of the nineteenth century, the Japanese economy has organized itself to use markets and private property for national development, but through a business dynamic that is different from China's and that has often befuddled and frustrated Americans trying to make a profit in Japan. Watching with envy Japanese success in the 1970s and early 1980s, Americans called the Japanese economic system "Japan Inc."

At the center of the Japanese cultural experience is a quality of life called *ninjo*.[7] Experiencing *ninjo* is to experience complete and unquestioned acceptance, as a mother emotionally supports a newly born child. *Ninjo* experiences occur in tight reciprocal relationships marked by *giri-on* mutual dependencies and symbiotic responsibilities for one another. *Giri-on* relationships link individuals closely through reciprocal favors and repayments of kindness.[8]

Companies built to sustain *giri-on* relationships form the distinctive Japanese Keiretsu groups of related companies—the Sumitomo group, the Mitsui group, the Mitsubishi group, etc.—each with their own banks and supplier networks. *Giri-on* relationships within Keiretsu groups require no more than limited amounts of equity capital and that from sister companies within the group. In the alternative, significant debt financing is provided by the group's bank. Insider boards are composed of executives from sister companies within the group. Keiretsu companies live by group decision-making processes. Strategy becomes inflexible once group consensus has been reached, but great opportunistic flexibility in tactics are used to secure group advantage.

When these standards of business practice are applied to interactions with stakeholders, a unique pattern of corporate behavior results. Foreigners have long been frustrated by their inability to establish significant business relations within the world of *giri-on* relationships. No wonder the Japanese economic system is culturally designed to exclude them.

The dynamic of the Keiretsu (before World War II they were called "Zaibatsu") is a capital structure light on equity and heavy on debt and without the possibility of bankruptcy, combined with a commitment of workers to the company in return for lifetime employment. This business structure brought splendid results for the Japanese until too much debt was accumulated thanks to the boom in property prices in the mid to late 1980s. Since that credit bubble burst in 1989, the Japanese economy has been in the doldrums, kept afloat by taxation and massive government spending. Seeking to protect the important value of *ninjo*, Japan's business and political leadership has been very hesitant to seriously tamper with Keiretsu structure and practices.

Figure 2.2 illustrates the cascade of the *ninjo* ideal down into benchmarks for processing the relationship of a typical Japanese company with its different stakeholders:

Japanese Corporate Value Pyramid

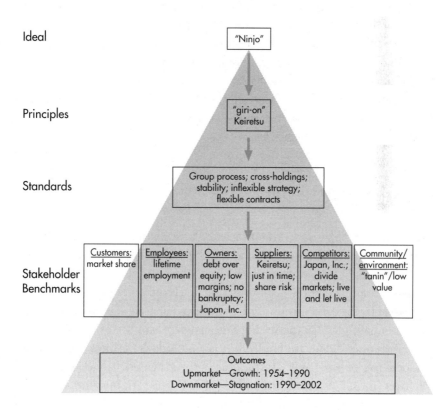

In the Keiretsu structure of Japanese capitalism, companies push for market share rather than higher profit margins per sale. Since their cost of capital—mostly interest on debt—is lower and fixed, they need not concern themselves so much with seeking high returns for equity investors. And, much of the equity they use comes from other companies in the Keiretsu group, which collectively seek market share for the group over high returns on their equity capital.

Japanese companies are often given fixed market shares domestically and divide world markets among themselves. Market shares are frequently established by government arrangement or by inter-Keiretsu agreement. Customers must, accordingly, accept their lot. Employees are in *giri-on* relationships and receive lifetime employment and many benefits from the company. Bankruptcy, causing the destruction of *ninjo* and *giri-on* relationships, is not permitted. Suppliers are most likely part of the Keiretsu group. In any case, they share in the business risks of their purchasers and deliver their inputs on a "just in time basis" to function as an extension of their customers' manufacturing process.

Japanese business leaders do not worry much about the needs and desires of those outside the Keiretsu. They are considered as people beyond the reach of any *giri-on* reciprocal concern. For example, the environment and other community needs receive low-priority attention because they have the status of *tanin,* or outsider, to the Keiretsu group. Special protest efforts by concerned citizens worried about the environment or the impact of corrupt collusion between business leaders and politicians are therefore needed to bring about higher levels of corporate responsibility.

MEXICAN BUSINESS VALUES

Mexico offers still a third variant of market capitalism, one deriving from Spanish colonial traditions of conquest and achieving high social status. The ideal sought by Mexicans, even in their business dealings, is a kind of status, the ability to be a "chief honcho" or "big boss," sort of a feudal barony supported by the company's business endeavors instead of by landed estates as in colonial times. Culturally, the Mexican company serves its owner like a *hacienda* once did for the landed gentry, and today's business owner plays the social role of *hacendado.* The Mexican business owner often seeks "dominion" over (mostly) his company and its subordinates. The business structure is very hierarchical, with much honor and respect shown to the owners.

Class distinctions are important, and upward mobility in society turns on becoming a "padron" in your own right ruling over your own "fief."

A Mexican company is considered to be the "territory" of the owner who has discretion over events within his domain. His permission must be obtained before entering company precincts. Success in business is measured, therefore, not so much by money earned, but by the social status and power derived from company position, by the respect one receives as an owner or manager (respect shared with one's immediate family as well), and by the number of people who pay one honor and deference.

Figure 2.3 illustrates the Mexican pattern of business enterprise. The results of business enterprise in Mexico are different from those achieved in China and Japan.

Suggested Mexican Business Value Pyramid

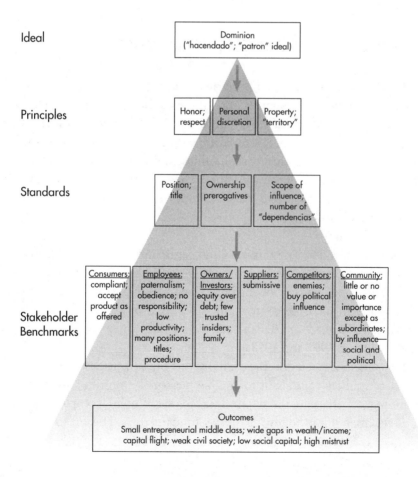

How the different stakeholders of a typical Mexican business relate to the enterprise is shown in Figure 2.3. Employees are treated paternalistically, and expectations about their performance and productivity are low. Ownership is concentrated, and family ownership is preferred. Outside financing is not really welcome, unless it accepts a deferential subordination to the owner. Consumers are treated as if they are a necessary evil, and they are imposed on to the extent possible. There is relatively little respect for community or the needs of civil society, unless the owner is given a position of public leadership. For example, owners tend to have their own private security forces and to live in guarded, walled compounds. Public security forces— the police—on whom most citizens have to rely for their security and protection, have low pay and low status. Although many wealthy families don't like to pay taxes for public purposes, they are not opposed to spending money in return for preferential treatment on the part of government authorities.

A WIDELY USED VARIANT OF MARKET CAPITALISM

Rights of private property and restricted market trade in goods and services are combined in many national economies in a system widely referred to as "crony capitalism" (Figure 2.4). The ideal of this business system is more political than economic in that powerful players set the rules to keep themselves and their families, and their family retainers, at the top of the social power structure. These architects of crony capitalism may be old established landlord families, but in many cases they are new arrivals in wealth and power, using cronyism to obtain both money and status.

In this connection one thinks of the Ferdinand and Imelda Marcos regime in the Philippines, Suharto's "New Order" in Indonesia, Mobuto in Zaire, "Papa" Doc/"Baby" Doc in Haiti, along with many other caudillos in the Caribbean and Central and Latin America. Crony Capitalism set up the financial structures of Thailand and Indonesia for their rapid and dramatic collapse in 1997 and 1998.

This system is not a genuine capitalist one but only uses some mechanisms of market capitalism to further personal ambitions over the common good. In gross, the system is more one of political exploitation of markets than it is of following market fundamentals. The key to crony

Crony Capitalism

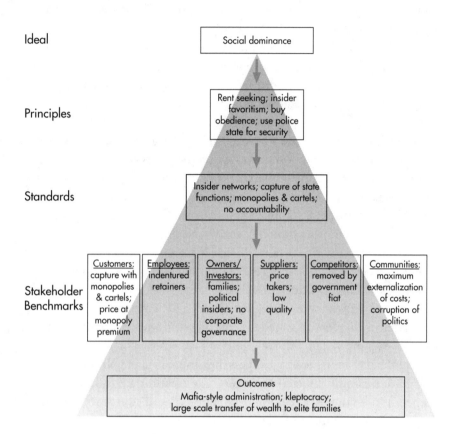

capitalism is control of the police and the military force of the state in order to back up concentration of economic opportunity in a few reliable hands.

In crony capitalism, economic advantage is sought through protected "rent seeking" rather than through free and open competition. Genuine competition is dysfunctional in such a system as it jeopardizes the future economic security of those taking rents out of the economy through access to political power. Competition, which brings new entrants into the market and moves prices to lower and lower levels, drives non-economic rents out of the market. Crony capitalism expressly sets out to accumulate just those privileged non-economic rents.

The "rents" sought to be charged by crony capitalists in return for their control of political connections are accumulated through the exercise of monopoly power, either in monopolies such as Suharto and Marcos granted relatives and political supporters or in small cartels where the valuable rent premium to be charged by the favored business over its marginal costs is shared among only a few.

The principles of this system include the use of favoritism, the purchase of government decisions, and the ultimate reliance on the police rather than markets and elections for control of the economy and the government. Crony capitalism has no standards of public accountability by which to be judged. Only insiders are privileged enough to have their preferences taken into consideration by those who run the system. The trade of customers is "captured" through monopoly or cartel market position. And because so many firms have excessive market power, pleasing customers with better quality of goods and services or with lower prices is unnecessary. Employees have few alternatives for finding employment, so they become dependents, living at the sufferance of the owners. Ownership is kept in as few hands as possible, mostly within families under the supervision of patriarchs. Banks allocate credit not with regard to sound lending principles but as a reward for gaining political influence.

Minority investment in crony capitalism is treated as a gift, a preferential sharing of rents allocated to those who will work diligently to maintain the existing system of privilege.

Suppliers have no leverage unless they, too, can gain political influence and have business directed their way, like obtaining a monopoly over cement production in a country. And, unprivileged competitors are kept in check by government regulation or harassment.

Crony capitalism pushes off on the community at large all the costs of doing business, such as pollution, treatment of injured workers, and social security, that it possibly can. And it thrives by corrupting political decision making.

CONCLUSION

In one sense, capitalism is similar across nations. But, in another and more important sense, different cultural values create different outcomes for capitalist enterprise. A cultural system's core values, like *tai he* in China, *ninjo* in Japan, or dominion in Mexico, create a field of power not unlike the energy field emanating from a magnet that aligns all iron filings within its reach. The power field of values flows down through an organization to influence those within the system, giving them clarity of purpose and direction. The values impress a particular quality on organizational life, influencing individual behavior in predictable ways.[9] Higher values do matter, even in business. Whatever we choose to believe in at the abstract level of normativity will influence our lives at the material level of facticity. Chapter 3 now exposes the values that predominate when markets turn brutal.

CHAPTER 3

BRUTE CAPITALISM: SURVIVAL OF THE FITTEST?

Greed is good. Greed is right. Greed works. Greed cuts through, clarifies, and captures the essence of the evolutionary spirit.

—Gordon Gekko
(played by Michael Douglas) in the movie Wall Street

Veni, vidi, vici.

—Julius Caesar,
as reported by Suetonius in The Twelve Caesars[1]

It will not be denied that power is of an encroaching nature, and that it ought to be effectively restrained from passing the limits assigned to it.

—The Federalist No. 48, Feb 1, 1788

THE VALUES WE CHOOSE TO LIVE BY have some say in determining our fates. Chinese, Japanese, and Mexican cultural priorities, to name only three autonomous value sets, bring about three shades of capitalism. A fourth variety of capitalism, which many assert to be the highest and best form of capitalism, replaces cultural norms with individual self-interest as the highest good.

This libertarian form of capitalism does not seek to apply moral character in business, leaving very open the probability that the powers of market capitalism will be abused by those who hold such power in their hands. A more brutish market environment then emerges to torment the weak, the trusting, and those in great need.

This vision of market capitalism belittles the need to be sensitive to responsibilities and duties. It would place all businesses beyond effective social constraint, in some antisocial circumstance of cutthroat competition for survival. This free-market extremism pushes the logic of individual autonomy as far as it will go, beyond all constraints save those of law. And, it argues, even laws regulating business and markets should be kept to the minimum. Unfettered freedom to buy and sell is best, we are told, for only in the forge of the hottest competition can society smelt maximum benefit for itself.

Here the goal is dominion over others; there are no social offices of service to perform, no need for fiduciary responsibilities. The spoils of conquest, not a vocation, are the rewards of work and investment. Self-interest without consideration of the whole set of circumstances is all we need; self-interest is to swallow virtue whole. Simplistic calculations of financial profit are deemed sufficient criteria for ethical decision making. To win over all the others, as Caesar did, is taken for the philosopher's *summum bonum* of the life to be well lived. Veni, Vidi, Vici!

This position is urged on us by Libertarians, followers of Ayn Rand, and Social Darwinists like Andy Fastow, the chief financial officer of Enron before its collapse and before his arrest for fraud.

Yet Caesar's life ended not as he had wished it would, but prematurely from assassination.

Some critics assert that this brute form of market capitalism is the true and necessary face of all capitalisms and that, therefore, no capitalism can ever serve the common good.

The first great proponent of free-market capitalism as a social good, Adam Smith, valued adversarial accomplishments of competition; he asserted that individuals seeking what was best for themselves could create wealth for others and that many individuals so acting would create wealth for many more. But Smith also presumed that individuals going into business were capable of acting from self-interest considered upon the whole. In fact, Smith wrote a complex and overlooked masterpiece, *The Theory of the Moral Sentiments*, on how we can acquire the capacity to consider our self-interest taken upon the whole.[2] Smith actually proposed creating a moral capitalism, not a rapacious one. His theory was separated into two books, the better known *An Inquiry Into the Nature and the Causes of the Wealth of Nations*, written in 1776, and his earlier book of 1759 promoting moral character as essential for a just society.

Belief in everyone's capacity for moral awareness justified Smith in his willingness to trust private enterprise when he came to write his second book in 1776. He did not fear that capitalists would run roughshod over society, necessitating in response government regulation of enterprise. Business investors would be prudent, he expected, and would learn from experience the discipline of the market.[2]

But the process of early industrialization did not fully comport with Smith's optimism about capitalism. By the 1830s, in England, France, and the United States, the first generation of factories and mills were producing great wealth for a few capitalists and miserable working conditions for a new class of proletarians. Factory and mill towns were dirty and smoky. Some called them "Satanic." Railroads were laid and rural lives were disturbed. Cities grew along with working class slums; a middle class found its political voice; aristocrats were offended and frightened by the decline of traditional social hierarchies.

Demands by capitalists and others in the middle class for more market freedom, along with democratic political reforms, set off a culture war over the value of capitalism. Out of this political and intellectual ferment, the vision of unfettered free enterprise would emerge. Initially, the proponents of legal and economic change won the argument: in England, the Corn Laws restricting trade were abolished, the right to vote was extended, and aristocratic and gentry control of the Parliament was reduced. Modernization began in earnest.

There followed a reaction against free markets. Aristocrats like Lord Byron, accompanied by other romantics like Shelley, disparaged the work ethic and other social conventions of the rising middle class. In France, with a culture always more theoretically inclined than that of England, aristocrats like Saint Simon, accompanied by intellectuals like August Compte and Proudhon, invented socialism and anarchism as critiques of the money power growing ever stronger in society. For a new Bohemian element of writers and cultural commentators, "bourgeois" values were subject to scorn and derision. Defense of capitalism, then spoken of as "free trade," fell to economists like David Ricardo and Whig essayists like John Stuart Mill and Thomas Babington Macauley.

The raw economic power of capitalism grew; newer, larger factories were built; the urban proletariat became a social force; and new technologies and conveniences—such as underground sewers and flush toilets, which improved London's health amazingly—were again and again brought to market. Money alone, not land or title, talent or grace, provided access to the goods of this new civilization. In the 1840s, Charles Dickens wrote his classic rebuke of capitalists—*A Christmas Carol*—to demonstrate in the persona of Ebenezer Scrooge just how far from Christian virtues businessmen responsible for the new civilization had fallen.

Scrooge, the poster boy for brutish capitalism, was created as emotionally stunted, an aging bachelor having locked love out of his heart and living only for his money. It took fear to break through his callousness, along with intervention of the supernatural. Dickens, who opposed the reform movement, wanted us to believe that at the center of capitalism were people like Ebenezer Scrooge, beyond all hope of social redemption and not capable of wise economic stewardship.

Karl Marx and Friedrich Engels published their call for Revolution, *The Communist Manifesto*, in 1848, picking up on nearly thirty years of growing objections to what Marx now called "the capitalist mode of appropriation." Into the fray to defend free trade and refute Marx stepped Herbert Spencer. In 1851, Spencer offered up a new intellectual discipline—sociology—as a way to think about social justice. In an age of scientific discovery and technological innovation, Spencer advocated scientific paradigms for social decision making. One of the most profound revolutions in thought was about to take place: Charles Darwin announcing his theory of evolution. After Darwin, God would no longer be so necessary as a source of conviction and right conduct, and could be replaced by human ingenuity, which was presented as more and more Godlike in its powers to do good for humanity.

As Darwin would just a few years later, Spencer argued scientifically that humans were an extension of animals and that, therefore, the rules of the animal kingdom should apply to human activity as well. Each human should be valued as a biological solitary and as inevitably locked in a struggle for survival with all the other human and animal solitaries. As Darwin assumed for the animal kingdom, so Spencer posited for human society that only the fittest individuals would survive. Competition was natural law and the basis for natural selection. The devil could take the hindmost of animals, of races and tribes, and of individual homo sapiens as well. Adam Smith's idea of human competition as taking place within society and therefore as a force for the creation of good was, in Spencer's hands, taken out of that moral context and reformulated as essentially a new theory of brute capitalism.

Robust market capitalism with no Marquis of Queensbury rules seemed for Spencer the perfect analogue among people to natural selection in the wild. Here was to be freedom and power for the alpha male of the species *homo sapiens*, the breadwinner and conqueror of that species. Spencer, for example, denied the wisdom of ever having a legislature regulate business activity. Instead, let businesses fight it out in the marketplace, he said. The winners will be better and stronger and more able to contribute to society. Losers deserved no sympathy and little respect.[3]

The rise and sudden collapse of Enron is a study in applied Social Darwinism as Spencer's theory came to be called. Andy Fastow, a principal architect of Enron's techniques of "aggressive" accounting, who hid billions of dollars in liabilities from investors, prided himself on being a Social Darwinist. The business value chart in Figure 3.1 displays the libertarian values trumpeted by Herbert Spencer and other Social Darwinists as carried out at Enron by Fastow and his colleagues in that company's senior management—all under the permissive and admiring gaze of Enron's board of directors.

In Figure 3.1, the value to be infused on corporate action is, simply, greed: the extraction from society of as much as possible for oneself, or, of whatever is needed to please one's desires. Moving down the Social Darwinist value pyramid toward the level of action and results, the principle to be applied in business is maximization of wealth without regard for others. The standards by which one can measure success in this enterprise are the familiar financial goals of "return on investment," "total compensation" (here mostly for senior corporate managers), and the price of the company's stock. Fidelity to these standards will focus attention on increasing the money that can be extracted from the enterprise in the short run. Application of the standards to the different stakeholders of Enron results in marginalizing their concerns and increasing their risks.

Once the consequences of living out Enron's core values and its operating principles were exposed, Enron was quickly driven into bankruptcy.

Spencer's Social Darwinism does provide a theory of capitalism, but not one that is cost-free.

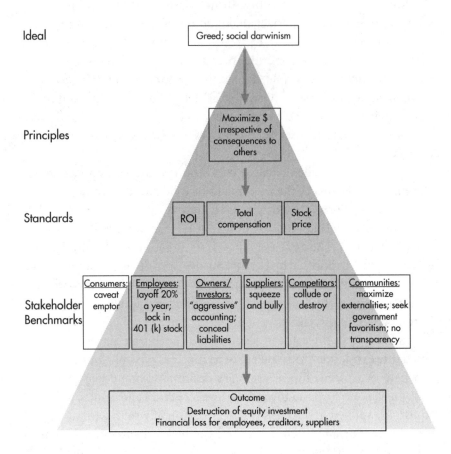

The Irresponsible Corporation—ENRON

Ideal	Greed; social darwinism
Principles	Maximize $ irrespective of consequences to others
Standards	ROI | Total compensation | Stock price

Stakeholder Benchmarks

Consumers: caveat emptor	Employees: layoff 20% a year; lock in 401 (k) stock	Owners/ Investors: "aggressive" accounting; conceal liabilities	Suppliers: squeeze and bully	Competitors: collude or destroy	Communities: maximize externalities; seek government favoritism; no transparency

Outcome
Destruction of equity investment
Financial loss for employees, creditors, suppliers

THE COST OF BRUTE CAPITALISM

Consider these recent achievements of corporate boards of directors and the senior officers they hired and supervised:

- Enron: accounting/off balance sheet contrivances; chief financial officer indicted; company bankrupt; billions of equity value lost

- Enron and other energy companies: manipulated power markets during California's 2000–2001 energy crisis to overcharge California by $3.3 billion

- Tyco: chief executive officer charged with tax evasion, waste of corporate assets; massive charge of $6 billion to earnings after disposal of CIT unit

- WorldCom: $3.8 billion fraud; loans to chief executive officer; bankruptcy

- Adelphia Communications: Off balance sheet loans to senior officers

- Dynegy: sham energy trades; chief executive officer resigns

- Xerox: accounting overstates profits by $1.4 billion

- Sotheby's and Christie's: price fixing

- CSFB: initial public offering allocation practices; shares in "hot" initial public offering's offered to 300 "Friends of Frank Quattrone" technology executives in return for investment banking business

- Merrill Lynch: $100 million settlement over analyst conflict of interest; market capitalization cut in half from January 2001 to September 2002

- Global Crossing: filed for bankruptcy after fiddling accounts

- Qwest Communications: chief executive officer resigned; profits restated, assets cut by 50%, or $34 billion; share price down

- Health South: $1.4 billion fraud; false entries created in income statements and balance sheets

- ImClone: chief executive officer charged with selling company stock due to inside information

- Ford: $3 billion recall due to rollover of Explorer SUVs

- Citigroup: $240 million settlement of Federal Trade Commission charges of predatory lending

- Salomon: fined $5 million; stock analyst Jack Grubman faces legal action

- Wall Street investment banking firms, including Merrill Lynch, Citibank, and CSFB: pay $1.4 billion to settle claims that they manipulated advice given to investors; civil litigation to follow

- Robertson Stephens: fined $28 million for taking kickbacks in exchange for access to "hot" initial public offerings

- JP Morgan Chase: incurred a fourth quarter 2002 loss of $387 million due to a $1.3 billion charge covering losses on Enron, regulatory penalties, and a charge for the potential costs of civil litigation

- $110 billion merger of AOL and TimeWarner cemented with inflated accounting of AOL revenues; within eighteen months, company value declined 75%, and massive write-downs of asset values were taken—AOL's 2002 earnings were written down by $98.7 billion (a figure only slightly smaller than the European Union's budget for 2003); civil litigation ensued for damages to investors

- Bristol-Myers: restates $2.5 billion in sales and $900 million in profits after inflating distributor's stock levels; settles antitrust lawsuits for a cost of $670 million

- ABB in Sweden: bonds trade at half face value; stock price drops from fifty-five to three Swedish kroner; credit rating drops to near junk levels; customers abandon ship, and major lines of business are sold off

- Vivendi-Universal in France: failure of strategy; loss to shareholders; class action suits filed alleging misrepresentation of company's financial realities

- Ahold in The Netherlands: chief executive officer fired and stock price collapsed after American subsidiary was found to have falsely reported earnings

- HIH insurance group in Australia: failed with debts of $3.1 billion after consistently underestimating claims liabilities; chief executive officer, among other things, spent A$340,000 on gold watches in one year; criminal and civil charges pending against several directors

- Insider control group at SAirGroup brings Belgian Sabena airline into bankruptcy; claim for recovery of $8.1 billion filed in Swiss courts by Sabena's bankruptcy administrator

- SK Global in South Korea: overstates 2001 earnings by $1.2 billion; liquidity crisis caused for credit card companies; $10 billion pulled by investors from investment trusts

Further costs to the American economy from this short-term, brutish pattern of corporate management include a charge of $2.8 billion taken by the insurer AIG to boost reserves for future casualty claims arising from insurance policies issued to corporate directors and officers. Stocks of the insurance sector were trading down at that time. The cost to GE of its directors' and officers' insurance rose 400 percent in one year after the scandals to $22.1 million.

Ordinary investors left Wall Street. This imposed a huge cost on the American economy. If equity markets lack buyers and stock prices accordingly founder, the cost of capital to corporations increases and new enterprises are prevented from raising funds to grow and prosper. In 2002, ordinary investors pulled $27 billion from American equity funds and put $124 billion into taxable bond funds. And, in January 2003, there were net redemptions from individual retirement accounts, pensions, and 401(k) plans for the first time since 1990. The net redemptions amounted to $1 billion.[4] As stock prices dropped, many companies had to divert profits into pension plans, causing further injury to the interests of shareholders.

Brute capitalism does not lead its conquistadors to El Dorado. By removing us from the security of society and cultural norms, Social Darwinism increases our risks of defeat and failure. Under the aggressive economic warfare proposed by brute capitalism, finding win-win equilibria that provide some small victories for everyone becomes more and more difficult.

THE CULTURE OF BRUTE CAPITALISM

Perhaps in the excitement of his conceptual breakthrough, Spencer overlooked just how inconsistent his theory was with the insights of Adam Smith. Where Smith had seen specialization and accelerating divisions of labor producing more and more cross-dependencies and interdependencies as capitalist economic growth expanded, Spencer only saw more and more autonomy, independence, and conflict to get one's way in the world.

One reads Spencer in vain to find recognition of the need for responsibility, for working out sustainable relationships, or for some enlightened quality applied to the struggle for life. Spencer did not see any value in symbiosis. Neither did he value the self-evident realities that the people who drive any form of capitalism are products of social conditioning, that they think and work through language and culture, and that they have a moral sense, all of which Adam Smith took for granted. To analogize people to animals in every important sense, as Spencer did, is a mistake.

At the height of the American era of the robber barons, in the late nine-teenth century, one of the greatest barons of the time, Andrew Carnegie, used Spencer's reasoning to defend American capitalism and his role in building it. In 1888, Carnegie wrote *Triumphant Democracy*, a hymn to American national success. He ascribed that American success, especially in contrast to his native land of Scotland and England, to the "freer play" America gave to the Darwinian axiom of "natural selection."[5]

Carnegie opined that "...men differ from each other—no two alike but all equally determined to live each his own life in his own way, this being his nature. This is the law of progress of his race, as it is of plant and animal life." He believed, "The 'survival of the fittest' means that the exceptional plants, animals, or men which have the needed 'variations' from the common standard, are the fructifying forces which leaven the whole."[6]

With the stock market crash of October 1929, and the ensuing great global economic depression, faith in the Robber Barons of brute capital-ism was hard to come by. One bitter commentator spoke sharply what many felt to be the case about brute capitalism: "I oppose modern capi-talism because by its very nature it cannot and will not function for the common good. ...Modern capitalism as we know it is not worth saving, In fact, it is a detriment to civilization. ...Capitalism has become so iden-tified with abuses which encumber it that its nature is merged with the abuses. Their removal means the burial of capitalism."[7]

But, oddly, the Spencerian thinking behind Carnegie's form of capi-talism still has continuing appeal 70 years after the Great Depression. Frankly, for many it is not hard to conclude that life really is a kind of jungle beyond the bounds of what we want for humane civilization. Neither is it hard to feel that few out there truly care for our welfare, that the race of life indeed is to the swift and the battle to the strong. We lose out on pro-motions and opportunities; people oppress us for their own good; our solace often is found not in business success but in religion or in mental escape from the "slings and arrows of outrageous fortune." To cope with reality, many of us succumb to dysfunctional relationships and various other addictions to numb the pain of being alive.

Why not, therefore, listen to Andrew Carnegie and Herbert Spencer? Why not strike out and take on the world, warriorlike, to leave behind our own saga of triumph or of glorious defeat, as did Beowulf, Odysseus, Caesar, Alexander the Great, Napoleon, and the other heroes of myth and history? Why not strive as did Richard Nixon, who, on resigning the presidency of the United States, took comfort in the rugged words of Theodore Roosevelt on the honor of being the man who had been "in the arena" even though having been defeated in the contest?

American images of Minutemen on Lexington Green, frontiersman like Hawkeye, the "Deerslayer," the mountain men and the cowboys of the wild west, the pioneers and homesteaders, the immigrants like Andrew Carnegie or James J. Hill who made fortunes in their new homeland, have given life and excitement to Spencer's sociology in America. And, for many men everywhere, there seems to be a genetic predisposition towards warrior values, to the hunt, and to hand-to-hand confrontation with destiny. The Promethean urge to win out takes over from time to time in all of us—men as well as women.

The culture of suburban America, built by men who suffered through the depression as children and who fought World War II, and by their wives and children, centers on personal autonomy. Every family there lives apart, on its own small estate; every family there owns one or more automobiles and shuns mass transit. Rugged individualism has at least aesthetic appeal in this contemporary setting.

Next, life for teenagers these days is very Darwinian in some ways; it can be a struggle for psychic personal survival—in the midst of peer competition, in the search for sex and, perhaps, love, and against the constraints of social norms. To the winner go the spoils of individualism.

After World War II, American Social Darwinism evolved into the conservative movement seeking to restrain the regulatory state. Spenser's theme of primacy for the individual in a struggle for existence was picked up by Fredrick Hayek, Russell Kirk, James Burnham, and Leo Strauss—the intellectual founders of modern conservatism. The influential magazine of opinion, the *National Review*, and Washington think tanks such as the Cato Institute, the American Enterprise Institute, and the Heritage Foundation, kept conservative and libertarian ideas alive and vital. In economics, Professor Milton Friedman and others at the University of Chicago made rigorous cases for the elimination of regulation and for sole reliance on market forces as the best way to achieve social justice.

In politics, Barry Goldwater's campaign for the presidency of 1964 threw Spencerian thinking in the face of America's political establishment. Sixteen years and four elections later, Ronald Reagan won the presidency on an attenuated Spencerian platform of freedom from regulation and low taxes, along with his zeal to defeat communism and save world civilization for individualism and free-market capitalism.

Ironically, the counterculture of political protest, hippies, sex, drugs, and rock and roll, which the children of suburbia and small towns brought to a boil in the late 1960s, has its own Spencerian aspect. The demand of that counterculture, especially in protest against military service in Vietnam, extended the dynamic of "teenage" self-absorption. The baby boomers sought self-expression to free themselves from social constraint; they sought conflict with authority figures, especially their parents; they espoused new roles for women and less repressed sexual behaviors; they promoted moral relativism the better to validate whatever their inner preferences turned out to be.

In all this there was something natural, something wild, even brutish, seeking to break in on the formalities of civilization. There was, at bottom, only assertion of the self against the world as it was. Spencer would have understood.

Brute capitalism still has its appeal. In his recent handbook for corporate success, *The 48 Laws of Power*, Robert Green gives comfort to the perspective that only the cunning and the manipulative survive in the competition for life's trophies.[8] Greene advises us that instead of struggling against the inevitable, instead of arguing and whining and feeling guilty, it is far better to excel at power. This mastery comes from the arts of indirection he says; learning to seduce, charm, deceive, and subtly outmaneuver your opponents will bring you to the heights of power. Nothing here about reciprocity, enhancing the moral sense, or doing your duty well and with fidelity as desirable or necessary success skills.

Brute capitalism limits the role of law and regulation while simultaneously diminishing the role of moral self-restraint and concern for others. It belittles the necessity for ethics, relying solely on the checks and balances of competition to modulate intense self-absorption into something of benefit for the whole. But achieving that common good has proven to be a difficult task in many settings where moral norms are ignored.

One can think of brute capitalism as a special case of market capitalism, an extreme one, not entirely irrational in the short run, but lacking the fundamentals necessary for sustainable profitability. By neglecting the moral dimension, brute capitalism opens the door to abuse of power by those running the engines of business, to people like Andy Fastow of Enron and others who think as he did.

CONCLUSION

Brute capitalism is one extreme position on private business behavior. It advocates the triumph of interest over virtue. At the other extreme is communism—the militant rejection of markets, private property, and individual human dignity—seeking to impose a vision of pure virtue over the dictates of self-interest. As we will see in Chapter 4, moral capitalism lies between the extremes, providing for us a dynamic symbiosis of virtue and interest.

CHAPTER 4

MORAL CAPITALISM: USING PRIVATE INTEREST FOR THE PUBLIC GOOD

... he intends only his own gain, and he is in this, as in many other cases, led by an invisible hand to promote an end which was no part of his intention. ... By pursuing his own interest he frequently promotes that of society more effectually than when he really intends to promote it.

—Adam Smith, *The Wealth of Nations*[1]

Where there is no vision, the people perish.

—Proverbs 29:18

THE ARGUMENT FOR MORAL CAPITALISM has two parts. First, as Adam Smith asserted in *An Inquiry into the Nature and Causes of the Wealth of Nations*, free markets have an inherent tendency to bring about a convergence of virtue and interest. In other words, the logic of self-interest considered upon the whole when applied to business over time leads to betterment for the individual as well as for society. Second, moral capitalism is advanced and accelerated by a sense of service, a fiduciarylike sensitivity to others.

FREE MARKETS PROMOTE VIRTUOUS CONDUCT

Property: the Basis for Living an Ordinary Moral Life

The German philosopher Hegel concluded that private property was necessary for morals. Without seizing hold of some touchable part of the cosmos, no person could fully bring his or her values into being.[2] In Hegel's terms, to objectify a subjective intent, to move from mental states to physical being, to incarnate value into the evolution of the world, something tangible had to be transformed according to the dictates of our own will. Only speaking of our intentions would not always fully bring our personhood into palpable being for others to take into account and accord us the dignity we seek. People have a need, Hegel assumed, to leave their mark on the world. That happens only once some part of the world is appropriated as being especially ours, to the exclusion of control by others. Ownership of things—a right to private property—therefore, has an important place in the theory of morals in that ownership of property enhances the living presence of our dignity.

Moral choice presumes that people are in a position to choose, that they are in command of some force or power that can make a difference. The rich have many options before them, the poor very few. Is this not why we so often expect more responsibility from the rich than we do from the poor? Those with money can always make a difference, do things right, stand against bad tidings and unhappy events, and go out of their way to help others.

Those without property are more easily overlooked. Frankly, fhey get stepped on by others more often than not. Rights of religious conscious, free speech, political participation, have less traction for those without money and property. Hernando de Soto, a Peruvian advocate for capitalizing the poor, now calls for giving the poorest of the poor titles to their shacks and hovels as a first step in improving their lives.[3] Give them capital, give them access to mortgage credit, he says, and then they can make something of their lives. Keep them in laboring servitude and less good will come of their lives and of their children's lives.

The advantages of wealth are not to be disparaged. Mae West was poor and she was rich; she concluded that "rich is better." Having money and possessing property brings self-confidence, promotes tolerance, permits individualism, and makes moral choices possible in life, actualizing personal values.

One can, however, choose an ascetic life over a life of property ownership. Buddha, Jesus, and Gandhi did so. Monks, priests, and nuns like Mother Theresa do so regularly. In his Rule for a Monastic Life, St. Benedict referred to the ownership of private property as a "vitium"—an evil practice.[4] St. Benedict was opposed to private property because it furnished occasion for the exercise of individual will in the pursuit of individual identity.

Yet, the ability of a Mother Theresa to serve so many of the poor and destitute in Calcutta depended on her ability to attract donations from others. Wealth was a precondition for her charitable accomplishments. To implement her will, she required the property of others. Mother Theresa's subjective intent to change the world as she felt would be necessary and proper was achieved through persuasion of others to implement her ideals with their actions and property. The impact of a Jesus or a Buddha on our lives unfolds inwardly, in our psychology where we choose our values and virtues. The ascetic life they embodied cultivates personhood at the level of their inner, personal subjectivity, often to the exclusion of more objective worldly accomplishments like military conquest or political success.

They express themselves through requisition of charisma, not material wealth. By making it more and more possible for ordinary people to gain the means of expressing their values and moral inclinations in this world of facticity, capitalism serves a moral end. It enables people to bring the world more and more into accord with their preferences.

Promoting Moral Behavior

Free markets actually promote moral behavior among buyers and sellers. This tendency provides a second ethical basis for capitalism, bridging the potential gap between virtue and self-interest.

Markets will not survive without trust. Reliance on the word and good faith of others sustains markets. The adage is, "Every dog gets one bite." Where experience shows that a party is not to be trusted, we will no longer send our trade his or her way. The law voids contracts procured by misrepresentation and fraud or obtained by means of inequitable dealings and punishes breaches of warranty. These rules of law, common to most cultures, bring communal power to bear so that trust is promoted in market transactions.

Where cheating and mistrust and broken promises prevail, markets are shrunken and reduced to barter and economic minimalism. Only sellers who establish a reputation for fair dealing can grow their customer base. Only they can borrow money or trade goods on reasonable terms. Immoral people are, over time, driven out of markets because fewer and fewer people will risk the consequences of buying their goods or accepting their "deals."

When the truth about Enron's finances and WorldCom's falsified earnings was made known, investors and lenders immediately drove both companies into bankruptcy. When Arthur Andersen's connivance in misleading the public regarding the financial condition of a number of high-profile clients became an accepted fact, the firm lost customers, imploded, and self-destructed. The markets punished all this misconduct very harshly.

The advantages of trust among market participants cannot be overstated. Capitalism asks us to bring the future into the present and judge—now—as to how much to risk our labor or our capital today that we may be better off tomorrow. Wanting maximum security of judgment in making that leap of faith as to the outcome of future contingencies encourages us to reward those who deserve our trust and to avoid those who do not. Trust reduces risk-aversion, enhancing economic activity. Self-interest promotes our rewarding the trustworthy, thereby adding to the moral quality of our society.

Promoting Individualism

Free-market capitalism welcomes individualism. It rewards innovation and state-of-the-art skill and sensitivity in meeting the needs and demands of others. It makes room for new values, products, and services. It responds to change. Its open architecture harmonizes with the many faces of human dignity. Tastes are not the same; needs are different. Capitalism can provide for all, if buyers have enough market presence to invoke the attention of sellers, or if sellers bring to the market something that then attracts buyers.

Even the mass consumer markets of advanced nations like the United States are not static. Fads come and go; products become obsolete. New products, better service and lower prices will draw customers away from their buying habits. Innovations enter the markets every day. If more healthy foods become attractive, grocery stores will provide them. If fuel-efficient vehicles come into demand, gas-guzzling SUVs will join stage-coaches in the ash can of history. People express their values through their purchases just as they do through acquiring property rights.

It is the same for workers. Labor markets can provide a profitable fit for individual talent. The more advanced and developed a market economy, the easier it is for a person to change jobs or careers. New skills, seniority, and imaginative use of old skills open up opportunity. Frustration often comes when the markets for labor are inflexible or when workers have insufficient capital to invest in more education or to buy time in which to seek alternate employment.

At the core of human dignity is individuality. To respect another person is to make way for that spark of special vitality that sets a person apart. Seeing another as limited by the traits of a class or race or tribe does not do full justice. At all times, we each know to a point of moral certainty that we are alone, unique, and different, even though we partake of class and ethnic identities.

By offering new possibilities for work, for ownership, for possessions, for self-expression, capitalism can provide a framework for existential human freedom. In doing so, it serves a moral end.

Promoting Mutuality

The rational, calculating mind that drives markets and capitalism leads to moral outcomes as well. As game theory has established, calculated pursuit of self-interest brings individuals into arrangements that have benefit for others as well as for themselves. The point of equilibrium—the terms of the "deal"—arrived at by calculating persons must have some significant positive value for the preference functions of each person in the negotiations. Otherwise, participants would cease to play the game.

Confronted with other calculating, self-interested people in bargaining situations, people do, over time, work out the best for themselves by providing others with something of advantage to them. John Nash, of *The Beautiful Mind* movie fame, won a Nobel Prize for that insight.

Through interaction, pursuit of self-interest arrives at a common good, a stable equilibrium of mutual benefit. There is give and take in game theory. If it were all take for one side and no give, then no equilibrium would result. The game would end.

When the Pilgrims landed in Plymouth, Massachusetts, the rules of their colony imposed community property as the reward for their efforts. Members of the colony were, in effect, on equal salaries, working for a common master. Governor William Bradford wrote: "[T]he young men did repine that they should spend their time and strength to work for other men's wives and children without any recompense. The strong has not more in division than he that was weak and not able to do a quarter the other could; this was thought injustice. The aged and graver men to be ranked and equalized in labors and victuals, clothes, etc., thought it some indignity and disrespect unto them. And the men's wives to be commanded to do service for other men, as dressing their meat, washing their clothes, etc., they deemed it a kind of slavery, neither could many husbands well brook it."

"For this community of property," Bradford continued writing, "was found to breed much confusion and discontentment and retard much employment that would have been to their benefit and comfort all being to have alike, and all to do alike if it did not cut off those relations that God hath set amongst men, yet it did at least much diminish and take off the mutual respects that should have preserved them."

Whippings were resorted to as an inducement to greater productive efforts in service to the community.

In the spring of 1623, members of the colony agreed to let people produce for their own benefit. With this result: "This had very good success, for it made all hands very industrious, so as much more corn was planted that otherwise would have been by any means the governor or other could use, and saved him a great deal of trouble, and gave far better content. The women now went willingly into the field, and took their little ones with them to set corn, which before would allege weakness and inability, whom to have compelled would have been thought great tyranny and oppression."[5]

In pursuit of their own private well-being under the new rule of private appropriation, members of the Plymouth colony increased the wealth and happiness of all. Reward brings forth enterprise as a general rule. The piper who is paid plays regularly to our satisfaction.

At times, acting out of interest stabilizes the expectations others have of our future behavior more forcefully than if we act only from charitable impulses. The others look to our interests, not to our will, to calculate how true our conduct will be to our word. Thus at times does self-interest promote higher levels of trust. Impulses to do good for another may quickly come and may just as quickly go should our mood change, whereas our interests are more permanent, our circumstances being constant. Counting on someone's interest in making a payment, for example, may be more dependable than trusting only to their promise to do so in return for giving them our possessions. Their self-interest becomes a power in our hands, giving us greater confidence that they will act as we desire and expect.

Pursuit of interest permits agreements to be reached where adherence to principle often promotes pride and hubris, both destructive of mutuality and compassion. Interests may be easier to compromise than points of honor, demands for self-esteem, or vindication of religious and ethnic identities in the eyes of others. Standing on ceremony or insisting on validation of one's moral superiority have little place in the realm of commerce and finance. In business, money is a solvent, dissolving social and ideological rigidities to open up possibilities for cooperation. Throughout recorded history, peoples and nations with little fondness for one another have nonetheless managed to engage in trade and commerce where it was in their separate, but reciprocal, interests to do so.

Of course, if the circumstances dictating the direction to be taken by self-interest change, a person will quickly decide on a corresponding change of course if necessary. Reliance on self-interest alone can be deceptively secure, for the world is mutable. Further, we may not accurately perceive how others calculate their interests.

In his famous observation that capitalism cleverly took advantage of self-interest, and did not rely on altruism to further the common good,

Adam Smith had in mind a game theory of negotiated outcomes. Markets, he saw, were the products of negotiations, of bargaining. He knew they served social well-being in the creation of jobs and income, and he observed that self-interest did not undermine this service. Rather, like an invisible hand, self-interest of the calculating individual incorporated social virtue into personal advantage. At the end of a market or an investment process, the selfish inclinations of individuals could be seen on a more level of perception about reality encompassing into a common good.

Smith wrote: "I depend for my dinner on the self-interest of the baker and the butcher, not on their love for me." He might equally as well have written: "The baker and the butcher depend for their income on my self-interest in eating well, not on my love for them."

Buyer and seller depend on the other; neither has power to abuse the other without paying a price. Checks and balances controlling base manipulations are in place. If the baker or the butcher provide unwholesome food, or charge excessively, I will take my trade elsewhere. Likewise, if I fail to pay them fairly, they will refuse to sell me what I desire.

As economies moved beyond agriculture and simple crafts into industrialization and international trade, Smith saw that division of labor into specialized tasks could occur with the application of capital to production. As societies specialize more and more and labor subdivides into ever more unique niches of functional accomplishment, individuals everywhere become more and more dependent on one another. No one can be self-sufficient. Obtaining what we need and what we want requires participation in a network of exchange relationships. To please others, we need to meet their terms; and for others to please us, they need to meet ours. Our selfishness is constrained by our evident need to please those on whom we depend. In this context, Smith understood, selfishness would be guided to mutually advantageous outcomes. Where selfishness leads to mutual satisfaction, it has accomplished a social, and therefore an ethical, result.

FINDING AN OFFICE TO PERFORM: ACHIEVING THE MORALITY OF CAPITALISM

Free markets may have a tendency to accomplish laudable moral ends, but they may not always be able to offset the countervailing impulses set loose by advocates of brute capitalism. A proper state of mind among those in business is very necessary for moral capitalism to fully flourish.

We know from the discussion in Chapter 1 that people everywhere have a moral sense, a capacity to bring moral capitalism into robust reality. Now we focus more narrowly on the precise frame of mind they should bring to that social and civilizing task.

Cicero had a word for the responsibility encouraged by market capitalism: *officis*. This Latin word is usually translated as "duty," but this English word is not an equivalent of Cicero's *officis*. Use of the English word "responsibilities" is apt as well. Cicero's word shows up in our word "office," as in "to hold an office" or "a public office is a public trust." One who holds an office—one who is an "officer"—has duties and is expected to be responsible. Officers are entrusted with the powers of a position. Accordingly, we expect them to be "dutiful" in the exercise of those powers and to act responsibly with a view to the advantage of others.

Cicero's advocacy of *officis* as a template for our conduct is most relevant to the morality of capitalism. Cicero's *officis* combines virtue and interest, leading to the inference that one can be self-interested as befits the game-theoretical dynamic of capitalism and also play virtue's part at the same time.[6] For Cicero, one could do well and still be good. The early Quakers were alleged to have achieved such dual results in their business pursuits. They were godly and financially successful as well.

But, can notions of good behavior in office embrace us when we are trapped within the relentless competitive pressures of the market? If we think of ourselves as having a station in in the world of commerce, industry and finance, the answer is yes. Having economic power of any sort can easily bring upon us the obligations of office within the structure of market capitalism.

Our particular station need not be so grand as president of the United States or chief executive officer of General Motors; acting as worker or consumer, as parent or child, will do as well. This insight we can take from Confucius. He envisioned people always as living in relationships with one another, with everyone having some office to perform for the benefit of others. His famous definition of government held that we would need no more for justice to obtain than for lords to lord rightly, ministers to minister rightly, fathers to father rightly, sons to son rightly, and so on through the entire range of reciprocal human relationships.[7]

A curious insight into the requirement that we think of ourselves as holding an office arose when a federal court considered an indictment for murder in 1842.[8] In the north Atlantic the previous year, the ship

William Brown struck an iceberg and sank. Forty-one survivors managed to get aboard the long boat, which was then over loaded and in danger of sinking as well. After two days, to increase the chance of rescue for some survivors, crew members rowing the long boat threw over fourteen male passengers, saving two married men, a small boy, the women, and themselves. The court noted, "Not one of the crew was cast over. One of them, a cook, was a negro."

Amazingly, the long boat was rescued, permitting those still on board to survive the ordeal. One such surviving member of the crew, Holmes, was later indicted for murder at the request of relatives of those thrown overboard to their death. Holmes's counsel argued that the sinking of their ship on the high seas had returned all survivors to a state of nature, where each was permitted to defend his or her own life and need not be concerned any longer for the responsibilities imposed by civilization. Holmes, in protecting himself, had done no wrong in those strange and compelling circumstances when he had thrown passengers to their deaths in the cold waters.

The judge disagreed. Sailors had a duty, which went with them even back into the state of nature. "… the very nature of the social constitution," wrote the judge, " places sailors and passengers in different relations. … we may safely say that the sailor's duty is the protection of the persons entrusted to his care, not their sacrifice." Some punishment should therefore be imposed on a sailor who failed in doing his duty. Holmes was given six months at hard labor and fined $20. President Tyler was petitioned to pardon Holmes, but refused. Holmes's punishment was subsequently remitted.

The policy of the law to assert that responsibility to others firmly stood as the sine qua non of civilization found able expression in two well-known English cases. In *Heaven v. Pender,* the judge declared, "Whenever one person is by circumstance placed in such a position with regard to another that every one of ordinary sense who did think would at once recognize that if he did not use ordinary care and skill in his own conduct with regard to those circumstances he would cause danger of injury to the person or property of the other; a duty arises to use ordinary care and skill to avoid such a danger."[9]

Then, in the case of *Donohue v. Stevenson,* Lord Atkin held, "The rule that you are to love your neighbor becomes in law, you must not injure your neighbor; and the lawyer's question, "Who is my neighbor?" receives restricted reply. You must take reasonable care to avoid acts or omissions which you can reasonably foresee would be likely to injure your neighbor. Who, then, in law is my neighbor? The answer seems to be—persons who are so closely and directly affected by my act that I ought reasonably to have them in contemplation as being so affected when I am directing my mind to the acts or omissions which are called in question."[10]

Merely by being ourselves we always have an office to perform in the markets of capitalism. In that office—be it buyer or seller, worker or investor—we need to be honest and reliable and to assert our self-interest with a view toward the whole. The Caux Round Table Principles for Business provide a simple but comprehensive guide to the responsibilities incumbent upon those who take up any business opportunity.

A better way, perhaps, to appropriate for ourselves Cicero's recommendation that we always live morally is to think of his *officis* simply as reaching adulthood. The trajectory of a human life aims at adulthood, to the assumption of power and responsibility in society.

We expect from adults maturity of judgment, the capacity to master their passions and to balance interest with the social advantages of duty. In short, adults are esteemed for their character. Such individuals, when thrown into the maw of commerce and industry, will hold out for higher standards. They will engender those levels of trust necessary for the robust growth of markets. They will accentuate the inherent tendency of free markets to evolve into a more novel form of capitalism.

THE FIDUCIARY IDEAL

Humanity is better off with markets and capitalism than with poverty and feudalism. Yet markets and capitalism facilitate abuse of the very power they create. For all the inherent preferences of markets for high levels of trust and reliability, for all the social good they can wring from individual pursuit of self-interest, capitalist markets have no cure for the hardness hiding in many human hearts.

Callousness, exploitation, and even oppression come into the world through human hands. Economic power is but one kind of leverage people use to impose their own advantage on others. If we could but reduce abuse of such power, capitalism would become more thoroughly beneficial for all.

Law is one measure by which we can reduce abuse of market power: we can regulate conduct in advance to prevent abusive actions and we can promise punishment in retrospect to counter the seductions of greed. Antitrust laws, contract enforcement, food inspection, limits on water and air pollution, licensing requirements, disclosure obligations in the sale of securities, rules for governance of corporations—all these and more have been adopted to improve the moral quality of capitalism. And yet, shortcomings abound: capital still does not flow to poor nations, investors are still manipulated through creative accounting, short-sightedness prevails, and, where taking advantage of others comes with little or no cost, it readily occurs.

Government can also use laws and regulations to align our incentives so that self-interest considered upon the whole will lead market players toward socially beneficial outcomes.

For incentives to be properly aligned, governments must do their part. Title to property and marketable interests, such as ownership of inventions, must be secure; contracts must be enforced; currencies must be stable; corruption must be prevented; bankruptcy laws must permit smooth realignment of interests after misjudgments have brought on business failure; information necessary for accurate valuation of assets and correct pricing must be provided openly; and financial institutions must be prevented from funding speculative bubbles.

Businesses must then not interfere with these structured incentives to steer selfish advantage. Adam Smith recorded his observation that whenever businessmen gather, they plan to subvert the competitive pressures of markets with collusion to fix prices. If we advocate the social justice of a moral capitalism, then we must insist that its rules be followed by all who seek to benefit from the system.

The question whether business decision makers can act from self-interest considered upon the whole is not completely answered in the affirmative by use of legal regulations, criminal punishments, or structured incentives. We must, in addition, move beyond the law into realms of voluntary calculation of how best to achieve the good.

As set forth in Chapter 1, our so acting upon principle happens most naturally when it arises out of habit and mental discipline. The foundation of good judgment lies in good character, in the choices we make of the values that we put in place to command our value pyramids.

Confucius advised in this regard, "Fine words and an insinuating appearance are seldom associated with true virtue"[11]; "See what a man does; mark his motives, examine in what things he rests. How can a man conceal his character?"[12]

Moral responsibility is a form of stewardship, of agency, of fiduciary undertaking. It asks how do my decisions affect others, especially those who have the power neither to reward nor to punish me for my decisions? It is a vision of mutuality, of service, of both self and others.

The Dalai Lama writes that ethics is the "indispensable interface between my desire to be happy and yours" and that "there is no self-interest completely unrelated to others' interests."[13] A fixation on the self distracts the mind from reflection on right principles. As the Dalai Lama teaches in the Buddhist tradition, to rise above the anxieties of the self, we must begin with examination of the self. In this very way, a moral capitalism demands that self-interest be properly understood as infused with values arising from an awareness of creation.

The world's religions, great and small, generally recommend this ethic of stewardship. The Old Testament said, "Woe unto the shepherds of Israel for they have fed themselves and not their flocks."[14] Pope John Paul II, in his Encyclical *Centesimus Annus,* spoke of avoiding a deep error: power of ownership "becomes illegitimate, however, when it is not utilized or when it serves to impede the work of others, in an effort to gain a profit which is not the result of the overall expansion of work and the wealth of society, but rather is the result of curbing them or of illicit exploitation, speculation, or the breaking of solidarity among working people. Ownership of this kind has no justification and represents an abuse in the sight of God and man."[15]

Confucius and Shinto call for sincerity to others to moderate the scheming of the calculating mind. Hinduism asks that householders act with a sense of duty. Buddhism teaches mindfulness, which builds awareness of others.

The Dalai Lama advises, "We find that the spiritual actions we undertake which are motivated not by narrow self-interest but out of our concern for others actually benefit ourselves." This he calls the capacity for "wise discernment." "Employing this faculty ... involves constantly checking our outlook and asking ourselves whether we are being broad-minded or narrow-minded."[16]

Moral capitalism presumes that people can subordinate themselves to higher ends, that they can find a calling or a vocation that energizes them with the conviction that their lives are in service of something hugely purposeful. This personal consciousness of being in an agency relationship vis-à-vis others bears directly on how we will use our power; if we are

AU: "others" correction not clear in MSP.

morally alive and aware of our status as an agent of higher purposes than our egocentric drives, we will tend not to abuse our position. Moral capitalism asks for a presence of mind, an orientation, a way of thinking. The failures of Enron, Arthur Andersen, and Wall Street were failures of individuals to remember that they needed to act, above all, from a sense of agency responsibility.

The common law of England and America has long provided a basis for moral capitalism. It is to be found in the fiduciary responsibilities imposed on agents, partners, trustees, and corporate directors and managers. The fiduciary must take into account—as if the other were an extension of the self—the interests of those who stand to benefit from the proposed action. The fiduciary must inwardly fuse consciousness of the other into consciousness of the self to then act from awareness of a wider circumference of needs, interests, and values.

The fiduciary ideal of agency responsibility does not give us an ethics of rules, like a set of precisely delineated instructions sent down by our superiors. We are not told by this office of self-restraint whether or not to drive an SUV, smoke tobacco or drink whiskey, divorce a spouse, or promote abortions. Fiduciary standards are not some ideal Kantian categorical imperative, a rule of mathematical certainty true for all times and in all places.

Fiduciary obligations flow from a principle within the moral sense that sensitizes us to the use of power when others come into view. Fiduciary thinking gives us a morality for decision making, an ethics of character, and wisdom. Fiduciary thinking makes us trustworthy, enhancing thereby the moral quality of that society in which we live and work.

CONCLUSION

Where the responsibilities of office are kept in mind, then a moral capitalism can supplant its more brutish cousin. Chapter 5 explores next how moral capitalism, as part of its work, proposes to overcome poverty.

CHAPTER 5

MORAL CAPITALISM AND POVERTY: MUST THE POOR BE WITH US ALWAYS?

When my pockets were full of money, all my friends were standing round;
Now when my pockets are all empty, not a friend on earth can be found.

—*"Rambler's Blues," American folk ballad*

Plate sin with gold, and the strong lance of justice hurtless breaks; Arm it in rags, a pigmy's straw does pierce it.

—*King Lear, act 4, scene 4, William Shakespeare*

MARKET CAPITALISM AND THE PRIVATE PROPERTY it uses to create an endless flow of wealth bring great benefits. But, within national economies and in the world at large, not everyone shares in this wealth. Consider the facts on global poverty even after a decade of dramatic economic growth, during which time private sector market activity created the controversial phenomenon known as "globalization."[1] Communism committed suicide, and free markets were finally recognized as the economic system that best produces goods and services.[2]

One billion people in the world are doing well, mostly in the European Union, the United States, Japan, Canada, Australia, Singapore, Hong Kong, Korea, and in a few other countries. The face value of stock market capitalization in these wealthy countries rose from roughly some $9 trillion in 1990 to some $35 trillion before the market downturn of 2000. These stock markets hold more than 95 percent of the world's equity capital. By the end of the decade, on the other hand, half of all our humans—three billion

61

people—live on less than three US dollars a day. Another two billion people are poor but live in countries that are making some economic progress.

The gap between the incomes of the poor and those living in wealthy countries is widening. In the European Union, agricultural subsidies pay farmers $2.25 a day for each cow they feed, nearly enough to fund daily subsistence for many of the three billion people who live in poverty. Only a small amount of the wealth available in prosperous nations finds its way to the less-developed countries. In fact, money is leaving poor countries every day to be invested safely and for good returns in the money centers of New York, London, Switzerland, and Singapore.

Having no money and possessing no property impose much hardship on people. Generally, over the span of nations, poor people want more money and property to call their own. They do not seek some communist utopia. Revolutionaries like Mao Tse-Tung, Che Guevara and Pol Pot never properly understood this human reality. Workers and peasants don't want to destroy capitalism; they want more of its wealth for themselves, instinctively sure that private property will better empower them. It has been rather the intellectuals, usually of middle-class origins, who seek to destroy markets and replace them with economic dictatorships managed by loyal members of the ruling party.

In the most ideal communist system ever attempted, Pol Pot abolished money when he ran Cambodia as a killing field. His cadres told people how many fish to exchange for a bushel of rice. His organization, Angka, provided Cambodians with daily meals, clothes, housing, tools, and everything they needed. Angka was everything; the people counted for nothing. They toiled as if they were machines with no right to complain, always fearful of execution at the hands of trained teenage killers for minor infractions of Angka's orders and regulations.

The wealth produced by capitalism is beneficial. Busy markets and bustling capitalism promote political and social progress. Markets insidiously undermine traditional societies and social practices; they subvert elites and promote the nouveau riche to social and political prominence. Markets give life to science and technology, which change lives. The steam engine, electricity, the car and the airplane, the cellular phone, fax, DVD, and more all arose out of capitalism, which works consistently to improve our lives. The dour economist Joseph Schumpeter called this process the "creative destruction" genius of capitalism. Adam Smith saw it as the origin of the "wealth of nations."

Consider the implication for cultural achievement of the historic fact that commercial cities have been centers of wealth as well as centers of sophistication, new thoughts, and cultural movements. Recall the contributions of Athens; the Florence of Leonardo and Michelangelo; Venice; Amsterdam; the London of Shakespeare, Newton, and Samuel Johnson; the Vienna of Mozart and Beethoven; and the Paris of Victor Hugo, Monet, Van Gogh, and Picasso. Commercial urban settings, rather than villages, tribal centers, and rustic backwaters, have led civilization forward.

Democracy arose in commercial cities; the freedoms offered by the cities put a check on the oppressions of feudal lords and kings. London took the lead in opposing royal power in seventeenth-century England, giving us the constitutional tradition. Cities created the middle class, the social foundation for democratic political institutions. From the beginning, markets, trade, and manufacturing went hand in hand with popular government, undermining aristocracy, feudalism, and monarchy.

More recently, in Asia, growing urban middle classes brought about the end of dictatorships in Thailand, South Korea, Republic of China/Taiwan, the Philippines, and Indonesia. The most successful and productive societies in Asia—Hong Kong and Singapore—are city-states.

POVERTY IN THE MIDST OF PLENTY

There are poor people who live in wealthy societies. Like the majority of those who live in poor countries, those who are poor in the midst of plenty are not effective participants in the market economy, often barely getting by on subsidies or living fitfully from hand to mouth, some in degrading conditions not respectful of human dignity. For many people of goodwill and compassion, this continuing existence of the poor refutes the possibility of ever having a moral capitalism.

Could it be different? Can the poor have any realistic hope for betterment of their conditions in a market economy?

From the perspective of human dignity, we must presume that the poor are not the intended victims of a harsh cosmic order from which there is no appeal to a higher conscience for a change in their circumstances. To so ignore the possibility of moving people out of poverty is more the cold view of brute capitalism with its preference for winners. Nor may we conclude that the poor must remain permanent victims of human social orders frozen in time. Capitalism at least brings change to human societies, constantly upsetting settled ways and opening doors for new ventures and new arrangements, even for the poor.

In its process of seeking customer satisfaction, capitalism always responds favorably to new inputs that will accomplish its goals. It welcomes goods and services that are of use to others. Providing such goods or services, then, is the road out of poverty for individuals as well as for nations. To be sure, a just society seeking to assist those living in poverty in "bettering their conditions" needs to honor the right of competition. The right to use one's wealth in order to gain more market power brings the greatest moral benefit to the poor, empowering them to make palpable their values and desires in the eyes of others. But the poor, you may say, have little or nothing to bring to the tables of market competition. Or, that what they bring to market often doesn't earn them enough to finance escape from their distressed condition. Both observations are true and explain why the poor tend to remain poor.

Capitalism, nevertheless, does offer a way out from the poverty trap. Unlike all bureaucratic and traditional peasant and feudal economic arrangements, capitalism brings time future into time present. The investment of capital converts a future sequence of market contingencies, one event following upon another, into present economic advantage. By using time in capitalist fashion, the poor can gentle their condition. Becoming prosperous, for nearly everyone but especially for the poor, never happens all at once; it is a step-by-step process.

The most dramatic capitalist use of time occurs in savings made possible by the invention of money. Money saved at compound rates of interest, over time, accumulates nicely. Consider that, during a forty-year working life, the annual investment of $2,000 at 6 percent, compounded annually, will accumulate to well over $1 million dollars.[3] Through systematic savings, a very ordinary worker could become a capitalist. Such annual contributions to a retirement account would be less than the yearly taxes placed by the United States Government on an income of $20,000 to support its public pension program for senior citizens.

High inflation, however, nullifies this ability of savings to accumulate into capital, which is why high inflation is the enemy of moral capitalism. Traditional pre-capitalist societies have rudimentary financial institutions and, as a result, high interest rates. Such societies offer their poor few means of financial advancement. Growing more sophisticated financial institutions and lowering interest rates are vital to overcoming systemic poverty.

The second way capitalism converts time into present value is through productivity enhancement. The learning of skills or gaining access to machines and better tools improves one's productivity. One person newly trained or equipped can do the work of several. The time formerly asked of many is compressed into the time spent by one, who therefore earns more than he or she did before taking over, so to speak, the earnings of others who are now no longer needed.

The third way capitalism moves time around is by its financial mechanisms. By having others entrust their capital to you, or by borrowing their funds, the time spent by them in accumulating wealth can be converted to one's advantage. One can use their financial strength to have a bigger impact in the markets.

The fourth way time can be converted to advantage in capitalism is through education. Well-chosen education sacrifices current time in exchange for enhanced market value in the future.

The policy conclusions for a moral capitalism from this analysis of time are straightforward. Societies should provide individuals, especially poor individuals, with institutions through which they can save at compound rates of interest, or for Muslims, at equivalent rates of shared returns on equity investment. Second, societies should have mechanisms of micro-credit and productivity enhancement for those who start life's competitive race with few material advantages. Third, societies need to place the social capital of education within reach of the poor.

In its approach to improving the position of the poor, moral capitalism asks a commitment from those who would better their circumstances. It asks that they, too, demonstrate the character that is rewarded with sustainable success. Moral capitalism presumes that all—rich and poor alike—possess a moral sense. Human dignity, moral capitalism believes, is common to both ends of the property spectrum. The office of the well-to-do is not to abuse their advantages and to contribute to the common good; the office of the poor is to turn time to their advantage that they might become more prosperous.

In its approach to ending poverty, moral capitalism stands on firm ground between the more extreme views of brute capitalism and socialism. Both brute capitalism and the various forms of socialism, in my judgment, deny significant human dignity to the poor. Brute capitalism looks on the poor as fate's carrion, little more than roadkill on the highways of trade and commerce. The corresponding extreme tendency of socialism is to look on the poor as being so without ability and opportunity, so hopeless in their poverty, that only life as permanent wards of the state will give them adequate comfort.

ENDING GLOBAL POVERTY IN AN ERA OF GLOBALIZATION

Governments alone cannot put an end to global poverty. Poor, developing, and emerging-market nations will not achieve sufficient economic development through government-funded official development assistance.[4] Much has been spent by governments and private donors during the past forty years seeking economic development in poor countries. There is little to show for all the money spent. Robust economic development has not become a general phenomenon around the world. Exceptions—in South Korea, Taiwan, Chile, Singapore, and Malaysia—are few and essentially used the private sector, capitalism, to improve the living standards of their peoples.

Obtaining new wealth requires investment of capital in order to expand market opportunities. There is no other way. Genuine wealth, the kind that funds sustained economic development, has its roots in private property. Government wealth is parasitic; it is taken from private wealth through taxation. And, further, where government seeks to acquire wealth by entering into business, the iron laws of bureaucracy take over and the efforts rarely are very profitable. But where private investment goes to work, real economic growth happens. When a country's growth rate improves, the standard of living for its people rises as well. It is hard to imagine how poverty could be abolished by any other means than by a program of private-sector investment. Government redistribution of wealth from rich to poor would subsidize the poor, yes, but would not create the necessary motors for self-perpetuating economic growth of any consequence. The poor would still be with us as wards of the state.

The money to fund the necessary private sector investment in poor and developing countries is readily at hand, that is, in private hands. The challenge is to move those funds into productive investment in poor, developing, and emerging-market nations. The great preponderance of humanity's wealth resides within the private sector. Private investment crossing national borders runs on average from $250 to $300 billion a year, five to six times as much as official transfers to poor and developing countries, which run about $50 billion annually. In 1999, before the global economic downturn, $865 billion of foreign direct investment moved between countries of the world. Seventy percent of this landed in the United States and the countries of the European Union. All of the other countries, which hold 90 percent of the world's population, received the other 30 percent, or $250 billion. Africa got practically nothing. And, total levels of world trade run about $7 to $8 trillion annually, leaving a net value added to world prosperity of some $300 billion.

Private trade can transfer significant wealth to poor countries. Farmers and workers in such countries have as much right to compete in world markets as do those producing similar goods and services in wealthy countries. The subsidies and other political barriers to trade imposed by wealthy countries to provide livings to their citizens—whose goods and services come with high costs of production—undercut the right of competition justly held by all the world's producers.

It is incumbent that wealthy nations conduct their financial affairs so that sums are transferred to poor, developing, and emerging-market countries without contributing to financial crises such as those that occurred starting in 1997 in Thailand, Malaysia, Indonesia, South Korea, and Russia and later in Argentina, with Brazil coming in for a close call in 2002. The rules for international lending need to be examined, especially the practice of withdrawing funds at short notice. At the same time, lending to poor and developing countries should be prudent and responsible, with proper monitoring of the use of the funds provided. It is not reasonable that the flows of foreign capital in and out of these nations should be conducted in a reckless manner that constantly puts these nations' economies at risk. Terms of these loans need to be examined, especially as to the rapidity with which capital can flow in and out of these countries, even though the appropriate terms may result in a somewhat higher cost of capital.

Only the global private investment community controlling most of humankind's liquid wealth—nearly $79 trillion in all the financial markets—has the means to significantly correct the dysfunction and inequity of global poverty. But do these investors have the will to act? Can they be counted on to build moral capitalism on a global scale?

WHY PRIVATE INVESTORS SHOULD CARE

Several considerations dictate that the present self-interest of wealthy nations, corporations, and individual investors, considered upon the whole, requires an effort to promote private-sector economic growth in poor nations. First, our twenty-first century world is interdependent. An action in one country has consequences in many other places. The resources needed by all of us—fish from the seas, lumber from the forests, oil from the ground—will depend on the production and consumption decisions taken by people throughout the entire world. The diseases to which we will be exposed, like HIV/AIDS and SARS, can spring from any country where public health is ignored and from there can easily find carriers to spread elsewhere. The repercussions of poverty will not be confined to the poor alone.

Second, poor economies will not develop strong, self-assured middle classes; therefore, such societies will find it hard to sustain democracy. They will more likely succumb to anarchy or resort to the terrorism of nuclear weapons and of biological and chemical agents, disrupting and impairing the lives of neighbors near and far.

Third, rising living standards and the education of women will make it easier to restrain population. Within this current century, humanity will double, with the increase in population occurring in the developing nations. It is imperative that we take care of water, land, and atmospheric resources before they are degraded beyond repair owing to use by growing populations in poor nations.

Fourth, currently wealthy, advanced, postindustrial nations need new opportunities for wealth creation. They face changing demographics. Their populations are aging and will be declining in absolute numbers. Aging populations will increase the costs of supporting those no longer working who are in retirement and who have growing health care expenses. Money paid by governments to subsidize those in retirement and for retiree health care or by companies into pension and health plans is not available for other purposes such as public works, education, national defense, wages, dividends, research and development, productivity enhancement, or working capital reserves. Aging and declining populations will not have sufficient consumers to sustain growing economic demand or to invest in the financial markets. Neither will such now wealthy economies have enough workers to earn the additional revenue necessary to finance the retirement and the health care needs of their senior citizens.

Within twenty years, publicly funded retirement and health care subsidies will be hard to finance. Private-sector pension plans, corporate and union, are already coming under stress as the number of retired workers increases. Just in two years from 2000, the projected pension obligations of American corporations rose 49 percent, far more than the increase in their earnings! The Pension Benefits Guaranty Corporation reported that 270 U.S. companies had reported deficits of more than $50 million each in their pension plans. As of early 2003, the Corporation had assets of $25 billion against liabilities of $35 billion, whereas the one hundred largest U.S. pension plans had fallen from a surplus of $183 billion in 2000 to a deficit of $157 billion, a swing to the negative of $340 billion.[5]

In every country, life expectancies are rising. People are living longer. By 2050, 35 percent of the populations of Spain, Japan, and Italy will be older than sixty-four years.

The number of younger people will drop. It is estimated that the working-age population of Japan will drop by 45 percent by 2050. Germany will lose 35 percent of its working-age population by that year. By 2050, Japan will have 1.1 persons aged twenty to sixty years for every person older than sixty-four years. Germany will have 1.5 persons, France 1.7, Italy 1.2, and Spain 1.1 Countries with more open immigration policies will do a little better. In the United States, by 2050 there will be 2.3 persons aged twenty to sixty years for each person older than sixty-four years, and in Canada the number will be 2 persons.

Immigration of workers from poor nations into wealthy societies would offset the coming population decline in those prosperous nations. Data from the U.S. census of 2000, when analyzed by the Center for Labor Market Studies of Northeastern University in Boston, revealed that during the preceding decade, recent immigrants were critical to American economic growth. In other words, the United States had not produced sufficient native-born workers to boost the economy. Immigrants accounted for all the growth among workers under the age of thirty-five. But such immigration is not popular with recipient countries. Pym Fortune was assassinated in The Netherlands for openly expressing concern over the introduction of Muslim values into his society through immigration. Only by growing the economies of what are now poor nations will pressure for immigration into havens of wealth be relieved.

Such investment in the growth of the poor but populous nations would earn returns for wealthy countries. These returns would be sufficient to pay for increasing costs due to aging and declining populations. Today's poor countries have the expanding populations to fuel rapid economic growth. But the system of investment by wealthy nations in economic growth in poor countries must be fair and just to be politically sustainable. Poor nations will not tolerate being exploited by the few and the rich.

CREATING SOCIAL CAPITAL

In Chapter 1, I argued that a society's social capital was a necessary capital input for a successful business. It follows, therefore, that nations with richer and more abundant social capital will experience more bountiful wealth creation from their private sectors.

Although business has a role to play in sustaining the vitality of a nation's social capital, government has the principal responsibility for creating this necessary input for growth. Moral capitalism cannot be expected to flourish wherever government is lawless or plays the thief with its people's money. A precondition for moral capitalism is government by principle seeking to implement reasonable norms of social justice. Overcoming poverty through private investment begins with responsible government.

Public authority is needed for the production and protection of social capital and social capital is needed for economic growth. For example, property rights—the social right to wealth—are created by governments and are protected by governments. Although government is not, and cannot be, the engine of wealth creation, for that is the role of private capital, government is nonetheless needed to give people the tools with which they can own and exploit property in market activity.

For example, Hernando de Soto writes that robust economic growth can only start with possession of legal title to property. Property rights create the basis of capital, even for the poor. De Soto wants governments, for example, in countries like Mexico and Egypt to introduce systems for the recording of ownership titles to slums and hovels. That step by government, he argues, would jump-start capitalism for the poor people who own those marginal dwellings.

Some of the important conditions of social capital necessary for successful development are:

1. *Political stability*. An environment with a high degree of personal safety is a necessity. Arbitrary rule must give way to accountable government.

2. *Government officials not tainted by corruption*. Government officials should also be careful to remain independent from commercial interests. Crony capitalism is anathema to the development of a prosperous economy.

3. *A basic infrastructure that will satisfy the needs of business.* This includes adequate transportation, electricity, communications, and banking systems.

4. *A well-functioning civil society.* Rule of law must prevail. Contracts must be fairly enforced.

5. *A certain level of education.* Eventually, it will be critical to have broad and deep educational achievement, particularly for women, for continuation of progress in economic growth.

As these elements are put into place, the opportunities for private business to create new wealth become more and more appealing. There is a virtuous circle between social capital and ending poverty. Improvement in the one makes it easier to achieve the other. For a developing country to transform itself into a prosperous nation is anything but a simple task. The process requires time, understanding, and unusual effort. Unless and until certain conditions—adequate social capital—exist, substantial, self-sustaining economic growth will not be achieved. Economic growth is not found in nature's order; it did not happen in the Garden of Eden. The creation of wealth and its subsequent distribution result from human effort. Culture and society are necessary foundations for economic prosperity.

CAUX ROUND TABLE PRINCIPLES FOR GOVERNMENTS

The Caux Round Table believes that although private business can improve standards of living through the creation of wealth, business only responds to opportunities for profitable exchange. The investment of capital waits on favorable conditions; such investment is reactive and selective, always searching for well-founded expectations of return as well as for security that those expectations of making a profit will come to fruition. Government must provide for sustained wealth creation through laws, enhancing social capital, and improving requisite physical infrastructures.

Bad government is a shortcut to endemic poverty. Four decades of venal and corrupt rule by military and civilian elites over Nigeria have little economic growth to show for the $259 billion in oil revenues the country has earned since 1960. From 1975 to 2000, Nigerians saw their real incomes decline 1.5 percent per year while a wealthy elite prospered. In Zambia, actual annual per capita income declined from 1960 to 1993, never growing higher than $500. But, if all the aid given to Zambia had been invested, and all the investment had gone into modest growth, by 1993 Zambians would have enjoyed annual per capita incomes of $20,500 in 1985 dollars.[6]

The Caux Round Table, therefore, recommends to governments that they live by the following principles.

Fundamental Principal:

Public power is held in trust for the community.

General Principles:

1. *Discourse ethics should guide application of public power.*
2. *The civic order shall serve all those who accept the responsibilities of citizenship.*
3. *Public servants shall refrain from abuse of office and corruption and shall demonstrate high levels of personal integrity.*
4. *Security of persons, individual liberty, and ownership of property are the foundation for individual justice.*
5. *Justice shall be provided.*
6. *General welfare contemplates improving the well-being of individual citizens.*
7. *Transparency of government ensures accountability.*
8. *Global cooperation advances national welfare.*

The full text of the principles for governments can be found in Annex II.

IMPLEMENTING PRINCIPLES FOR GOVERNMENT: THE TWELVE CORE BEST-PRACTICE STANDARDS

After the collapse of currencies for Thailand and Indonesia and financial crises in Malaysia and South Korea in 1997 and 1998, experts in international financial institutions cooperated in recommending twelve core best-practice standards by which countries could hope to avoid, or at least to minimize the negative impact of, future financial crises. Cooperating in the creation of these best practices were the World Bank, the International Monetary Fund, and the Bank for International Settlements, assisted by the

Organisation for Economic Co-operation and Development, the G-20 group of governments, the International Federation of Accountants, the International Accounting Standards Committee, the Financial Action Task Force on Money Laundering, the Basel Committee on Banking Supervision, the International Organization of Securities Commissions, and the International Association of Insurance Supervisors.

Once a market is sound and attractive for financial transactions, it has become healthy for private-sector investment. So, the application by governments of the twelve core best-practice standards would promote economic growth as well as ward off financial turmoil. With the twelve core best-practice standards in place, domestic capital would not leave, foreign capital would come, and both domestic and foreign capital would earn reliable returns. Growth would occur.

The following areas of financial and entrepreneurial activity are covered by these best-practice standards:

- Monetary and financial policy transparency
- Fiscal policy transparency
- Data dissemination
- Accounting for private firms
- Corporate governance
- Insolvency and reorganization of companies to minimize investor losses
- Bank payments and settlements
- Money laundering
- Banking supervision
- Securities regulation
- Insurance company supervision

Disclosure of the truth and accountable governance lie at the center of all these proposed best-practice standards. These two norms promote reliance and reduce risk.

When private capital and public power act responsibly in concert under the principles advocated by the Caux Round Table, the result is economic growth under conditions of just distribution of wealth, as illustrated in Figure 5.1:

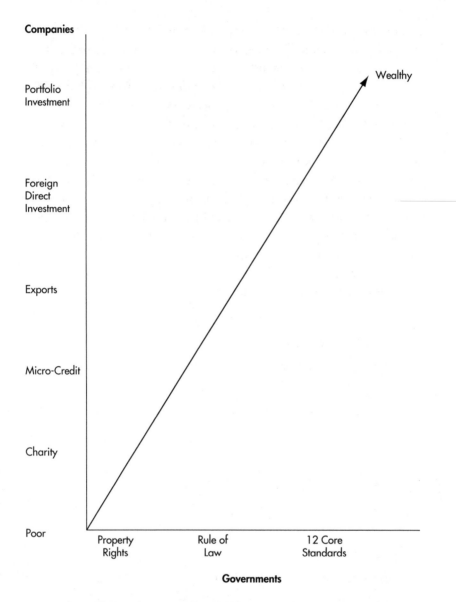

CONCERNS ABOUT GLOBALIZATION

Both the wealthy and the poor nations have concerns about globalization. The former fear unfair competition from poor countries owing to the indiscriminate depletion of resources, lack of enforceable environmental regulations, and substandard wages, all of which tend to reduce product costs and eventually eliminate jobs in the richer countries.

Malaysia's prime minister, Mohammad Mahatir, speaking for poorer countries, sees globalization benefiting the richer nations. He argues that the wealthy nations have created the World Trade Organization as their club to see that rules would be written and enforced to keep the poorer countries in their place. He doubts the sincerity of the wealthy nations when they profess to help their needy cousins while at the same time they deny such relatives access to wealthy markets for agricultural and textile products. Many poor but traditional societies are also afraid that their embrace of globalization will doom their traditions and cultural values as foreign commercial interests invade their countries.

Despite these concerns, investment from the private sector as part of globalization is the only way that poor nations are going to improve their living standards. For some it may not be an easy decision whether or not to abandon old ways in exchange for the promises and risks of globalization, but perpetuating the status quo is not desirable either.

The Caux Round Table promotes its Principles for Business to give business leaders around the world sensible rules for ethical behavior and good corporate citizenship. Global use of the principles promotes trust among businesses in different countries, encouraging the flow of capital and the exchange of technology around the world. The Caux Round Table Principles, if followed, will prevent many of the negative outcomes of globalization and so will lead to more equitable development among all of the world's people.

CONCLUSION

Moral capitalism asserts that ending global poverty is a joint venture between responsible governments and ethical businesses. The next chapter begins to explain how the Caux Round Table Principles for Business provide guidelines for moral capitalism.

CHAPTER 6

THE CAUX ROUND TABLE: ADVOCATE FOR MORAL CAPITALISM

Give just weight and full measure.
— *The Holy Koran, Surah Cattle, 6:149*

What Heaven has conferred is called the Nature;
an accordance with this Nature is called the path of Duty;
the regulation of this path is called Instruction.
— *The Doctrine of the Mean, Chap. 1*

MORAL CAPITALISM WILL NOT HAPPEN by the grace of God. Responsibility for the good rests on our shoulders.

Ideals and values, if they are important enough, can effect social action. Mind imposes itself on the world through will. As pointed out in Chapter 2 on Chinese, Japanese, and Mexican national capitalisms, some ideals or principles are so important to different cultures that they function like the axle around which all the spokes of economic action turn. Since moral capitalism cannot arise of its own will, people must be encouraged to adopt its axial principles and use them to turn the wheels of enterprise. Committing moral capitalism requires acts of culture. With this understanding, the Caux Round Table Principles for Business were published in 1994 to improve global business culture.

The Caux Round Table first gathered in 1986. That year, Frederick Philips, then head of The Philips Company, the firm founded by his family in The Netherlands making light bulbs and consumer electronics, invited Japanese, European, and American colleagues to confront the divisive xenophobias then rampant in the automotive and consumer electronic industries. It was the time of Japanese manufacturing triumphs. Philips sought through dialogue to temper the angry passions seeking to keep Japanese companies out of Europe and America and European and American companies out of Japan. Philips was joined in this effort by Olivier Giscard d'Estaing, vice-chairman of Insead, the prestigious business school in France.

Philips was idealistic but not naïve in this attempt at reconciliation. He believed that, in general, people could do the right thing when they thought about their true circumstances, that they could find within themselves "self-interest considered upon the whole," and that they could dedicate more of their commercial efforts to creating a greater good. After World War II, Philips had participated in many sessions in Caux—a little hamlet in the Swiss Alps—seeking reconciliation among French and Germans to prevent a future war between those two hereditary enemies. From those sessions came the trust and confidence to establish the European Coal and Steel Community. From that small success then came the Common Market, and finally the European Union.[1] So far, this very successful effort at regional integration has prevented repetition of general warfare in Europe.

At that first meeting of what was to become the Caux Round Table, Philips' guests conceded that xenophobia, with its appeals to prejudice, ugly emotions, and racism, was no basis for global business. If the Japanese made better products for a lower price than did the Europeans and Americans, they should reap the reward of that commercial success. Conversely, European and American companies should not be excluded by acts of politics from selling in Japan's domestic markets. Business should just be business, the group concluded, and to the winner on the merits of fair competition should justly go the spoils.

Participants found the collegiality of Caux contagious and returned once a year to reaffirm their sensibility about the international professionalism of business. Leadership of the group then shifted to Ryuzaburo Kaku, chairman of Canon, Inc. As a young boy, Kaku had survived the American nuclear destruction of Hiroshima, his home city. Ever after, he felt a special calling to make a difference for socially responsible undertakings. He was independently minded and something of an outsider during his career as a salaryman for Canon. And so, somewhat surprisingly for many Japanese and even himself, he had been named chairman and chief executive officer of the company. Kaku assumed that leadership position just when Canon's fortunes had turned sour.

To other members of the Caux Round Table network, Kaku claimed that he had turned Canon's prospects around and had built its sales up nicely by following a strategic vision he called *Kyosei*. Kaku took as his guide for action the Japanese virtue *Kyosei* instead of the more common Japanese goal of *ninjo*. Roughly translated, *Kyosei* means "living and working together for the common good." It is a vision of moral capitalism, a form of stewardship sensitivity, derived from Japanese cultural insights.

In one sense *Kyosei* is very Buddhist. It presumes that living beings are interdependent; that no self can exist totally cut off from other selves; that our actions have consequences that drag us, willingly or unwillingly, into the lives of others; and that the actions of others will similarly penetrate our experience of the world. *Kyosei* expressly rejects the factual basis for Herbert Spencer's theory of Social Darwinism which is used to justify brute capitalism.

In 1991, Kaku came to Minnesota to present his approach to business management using the principle of *Kyosei*. American business leaders there were arguing about their own American analogue to *Kyosei*. Some called it "business ethics," others called it "stakeholder theory," and still others spoke of "sustainability."

Kaku met with a warm reception from some Minneapolis business leaders, like Chuck Denny, chief executive officer of ADC Telecommunications, and Robert MacGregor, president of the Minnesota Center for Corporate Responsibility. Denny came from the old-family Minneapolis business tradition of good corporate citizenship, and MacGregor's Center had been founded to sustain that tradition. Minneapolis family companies like Dayton's, a department store company, started the 5 percent charitable contributions club. They supported the arts, the Citizen's League, and innovative local government reforms.

The Minnesota Center for Corporate Responsibility was then writing down guidelines for business managers reflecting the stakeholder concept of business ethics. Invited to Caux, Switzerland, for the 1992 global dialogue of the Caux Round Table, Denny and MacGregor brought with them these proposed Minnesota principles for ethical and socially responsible business. They challenged members of that year's Round Table to write global guidelines for companies.

Though initially skeptical of the American legalistic fixation that rules of conduct be written down, Kaku was up to the challenge of drafting guidelines for global business. And, several Europeans present supported the American initiative, most especially Jean-Loup Dherse, former chairman of the English Channel tunnel project—the "chunnel"—which would use modern construction technology to connect the United Kingdom directly to the continent of Europe for the first time in history.

Devout Catholics, Dherse and his friends were inspired by the recent encyclical of Pope John Paul II, titled *Centisimus Annus*, a powerful teaching of that Church coming to terms with capitalism after the collapse of both the Soviet Empire and the Soviet Union itself. *Centisimus Annus* contained a mixed message: capitalism could be just and equitable as long as it did not derogate from principles of human dignity. From the Pope's perspective, treating people as moral objects and not as insensible equivalents to machines was necessary if capitalism were ever to be morally acceptable.

The Caux Round Table participants set about blending the Minnesota principles of stewardship with regard to stakeholder concerns with Kaku's vision of *Kyosei* and, third, with the Pope's principle of human dignity. America, Japan, and Europe each contributed a moral vision to the final statement of global business principles. What resulted was historic—the first global code of conduct for capitalists written by senior capitalists from different moral traditions.

The Caux Round Table Principles—now most frequently called the CRT Principles—contain an introduction, a preamble, seven General Principles, and six sets of stakeholder principles, which are guidelines for a company's responsibility toward its customers, employees, owners and investors, suppliers, competitors, and communities.

THE PREAMBLE

The Preamble to the CRT Principles for Business states, "Law and market forces are necessary but insufficient guides for conduct." And "… we affirm the necessity for moral values in business decision-making."

The CRT Principles thus bluntly assert that the social philosophy of Social Darwinism provides a misleading guide to capitalism. The CRT Principles are a call to stewardship in business, finance, and commerce. They recognize the intangible moral responsibilities that come with possessing economic power. They are a guide for the implementation of moral capitalism. The full text of the CRT principle can be found in Appendix I.

THE GENERAL PRINCIPLES

The Seven General Principles:

1. *The responsibilities of businesses: beyond shareholders toward stakeholders.*

2. *The economic and social impact of business: toward innovation, justice, and world community.*

3. *Business behavior: beyond the letter of law toward a spirit of trust.*

4. *Respect for rules.*

5. *Support for multilateral trade.*

6. *Respect for the environment.*

7. *Avoidance of illicit operations.*

By following these Principles, a business can establish its credentials as a socially responsible enterprise.

THE STAKEHOLDER ETHIC

The CRT Principles forthrightly embrace the stakeholder ethic, finding it compatible with both *Kyosei* and human dignity. The Preamble to the Principles states that "… respect for the dignity and interests of stakeholders [is] fundamental." Most of the seven General Principles for business provide guidance for consideration of stakeholder interests.

General Principle No. 1 makes the case for stakeholder sensitivity: "Businesses have a role to play in improving the lives of all their customers, employees and shareholders by sharing with them the wealth they have created. Suppliers and competitors as well should expect businesses to honor their obligations in a spirit of honesty and fairness. As responsible citizens of the local, national, regional and global communities in which they operate, businesses share a part in shaping the future of those communities."

In specific implementation of the general injunction contained in General Principle No. 1, the entire contents of Section 3 of the CRT Principles for Business is devoted to the six stakeholder groups—customers, employees, owners and investors, suppliers, competitors, and communities. Furthermore, General Principle No. 2 focuses multinational corporations on the obligation to consider the needs of stakeholders in poor and developing countries.

And, General Principle No. 6 holds that the environment is really a stakeholder as well so that responsible businesses need to promote sustainable development and prevent the wasteful use of natural resources. The command of General Principle No. 2 that businesses must innovate in technology and production methods as part of their social responsibility guides business to increasingly sustainable use of the world's natural environment.

Pollution of the environment and heedless use of its resources were largely created by technology, production methods, and economic growth; these trends can be reversed in time by the very same forces that created them.

General Principle No. 3 ties it all together: businesses must conduct themselves with sincerity, candor, truthfulness, and transparency. And they must keep their promises. Enron failed to do this; so did the tobacco companies in their advertising about the dangers of nicotine addiction, Arthur Andersen in certain of its audits, and Wall Street investment firms in the advice provided to many of their trusted clients.

GENERAL PRINCIPLE NO. 1

The Responsibilities of Businesses: Beyond Shareholders toward Stakeholders

The value of a business to society is the wealth and employment it creates and the marketable products and services it provides to consumers at a reasonable price commensurate with quality. To create such value, a business must maintain its own economic health and viability, but survival is not a sufficient goal.

Businesses have a role to play in improving the lives of all their customers, employees, and shareholders by sharing with them the wealth they have created. Suppliers and competitors as well should expect businesses to honor their obligations in a spirit of honesty and fairness. As responsible citizens of the local, national, regional, and global communities in which they operate, businesses share a part in shaping the future of those communities.

This General Principle defines the social office of private enterprise. It is to create wealth and employment and to produce products and services at a reasonable price commensurate with quality. All business activity, and all business judgments, must keep this role in mind. To deviate from the role is to lose the right way of doing business. From the perspective of the CRT Principles, a business, therefore, is a social status with duties and responsibilities to the common good. It does more than make money for its owners and investors. This logic would apply as well to an individual who dedicates his or her capital to profitable enterprise. The CRT Principles apply to "business" not just to corporations.

General Principle No. 1 creates a duty to reduce poverty by increasing wealth and employment where conditions permit. The business approach to poverty reduction is doing more business. Subsidy of the poor and the funding of social capital expenditures are primarily the responsibility of government and public charities to which businesses contribute through taxes and charitable contributions. General Principle No. 1 also affirms that a business must maintain its own economic health and viability—business is not to be subsidized, but must pay its own way—in order to create more and more wealth for society.

GENERAL PRINCIPLE NO. 2

The Economic and Social Impact of Business: Toward Innovation, Justice, and World Community

Businesses established in foreign countries to develop, produce, or sell should also contribute to the social advancement of those countries by creating productive employment and helping to raise the purchasing power of their citizens. Businesses also should contribute to human rights, education, welfare, and vitalization of the countries in which they operate.

Businesses should contribute to economic and social development not only in the countries in which they operate, but also in the world community at large, through effective and prudent use of resources, free and fair competition, and emphasis upon innovation in technology, production methods, marketing, and communications.

The responsibility of business to build better lives for people throughout the global community is reinforced in General Principle No. 2, which says that businesses should "contribute to the economic and social development ... in the world community at large."

The CRT Principles acknowledge the power of multinational corporations to improve conditions in countries where they do business, calling on such companies to "contribute to the social advancement of such countries by creating productive employment and helping to raise the purchasing power of their citizens." Businesses, the CRT Principles assert, should also contribute to human rights, education, welfare, and vitalization of the countries in which they operate.

GENERAL PRINCIPLE NO. 3

Business Behavior: Beyond the Letter of Law toward a Spirit of Trust

While accepting the legitimacy of trade secrets, businesses should recognize that sincerity, candor, truthfulness, the keeping of promises, and transparency contribute not only to their own credibility and stability but also to the smoothness and efficiency of business transactions, particularly on the international level.

This General Principle calls for acting according to the standards of trust that moral capitalism requires and rewards. This General Principle ties the CRT Principles for Business to the foundations of moral capitalism. By acting with "sincerity, candor, truthfulness, and transparency" and by the "keeping of promises," businesses build social capital necessary for robust and sustainable economic growth. General Principle No. 3 calls for character in decision making, not just grudging compliance with the least requirements set by local laws and regulations.

GENERAL PRINCIPLE NO. 4

Respect for Rules

To avoid trade frictions and to promote freer trade, equal conditions for competition, and fair and equitable treatment for all participants, businesses should respect international and domestic rules. In addition, they should recognize that some behavior, although legal, may still have adverse consequences.

This General Principle on respect for rules provided another foundation for moral capitalism. Not every person in business likes to run the risk of failure. Those who fear genuine free markets are often disposed to go beyond the bounds of legitimate market competition to avail themselves of some external force or power with which to get their way with customers, workers, investors, or suppliers. Legal privileges (monopolies, licenses, rights to trade) can, and corruption and insider relationships do, interfere with ordinary market forces to turn them against ethical outcomes. By insisting on respect for rules, General Principle No. 4 would keep all those who seek to profit from market activity within the bounds of legitimate competition.

This self-restraint is most important for moral capitalism, for those without money or access to political power have little by which they can protect themselves from imperious, overbearing players. Power abuse converts moral capitalism into brute capitalism.

Finally, General Principle No. 4 points to a range of business decisions that, although strictly legal, are immoral or unfair. In the spirit of *Kyosei* and with respect for human dignity, this General Principle demands that businesses refrain from making such decisions.

GENERAL PRINCIPLE NO. 5

Support for Multilateral Trade

Businesses should support the multilateral trade systems of the GATT/World Trade Organization and similar international agreements. They should cooperate in efforts to promote the progressive and judicious liberalization of trade and to relax those domestic measures that unreasonably hinder global commerce, while giving due respect to national policy objectives.

This General Principle adds its voice to the other parts of the CRT Principles for Business that encourage investment and trade with poor, developing, and emerging-market nations. By implication, the Principle calls on domestic firms to broaden the scope of their purchases and sales to embrace a global business community.

Underlying this opposition to regulation of trade for reasons of political favoritism we can find a moral principle arising from the very premises of moral capitalism. Free access to business opportunity provides an economy with the freedom of action needed for enjoyment of a personal claim to enhance the value of one's property. The moral imperative that allows people expression of their personhood through the exercise of dominion over property goes beyond simple ownership to encompass active use of property in order to realize its potential.

Ownership without a chance to use one's property in commerce and enterprise would be a very limited kind of dominion, restricting development of one's potential to whatever allotment of wealth happened to fall one's way. The poor would stay poor and the rich, rich. No one could "better their condition"; incentives would evaporate and economies would stagnate. The full measure of human dignity would never be reached.

To avoid such immobility of personal destiny, owners need to compete in the marketplace. Restraints on trade imposed by legal rules or social customs truncate our freely chosen moral possibilities. General Principle No. 5

affirms this right of competition at the level of the global economy, giving particular deference to the moral claims of poor and developing nations to gain wealth by which to enhance the dignity and moral choices of their peoples in that they should be able to sell and trade what they own with all the countries in the world. The poor should not be denied use of rights that the rich so easily exploit for their economic benefit. Subsidies for the farmers of Europe, Japan and the United States that deny markets to poor farmers in developing nations are hard to square with the requirements of a moral capitalism.

GENERAL PRINCIPLE NO. 6

Respect for the Environment

A business should protect and, where possible, improve the environment, promote sustainable development, and prevent the wasteful use of natural resources.

This General Principle states in comprehensive fashion the obligations of a business to be mindful of the needs of our global environment. A business should, under this General Principle, protect and, where possible, improve the environment, promote sustainable development, and prevent the wasteful use of natural resources.

GENERAL PRINCIPLE NO. 7

Avoidance of Illicit Operations

A business should not participate in or condone bribery, money laundering, or other corrupt practices: indeed, it should seek cooperation with others to eliminate them. It should not trade in arms or other materials used for terrorist activities, drug traffic, or other organized crime.

This final General Principle reinforces the requirement of moral capitalism that businesses must avoid illicit and corrupt transactions in order to sustain the cultural framework supporting moral capitalism. This rejection of illicit means is one important way in which companies and individuals can contribute to the formation and growth of constructive social capital.

FROM ASPIRATION TO ACTION

Giving people mental constructs like the CRT Principles for Business to apply in their calculations of how best to gain business advantage will impact their behavior. The teaching of norms, although it is no guarantee that students will apply their lessons well, nonetheless is where we must start in building a moral community.

Great teachers like Jesus Christ, Confucius, and the Gautama Buddha gave us stories and principles by which we could, in their minds, so order our daily lives that we would become more worthy and find greater happiness. The end of their teachings was that we would apply in our own lives—by means of our own mental and emotional abilities—ideas and understandings that we have learned from them.

Such idealists and teachers of morality, however, are often dismissed by self-proclaimed realists or "practical people" as being excessively naïve in that their aspirations for humanity go beyond the apparent scope of the possible. We may note that sin is still with us, even among his followers, though Jesus preached against it.

Nowhere is this skepticism more vibrant than in business. Ideals and morality are often spoken of as virtual antimatter to the behaviors allegedly needed to maximize profits. Allegedly, brute capitalism is the way to go in business, so that any admonitions contrary to its teachings are dismissed as drivel. So the CRT has a problem: publishing principles does little to get them implemented.

The CRT understands that morality works in the business corporation through hierarchy, moving from vague but lofty ideals down through principles and standards, to objectives, and then to action. Consider Figure 6.1 illustrating the flow of ideals into accomplishments.

Figure 6.1 represents the value-action system of moral capitalism. It stands in contrast to the Enron Chart of Chapter 3 (Figure 3.1), which illustrates the more brutish version of market capitalism.

At the highest level of the moral capitalism chart (Figure 6.1), directing our principles, our standards, our management benchmarks, and our decisions we find our best ideals, our highest aspirations, and our vision of the common good. Setting these values and ideals in place for a corporation or a business is the responsibility of its owners, its board of directors, and its top managers.

Moral Capitalism

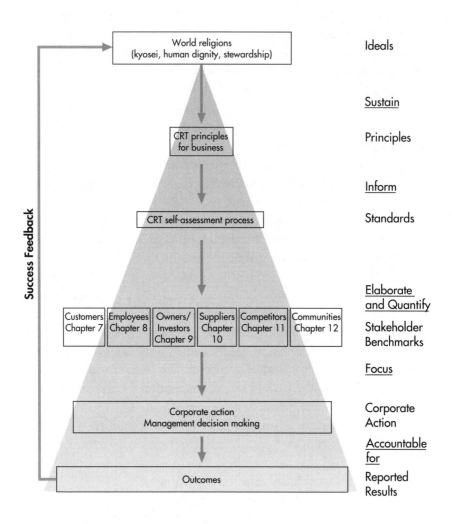

These governing ideals could be taken from religion, but they don't have to be found only there. People responsible for an enterprise could agree among themselves on a common goal, arriving at that end from different religious starting points. In just such a fashion did the CRT Principles for Business themselves arise from a blending of Roman Catholic teachings and American Protestant and secular traditions of stewardship with Japanese Buddhist and Shinto perspectives.

At the next level below our ideals, the socially responsible business should place a set of principles, like the CRT Principles for Business, or the nine principles of the United Nations' Global Compact.

Flowing down toward more objectivity and specificity, we next find standards and guidelines such as the self-assessment and implementation management process invented by the CRT and called "ARCTURUS."

At the level of stakeholder engagement, a company seeking to meet its proper responsibilities under a moral capitalism would apply to its decision making the considerations listed for each of the six stakeholder groups in Section 3 of the CRT Principles for Business. These specific stakeholder considerations are discussed in Chapters 7 through 12.

Then we come down to the most challenging level of all: the level of walking-the-talk—actual rubber-meets-the-road, shoulder-to-the-wheel, management performance. At this level, the devil is truly in the details. Judgment and intellectual effort are required to square-up the details with the company's standards, principles, and ideals.

Below the action level we find outcomes, which can be measured to see how much progress toward our goals and ideals we are making. In a successful company, its accomplishments will reflect its ideals.

THE CRT'S SELF-ASSESSMENT AND IMPROVEMENT PROCESS

Principles do not self-execute. Leaders must invoke them to set goals for managers, and managers, in turn, must be aware of the deeper purposes behind the tasks set before them and their subordinates. The Caux Round Table has, therefore, borrowed a page from business: management by objective. The CRT Principles for Business have been converted into management objectives suitable for executives in companies large and small. Corporate boards of directors, chief executive officers, and line managers all can now more easily and reliably become successful stewards of sustainable business value. Results of operations can be monitored against strategic and tactical risk profiles and for positive or negative contributions to various value drivers in the zones of capital factors, conversion of capital into product or services, the quality and price point of product and services, and customer satisfaction and loyalty.

Where risks or negative detractions from value are detected, changes can be made to improve enterprise results, lower risks, and enhance overall value. Improvement flows from present results first through assessment,

Assessment Framework—Criteria Matrix

Category	1. Fundamental Duties	2. Customers	3. Employees	4. Owners/ Investors	5. Suppliers/ Partners	6. Competitors	7. Communities
1. Responsibilities of Business	Criterion 1.1	Criterion 1.2	Criterion 1.3	Criterion 1.4	Criterion 1.5	Criterion 1.6	Criterion 1.7
2. Economic and Social Impact of Business	Criterion 2.1	Criterion 2.2	Criterion 2.3	Criterion 2.4	Criterion 2.5	Criterion 2.6	Criterion 2.7
3. Business Behavior	Criterion 3.1	Criterion 3.2	Criterion 3.3	Criterion 3.4	Criterion 3.5	Criterion 3.6	Criterion 3.7
4. Respect for Rules	Criterion 4.1	Criterion 4.2	Criterion 4.3	Criterion 4.4	Criterion 4.5	Criterion 4.6	Criterion 4.7
5. Support for Multilateral Trade	Criterion 5.1	Criterion 5.2	Criterion 5.3	Criterion 5.4	Criterion 5.5	Criterion 5.6	Criterion 5.7
6. Respect for the Environment	Criterion 6.1	Criterion 6.2	Criterion 6.3	Criterion 6.4	Criterion 6.5	Criterion 6.6	Criterion 6.7
7. Avoidance of Illicit Operations	Criterion 7.1	Criterion 7.2	Criterion 7.3	Criterion 7.4	Criterion 7.5	Criterion 7.6	Criterion 7.7

then to reflection, and finally, to action and better results in a continuous process. Implementing a comprehensive improvement process will bring a company more and more into effective alignment with the CRT Principles for Business and the practices of moral capitalism.

A similar management approach has worked through the Malcolm Baldridge Quality Award Program of the U.S. government to achieve quality improvements and increased sales, so why not employ it on behalf of moral capitalism?

Business people are goal oriented; give them the right goals and incentives to succeed, and progress comes along without a second thought. This Caux Round Table self-assessment and improvement process evaluates companies on forty-nine areas drawn from the CRT Principles for Business as they impact the six stakeholder constituencies. Figure 6.2 presents the complete measurement matrix of the forty-nine significant zones of value enhancement and risk possibility. Each cell in the matrix demands management attention if there is to be complete stewardship of the business.

Inquiry by senior management regarding each cell of the matrix as to whether the company has a policy for success in that cell, how each policy has been translated into goals, and what results have been achieved in reaching for those goals, will provide a 360-degree survey of the corporation or the enterprise. The concerns of every stakeholder will be addressed, and fidelity to each of the CRT's recommended seven General Principles will be assessed. Shortfalls will emerge for management attention; risks will press themselves on management for reduction. Acting on its self-assessment will make the company more profitable and more socially responsible.

CONCLUSION

In the nine years since their publication, the CRT Principles for Business have remained the *only* set of principles for corporate social responsibility proposed by business leaders. Second, the CRT Principles for Business remain the most comprehensive principles available for business decision making, thanks to the thoroughness of their consideration of stakeholder concerns. Those concerns are presented in the following chapters, each devoted to an extended discussion of one of the six recognized stakeholder groups.

CHAPTER 7

CUSTOMERS: THE MORAL COMPASS FOR CAPITALISM

*Treating people with respect will gain one
wide acceptance and improve the business.*

> —Second Business Principle, Tao Zhu Gong,
> Assistant to the Emperor of Yue,
> 500 B.C.E.

*I have wished a bird would fly away,
And not sing by my house all day;
Have clapped my hands at him from the door
When it seemed as if I could bear no more.
The fault must partly have been in me.
The bird was not to blame for his key.
And of course there must be something wrong
In wanting to silence any song.*

> —Robert Frost, "A Minor Bird"

CONSUMER SOVEREIGNTY

CUSTOMERS ARE ALWAYS THE HEART of market capitalism. A business without customers is only somebody's fantasy of how to make a living. The valuation of every business turns on its expected income stream, not its projected costs. Buyers, not sellers, keep a market going forward.

Markets move goods and services where supply and demand curves intersect. The demand curve set by consumer preferences—the elasticity of their needs and wants—drives capitalism.

And, the infamous logic of markets always forcing costs of production down is equally driven by consumers. All else being equal, consumers will buy where a supply curve intersects their demand curve at a lower price point. The high probability of such behavior occurring again and again in cultures all around the world reflects the motivational power of consumer self-interest, a universal aspect of the human condition. Consumers, rather than owners, are the cause of downsizing, layoffs, and other measures to cut production costs. Consumers are not in the business of subsidizing either workers or owners by buying at prices higher than necessary.

When we think about two hundred years of argument over capitalism, consumers have fallen, overlooked, between the two contending stools of capital and labor. For years, political passion and rhetoric defended either the claims of investors or the demands of workers as central to modern industrial production. From the time Karl Marx published his book *Das Kapital*—"Capitalism"—political struggle and violent oppression has muddied the waters of our understanding. Communism declared war to the death with capitalism. Millions then died before communism expired with a tired whimper, its pretensions refuted by the necessities of human nature. On the other side, opposed to communism, were the defenders of private capital: Social Darwinists, economists, political liberals, the middle classes, and, in the United States, inheritors of the Protestant Ethic.

The argument between the advocates of capital and labor was over the spoils of industrialization: who deserved more—investors with their capital or workers with their labor? Both sides forgot that unless there were happy consumers with money in their pockets ready to spend in the markets of capitalism, there would be no spoils to fight over. Customers—and only customers—provide the money out of which both wages and profits come.

Who, then, is responsible for meeting their needs and concerns?

Consider United Airlines: it filed for bankruptcy in December 2002 with the highest wage cost structure in its industry. It had been losing money in large amounts steadily for several years. One very important lesson to draw from its experience was that the company had failed to bring to the market a product that sufficient customers found worthy of purchase. Customers were looking for lower fares. United's workers enjoyed higher wages in the short run but lost out strategically for overlooking customer satisfaction.

Simultaneously, Southwest Airlines, a low-cost, no-frills operation, ran no risk of bankruptcy. The value placed on its stock by investors was much greater that the value assessed for its much larger rival, United. Workers for Southwest may make less than those at United did, but they have the satisfaction of contemplating continued employment and, for their retirements, sound pension plans.

Under principles of financial analysis, companies are given a capital value according to how much money they make. The hyping of the American stock market in the 1990s—from initial public offerings (*IPOs*) of dot-com companies, to unrealistic and misleading Wall Street investment advice, to Enron's creative accounting—all focused like a laser on investors' fixation with income projections. The more income reported in the present or expected in the future, the greater the company's value to investors. Stock prices rose or fell with income reports and projections.

Jack Welsh, chairman and chief executive officer of GE, reported higher earnings every quarter. GE's stock made great gains. Jeff Imholt, his successor, was not so lucky; he could not make such reports, and GE's stock price dropped appreciatively on his watch.

After the Enron, WorldCom, and Global Crossings scandals, many companies had to restate their reported earnings as actually having been lower than what had been previously reported to the public. The season of truth-telling began when Enron had to restate its past earnings, which over a weekend dropped by $800 million. Having lost real customer income, Enron had created an accounting illusion that it was still making a profit. Starting in 1999, Enron's earnings from sales of energy and from trading in energy were flat or negative. Customers were telling Enron that there was not great demand for the products and services it was bringing to the markets. Suddenly, Enron's prospects as a very profitable company, as a darling of investors, were not very bright.

Andy Fastow, the self-described Social Darwinist, was chief financial officer for Enron. He came up with a plan from the brutish side of capitalism: Enron would arrange transactions that would replace customer revenue with income look-alikes. Special-purpose entities would be funded with new investors to buy Enron assets. Enron would benefit in two ways: a profit could be recorded on the sale of assets, and the debt that Enron carried tied to those assets could be moved off Enron's books to the books of the special-purpose entity. In effect Enron was using capital—mostly borrowed money—taking the form of the investment in the special-purpose entities as if it were income from customers. Fastow deceived, for a time, the markets as to Enron's actual situation vis-à-vis customers and so violated a basic requirement of moral capitalism: tell the truth.

At WorldCom, a similar deceit was used for the same purpose but was less conceptually creative. When customer reaction to the massive increase in telecommunications capacity revealed that too much capacity had been put in place relative to consumer demand, telecom companies began to show losses. Revenue from customers was less than that necessary to pay company expenses, especially the expenses of debt. At WorldCom, the treasurer simply lied. Instead of reporting current expenses for leases of communications capacity, he created a new bookkeeping category for capital expenses of "prepaid capacity" and wrongfully recorded those current lease expenses as capital investment so that they could be entered on the company's balance sheet and not on its profit and loss statement.

In the end, business success comes back to customer satisfaction. Customers cannot be taken for granted. In the first quarter of 2003, for example, McDonald's reported its twelfth consecutive monthly decline in comparable sales. Customer preferences in fast food were shifting.

Moreover, sophisticated and demanding buyers will propel a firm into continuous innovation in order to have products and services of interest to those customers. The benefit of such innovation lies in enhancing the firm's competitive advantages in a global marketplace. These cutting edge customers press firms to meet high standards and so to consistently outperform the competition.[1]

No chief executive officer and no board of directors can overlook fundamental marketing questions: (1) do we offer a product or a service at a price that someone wants to pay, and (2) are there enough people willing to pay that price to give us gross income adequate for our needs?

SERVING HUMAN DIGNITY

Because of service to customers, markets create order out of change and variety. They replicate in human society the principles of chaos theory, the new post-Newtonian understanding of our universe. Markets are living systems—never resting structures that constantly seek their own self-renewal.[2]

Who is to say, then, that the order established, destroyed, and reestablished again and again by market capitalism is good or bad, moral or immoral? Every buy-sell decision—all of which when taken together constitute the interim patterns that continuously evolve one out of another through market activity—has different values when seen through the separate eyes of different participants. There is no common standard of utility or good for all those participants. How can the moral pluses and minuses of all those perspectives be reduced to a single state of good or bad? We find the moral core of capitalism at the level of all the different customers, not with the capitalist or the worker.

Customers bring their values—a wide variety of values, goals, interests, and desires—to the marketplaces of capitalism. Sellers come to those same market places hoping to match products or services well enough to at least some of those customer values that sales will take place. Capitalism does not impose any moral goals on the customers seeking products and services. Respect for human dignity, therefore, demands that we esteem capitalism for this very capacity of moral restraint. If we seek to dignify the human individual, then we must allow individuals to impose their own values on the chances they take in life. Their actions taken in subordination to their value choices constitute the very free will of human kind spoken of so favorably by moralists, especially in Christian theology.

By respecting customers, we vindicate their will, not our own. We therefore act as agents in a moral endeavor when we respond to them as the driving force of capitalism.

In Section 3 of the CRT Principles for Business, we find recommendations for consideration of the interests of customers. The CRT believes "in treating all customers with dignity, irrespective of whether they purchase our products or services directly from us or otherwise acquire them in the markets."

With regard to customers, the CRT Principles continue: "We therefore have a responsibility to:

provide our customers with the highest quality products and services consistent with their requirements;

treat our customers fairly in all aspects of our business transactions, including a high level of service and remedies for their dissatisfaction;

make every effort to ensure that the health and safety of our customers, as well as the quality of their environment, will be sustained or enhanced by our products and services; assure respect for human dignity in products offered, marketing and advertising; and

respect the integrity of the culture of our customers."

Capitalism has no cure for abuse of free will; it has no bleach which will wash away the stain of sin from human actions. Markets will sell sin if sin can find willing sellers and buyers. For some moralists, this lack of redemptive capacity on the part of capitalism condemns it.

CAN CUSTOMERS BE TRUSTED TO BE MORAL?

Markets do not control the morality and desires of the buyers who exploit them for personal satisfaction. Markets respond to the conditions and circumstances brought forth by buyers and sellers. Business, of course, follows the markets and, therefore, cannot impose its moral ends on unwilling customers.

Should tobacco be sold? To minors? To anyone? Should guns be manufactured because there is some demand and a profit can be made in the manufacture? Should business serve desires for pornography, prostitution, liquor, fatty hamburgers, heavily scented or richly perfumed cosmetics, SUVs?

If the morality of capitalism is to be measured by the morality of its consumers, then capitalism will always come up ethically short. From time to time, people have other things on their mind than moral perfection. Communities have long known of this human drag coefficient on morality, that people will seek the harmful and the exploitative over the just and the pure. And so, laws have been enacted to restrain human desires. Just as murder is proscribed, so are child pornography, harmful drugs, liquor to minors, prostitution, and many other products and services. The ethics of what the market may offer are defined by the law, with two exceptions.

First, there is a grey area of products and services that may be legally sold but that many feel in good conscience should not be sold, even if legal, such as SUVs, tobacco, and whale meat. Here, the morality of a company selling such products or services may be called into question because it seeks to serve certain objectionable desires of its customers.

Second, companies that spend money to create desires and customers for morally questionable products and services cannot defend themselves from moral criticism on the grounds that such sales are, after all, lawful. Allegations that tobacco companies knowingly used the narcotic effect of nicotine to capture customers, and so put money into advertising to intensify demand for the pleasure of nicotine addiction, tainted the tobacco industry and cost it billions of dollars.

Skillful advertising of heavily polluting automobiles designed to increase consumer demand for such vehicles, if it were a principal cause of such demand, would be morally questionable.

The CRT Principles for Business openly recognize the problem that the exercise of free will by consumers may cause abuse from a moral perspective of the power of decision making that has been placed in their hands by free markets. In the provision of products and services, the CRT Principles do not require businesses to be satisfied with just any level of consumer acceptance. There must be a quality component to goods and services; they must not detract from health and safety (tobacco, alcohol, junk food, and weapons come within this concern), and they must not detract from a sustainable environment (SUVs are vulnerable here, but genetically modified foods are a more complex case). And, having the human dignity of our customers in mind should keep us away from offering products and services that would degrade that dignity, such as pornography or aids and means to assist in crime and vice.

DEMOCRATIC CHOICE: THE ESSENCE OF MORAL CAPITALISM

Capitalism shares moral ambiguity with democracy. Both systems empower individuals. Both tolerate the application of personal values to life choices individual decision by individual decision from the bottom of society up, and neither imposes a theology, ideology, or agenda of social engineering from the top of society down. Neither moral capitalism nor democracy contemplates final outcomes for people because they are only procedures for the expression of personal power. They have open architecture and innumerable feedback loops built into their system dynamics, and they are most compatible one with the other for both rest on the same fundamental principle of respect for human autonomy and dignity. Moral capitalism and democracy are both process systems, where procedure and playing by the rules is elevated in importance over substantive goals and objectives.

So, as history has shown frequently from the English Civil War of the 1640s to more recent protests in South Korea and Thailand, political activists promoting democracy and human rights find allies in the middle classes raised up by market capitalism. Such advocates of democracy and human freedom are indeed well advised to promote capitalism as an additional means by which to attain their political ends. Conversely, those who promote the benefits of capitalism for relief of the poor and for the improvement of the human condition would be well advised to extend their efforts to implementation of the Rule of Law and constitutionalism. Moral capitalism is an extension of democracy by other means.

In democracy, people may vote as they please, even against their own interests as others may see those interests. In capitalism, people decide for themselves as to how to spend their money. Under the principles of moral capitalism, people may or may not agree with moralists, pastors, and mullahs or with deep ecologist environmentalists as to what constitutes the comfortable and advantageous life. In capitalism, people do not take orders on these points; they are empowered to create the life that only they find to be comfortable and advantageous. The markets are an open process respectful of pluralism.

In American republican democracy, church and state are expressly separated one from the other so that those inspired by religious revelation may not have access to the police powers of government to improve the fortunes of their religion. Values, even evaluations of ultimate good and evil, are not enforced by the state unless some open, participatory public process invoking discourse and persuasion has been completed by means of which certain values—perhaps religious in origin—are secularized and found fit for imposition on citizens generally.

THE MORAL NORM OF RECIPROCITY

Buying and selling in market transactions require reciprocity, for there can be no buyer without a seller, and vice versa. An efficient market creates mutuality, which is a moral condition between people. Independent wants and needs are matched one to another. Where such mutually beneficial reciprocity between various wants and needs is easily achieved, market networks of exchange and cooperation thrive for sustained satisfaction of human well-being.

By facilitating and perpetuating this exchange of goods and services, markets encourage the production of more and more goods and services.

This is, of course, why markets and not governments cause the wealth of nations to increase. Markets foster the division of labor as some create new products to meet possible demand and others create new demands by asking for new things they want to buy.

Mencius understood in ancient China that markets were a social good because they served people's needs through reciprocal exchange. He wrote: "If you do not have an intercommunication of the productions of labor, and an interchange of men's services, so that one from his overplus may supply the deficiency of another, then husbandmen will have a superfluity of grain and women will have a superfluity of cloth."[3] When asked to put all of human morality into one word, Confucius replied "reciprocity."[4] Customers bring this moral norm to capitalism.

GLOBALIZATION AND RESPECT FOR THE CONSUMER

In capitalism, therefore, business must respect consumers as the origin of morality and values. Business must not impose choices on consumers or deny them the freedom of moral choice as to what they want to buy.

Business can cross the line and deny consumers freedom of moral choice by use of fraud and deceit. Thus, CRT Principle No. 3 holds that "sincerity, condor, truthfulness, the keeping of promises, and transparency" are fundamental obligations of business.

Businesses need to provide customers with the highest-quality products and services consistent with their requirements. Note that the requirements are set by the customers, not by the businesses. Doing otherwise would deny customers what they want and so would quickly sabotage their moral independence.

From Paris to Beijing, customers buy fast food from McDonalds and KFC. Teenagers prefer blue jeans, Nike sneakers, and the other accoutrements of rock and roll culture, to the dismay of traditionalists everywhere. Cell phones and satellite TV bring world events to the most remote corners of ancient lands. Culture is gravitating toward shopping mall consumerism around the world. The spending preferences of young customers and women defining new identities for themselves through their purchases are driving market trends around the world.

Those who object to (1) the subversion of personal character through the measurement of a person's humanity by reference to his or her possession of "cool" commodities (the "commodification of personhood," as some theologians call this moral elevation of materialism), (2) the seeming end of the work ethic, (3) the cheapening of standards in the mass market, (4) the growing irrelevance of elders and religious instruction, and (5) the breakdown of family structures often blame global capitalism for what they dislike about this revolution in popular culture. Opponents of globalization want to prevent companies from meeting consumer desires, as if the companies were at fault or were responsible for those desires. The power driving globalization, in the final analysis, is the power of consumers.

A COMPANY'S OBLIGATIONS

Brute capitalism looks at customers mostly as prey. Aside from its immorality, this makes little sense as a business strategy. It fails the test of self-interest considered upon the whole because it proves injurious to reputation capital. Businesses need customers. Driving them away makes no sense. Abuse of market power and exploitation will do just that—drive customers away and damage the good will of the business.

To keep their customers coming, businesses need goodwill just as much as they need steady production of a desirable product or service at an affordable price. Goodwill is a bookkeeper's asset on the balance sheet of almost every company. A high level of goodwill, which usually means a high level of customer loyalty, is a value multiplier. It indicates that a company's income stream is secure into the foreseeable future. Goodwill lowers risk and increases the financial value of the enterprise. Only a fool would intentionally sabotage his company's goodwill.

Reputation capital includes goodwill and more intangible advantages that come with brand esteem. Branding a product favorably permits a company to avoid falling to commodity pricing for the goods or services it offers and instead to charge a premium over cost. Many consumers will pay more for Marlboro cigarettes or Centrum vitamins than for their generic competitors, for example. Branding has value in the market for human capital as well. Companies with poor reputations cannot compete effectively for high-quality employees.

As illustrated in Figure 1.1 in Chapter 1 on the self-sustaining successful business, reputation capital supports and enhances finance capital and human capital. When Arthur Andersen's reputation dissolved owing to Enron's transactions with special-purpose entities, which the accounting firm had blessed, Arthur Andersen lost customers and collapsed. For Enron, as the truth about its ability to earn real profits came to light, its reputation suffered and people sold its stock. As its stock price dropped, it could no longer obtain financing. Bankruptcy was the only course of action left open.

Aside from fraud on investors, mistreating customers is the fastest way for a company to lose its reputation. When Ford Motor Company experienced customer anxiety over rollovers of its Explorer SUVs due to use of Firestone tires, the company terminated its relationship with Firestone and spent hundreds of millions in remediation of customer concern. Keeping its customer base loyal was that important to Ford. For Firestone and its Japanese owner, Bridgestone, the loss of goodwill was monumental, threatening the survival of Firestone and the solvency of Bridgestone.

Keeping up customer goodwill requires attention to relationships and to reputation. Quality of customer relationships and building comforting reputations for quality and service are the intangible moral components of every successful business. Reputation capital cannot be bought, it can only be earned.

The barons of brute capitalism prefer shortcuts to customer loyalty. They would rather have raw market power like that given by a monopoly so that customers are so dependent on the company that they have no recourse to other products or services. Many brute capitalists pride themselves on thinking up ways to manipulate markets and deny customers the power of free choice. The gossamer advantages of evading accountability to customers seem so real and so attractive that brute capitalists will go to great lengths to minimize the market power of consumers. Even though it had a popular product in its Windows software package for PC computers—a product earning margins of 85 percent—Microsoft nonetheless resorted to tying and other anticompetitive actions to lock in customers and deny them market power

Under the iron rules of supply and demand interaction, where the demand curve of customers can be made more inelastic, sellers operate with more market power. Restricting sources of supply is one way of making customer demand curves more rigid. This is usually done with government regulation of consumer choice or collusion with competitors to establish cartels.

For example, public utilities were once legal monopolies. The result was arrogance on the part of managers and employees toward customers, poor service, higher prices, and growing customer annoyance. AT&T's monopoly of telephone service was finally broken by federal court action responding to customer dissatisfaction.

The CRT Principles require that customers be treated fairly. Such respect builds goodwill and quality relationships for a business. It is a necessary and just return on reputation capital. A business should not circumvent these obligations by seeking monopoly power, either through market dominance or by government intervention. Monopoly power undermines a business's need to respect its customers. As the relationship between customer and business loses the tension of mutuality, it becomes less and less moral. The business more and more dictates terms and decides for the customer, upsetting the moral basis for capitalism.

Avoiding long-term relationships with customers is another way of minimizing their market power. If customers are casual, one-time buyers, without intending to repeat their patronage, they can be ignored, told to "take it or leave it," or even hood-winked, with less adverse consequences to the seller. "Take their money and run" is the rule of brute capitalists everywhere. A favorite business model under the norms of brute capitalism is the rug bazaar: a one time transaction with a gullible stranger just passing through town.

There is a special potential for business denial of meaningful human choice in the areas of health and safety. Providers of goods and services often know more about the risks and consequences of using what it is they sell than do their customers. Thus, in these industries, an important aspect of mutuality between buyer and seller is missing. Risk of harm can be easily pushed off onto unsuspecting customers by closed-mouthed sellers, which violates a moral norm of respect for your customers.

Consumer protection laws specify what companies must do to disclose risks and consequences associated with use of their products and services. The CRT Principles go further and assert that companies should recognize that some behavior, although legal, may still have adverse consequences for customers. Sales under these circumstances should be recognized as coming burdened with a responsibility to be considerate of customer awareness and generous in disclosure of all material information.

In the case of Enron, its lawyers, Vincent & Elkins, and its accountants, Arthur Andersen, had obligations under this section of the CRT Principles to warn Enron of future risks and consequences. As professionals knowing more than Enron's board of directors did about what might go wrong with aggressively and secretly using special-purpose entities and hiding debt obligations, Vincent & Elkins and Arthur Andersen had a duty to look after the fundamental economic health and safety of their client. They should have advised the board of directors of the risks inherent in the push-the-edge-of-the-envelope steps proposed by management. In effect, they sold Enron dangerous products without making adequate disclosures and so abused their business relationship with the company.

CONCLUSION

The capacity for making moral choices gives dignity to humans. This capacity is our moral sense, the foundation of our being able to leave the Darwinian state of nature and live in civil society. If bad choices are made from time to time, that is the fault of individuals, not of moral capitalism itself. Once again, personal character suggests itself as the basis for an improvement in the outcomes of capitalism, for people with character will be less likely to abuse their power as consumers. Chapter 8 looks at how moral capitalism addresses the demands of employees for fair recompense.

ASSESSING YOUR COMPANY

How well does your company implement the CRT guidelines for interaction with customers? To make an assessment, complete the following questions:

SCORE

CRITERION 1.2 (Principle: Beyond Shareholders toward Stakeholders) How does the company provide quality products and services that maximize their value to the customer while ensuring respect for human dignity?

0   5   10
Lower Quality   Higher Quality

CRITERION 2.2 (Principle: Economic/Social Impact of Business)
How does the company ensure protection for its customers and demonstrate respect for their cultures in its marketing and communications?

0   5   10
Lower Quality   Higher Quality   _____

CRITERION 3.2 (Principle: Business Behavior)
How does the company elicit the trust of customers (e.g., through responsible advertising, warranty fulfillment, etc.)?

0   5   10
Lower Quality   Higher Quality   _____

CRITERION 4.2 (Principle: Respect for Rules)
How does the company manage compliance with the letter and spirit of national and international customer-related rules?

0   5   10
Lower Quality   Higher Quality   _____

CRITERION 5.2 (Principle: Support for Multilateral Trade)
How does the company support its customers throughout the world and improve the cost and quality of its goods/services through international trade?

0   5   10
Lower Quality   Higher Quality   _____

CRITERION 6.2 (Principle: Respect for the Environment)
How does the company manage customer-related environmental issues (e.g., health and safety, "green design," recycling, etc.)?

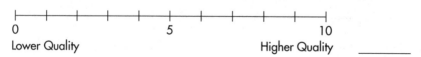

0   5   10
Lower Quality   Higher Quality

CRITERION 7.2 (Principle: Avoidance of Illicit Operations)
How does the company take action to prevent such illicit activities as deceptive sales practices and sales to inappropriate customers?

0   5   10

Lower Quality   Higher Quality   _____

TOTAL SCORE (maximum possible points = 70)   _____

CHAPTER 8

EMPLOYEES: PARTS FOR A MACHINE OR MORAL AGENTS?

Comradeship and trust will emerge naturally when discipline and high standards are enforced.
—*Eleventh Business Principle, Tao Zhu Gong, Assistant to the Emperor of Yue, 500 B.C.E.*

We few, we happy few, we band of brothers.
—*William Shakespeare, King Henry V, act IV, scene III*

GIVEN NEARLY TWO HUNDRED YEARS of worker agitation over wages and working conditions, of high-profile political antagonism between labor and capital, employees are the most volatile stakeholder constituency for a corporation. We have been conditioned to think of labor relations in business and in industry as naturally adversarial, rooted in the most objectionable practice of brute capitalism—the sacrifice of worker interests on the altar of profit. As a result of this history, asking labor and management to work closely together can often be counterproductive.

Management-worker relations have been conceptualized in a long debate as a zero-sum competition for money: what one side gets, the other must lose. So, wringing more profits out of the business for its owners demands lowering wages for its workers.

This vision of confrontation churning away in the heart of market capitalism came quickly on the invention of the factory in the early decades of industrialization. In the 1830s, nascent socialism pointed to the needs of capital and to private ownership of the factories as the causes of low wages and harsh working conditions for employees. Two remedies were therefore suggested: (1) organization of worker power to offset the power of capital and (2) abolition of private property. Unions, backed by the

109

strike on one hand and social revolution on the other, dominated the nine-teenth century's social agenda in industrial economies. The worker question was at the center of social controversy over industrial capitalism during its robber baron phase: how to get fair returns to workers while promoting the success of enterprise. By the 1930s, unions had carried the day in the industrialized countries, whereas social revolution had won out in preindustrialized Russia.

In England and America, however, the theme of adversarial conflict took hold in the law as well. As the industrial revolution produced a new economy, with a growing middle class, urbanization, workers, unions, and high finance, the courts of both countries embraced a vigorous doctrine of contract flexibility. Freedom for entering into contracts on one's own terms was the policy goal of the law. Economic actors were seen as autonomous, equal to one another, and able to bargain for their own best outcomes. Freedom of contract promoted autonomy and flexibility in the marketplace more than the accountability of older rules of law. Henry Maine, the noted legal scholar, wrote in mid-century to say that the progress of civilization was a movement from status to contract.[1] He was trying to say that duties for a person, or a company, no longer came with birth or high social position, but only with voluntary submission to an obligation. No more noblesse oblige; no more paternalism from well-meaning lords of the manor living in a Jane Austin world of proper social deportment. We see this change in the law in the Dartmouth College case of 1824, where the U.S. Supreme Court chose freedom of contract over traditional notions of a public servitude to free Dartmouth College as a private corporation from control by the State of New Hampshire.

Companies were therefore free to contract as they might with individual workers. This, obviously, left workers vulnerable to the economic power of the companies. Workers needed weekly wages; they had no capital with which to build their own factories or hold out on long strikes. And, American courts in the early twentieth century even went so far as to limit the power of government in seeking to help workers. The U.S. Supreme Court ruled that government regulation of wages and hours wrongfully restricted the contractual freedom of workers to contract as they wished for the sale of their labor.[2]

Legal doctrines of freedom of contract explicitly incorporated Herbert Spencer's principles of Social Darwinism. In particular, contract law embraced Spencer's preliminary understanding of the biological and evolutionary necessity for competitive individualism as the rule of life for human societies.

Ironically, both the Social Darwinist defenders of market competition and their strident Marxist opponents agreed that the relation between capital and labor was necessarily adversarial. Both agreed that labor power was hired or purchased for wages. Consequently, employers need have no concern over the lives of their workers once the wage was paid, along the lines of Ebenezer Scrooge's cold contempt for Bob Cratchit.

Marx railed against the "cash nexus" humiliating and oppressing workers and transforming them into commodities to be bought and sold like machines. His remedy was to terminate private ownership of the means of production, to free workers from "wage slavery."

Herbert Spencer, on the other hand, saw the "cash nexus" progressively in the light of human evolution, where it freed workers to sell their labor on the best possible terms and find employment suitable to their desires and talents. Rightly gone, he thought, were the days of guild apprenticeships, serfdom, and feudal subordination.

From this historical perspective of conflict, it may be hard now to shift one's thinking and consider employees to be a crucial stakeholder of enterprise, one necessary for its success. Although human capital may be bought, its full potential only emerges with application of care and respect. Workers who are treated shabbily give back shabby performance. W. Edward Deming's Total Quality Movement demonstrated the financial value to a company of a motivated and loyal workforce. Deming advised companies to improve their quality as a strategy to gain increased profitability. Improving quality, he argued, required the personal commitment of employees to quality workmanship.

Deming's recommendations can find a bisis in the old Common Law of status obligations. Expecting owners and managers to have a station with responsibilities toward employees—a status—while, simultaneously, expecting workers to have a station with responsibilities toward managers and owners—another social status—might seem more beneficial for the interests of both than is today's zero-sum rivalry under conditions of full contractual freedom. And, with both sides having an "office" to perform toward the other, the employment relationship would take on depth, becoming moral for both owners and workers and personally more fulfilling for the workers. Status has moral advantages in conferring protection against abuses of power that markets cannot provide.

The Common Law doctrines of agency, evolving over several centuries out of Old Testament and Roman concepts, ground the employer-employee relationship on mutual offices. The principal has duties toward his or her agent, whereas the agent has fiduciary duties toward the principal. Into the agency relationship enter notions of loyalty and mutual assistance, which do not appear in a "cash nexus" hire and sale of simple labor power.

There is another implication for moral capitalism hidden in the agency relationship. Agents are hired to do things their principals can't. Take a taxi driver or a surgeon: as a passenger, your life is in the hands of another, just as when the surgeon is working on your heart. As a principal, you are buying good judgment and professional skills from another and putting yourself under their power. They, not you, have control over an important part of your future. You are dependent on the quality of their work. You must trust their decisions. This is a relationship of dependency in which you want them to think about your best interests. It is fundamentally, therefore, a moral relationship and is so precisely for your benefit.

On account of this dependency of the enterprise on those in its employ— its agents, employees, and workers must receive due regard from their employers for showing loyalty and good judgment in serving the ends of enterprise. The ties that binds a worker to the success of his or her company are more moral than they are economic.

As a result of having a status of trust, agents, employees, and workers do not lose their moral autonomy when they accept to work for another. They retain in their various employments freedom of conscience and judgment, being held accountable for good use of those powers in the exercise of their office. They may, therefore, be critical of their working conditions and suggest new ways of work or ways to modify their relationships. This creativity on their part is an intangible capital asset of the firm of no small importance. Such constructive engagement with management is called for by the morality inherent in their position and should not be overlooked or discouraged by an employer. It is one of the benefits of hiring quality employees.

Aligning with the moral norms of agency law and seeking a way to fit the dynamics of management labor relations into a more constructive pattern, Deming proposed that in return for management's taking responsibility for quality and worker dignity, employees in return should:

- Absorb and live the company's mission, goals, and operating philosophy

- Look toward the long-term good of the firm, not solely toward short-term gains for labor; consider the needs of investors, customers, and vendors

- Show genuine concern for constant improvement of quality

- Know exactly what your job is and strive for improvement

- Not demand and create stultifying seniority and work rules

- Avoid adversarial and competitive behavior between and within shifts and departments or with management; act as part of a team for the common good of all[3]

The CRT Principles for Business adopt the agency perspective on employer-employee relations. The Principles posit a relationship of mutuality, of reciprocity, between the company and its employees. The Principles reject the premises of brute capitalism, with its insistence on adversarial conflict between management and workers as so many scorpions in a bottle struggling with one another to climb out and save themselves.

The CRT Principles hold that the company and its employees have a stake in each other. A company that is profitable for its owners and that attracts new investment most likely can pay its employees good wages and, more important, can enhance their productivity with new capital investment while bringing new products and services to the market through spending on research and development.

Employees depend on the company for their livelihoods. They need the company to be consistently profitable, but they also need to share in that success, otherwise their employment would be of little use to them. Moreover, the families of employees similarly depend on the company's commercial success. From the perspective of social justice, employees are just the tip of the iceberg. The wages they receive and the standard of living they enjoy flow on past them to impact many other lives—and set in motion standards of living for entire communities. It is at this point that the CRT Principles affirm that communities look to business to create wealth and to distribute that wealth. If businesses lack responsibility and do not treat employees fairly, communities suffer.

Conversely, and justly, companies are dependent on their employees. A dedicated, loyal, productive, and willing workforce—blue collar or white collar—makes all the difference for a company. Such workers are necessary for success. They produce quality products and services at the best cost.

They, not the chief executive officer, build goodwill for the company among consumers.

Southwest Airlines is one of the most considerate employers in its industry; it was the only large American airline not to lay people off after September 11, 2001, being the only American airline able to make a profit in those depressed conditions for air travel. In 2001, the company received 120,000 applications for 3,000 job openings. Southwest Airlines had its pick of the best applicants, gaining a significant competitive advantage over its rivals for human capital resources in a customer service-sensitive industry.

The dependency of companies on employees is growing with every technological advance. High-tech companies thrive on the brainpower of their highly educated employees; such companies are afraid of losing their resident geniuses. The very valuable income-earning asset of knowledge belongs to the worker, not to the company. The solicitous care and feeding of such technical and creative employee superstars is vital to the success of many chief executive officers. Recognizing this reality, most large companies invest in the overhead of human resource departments in order to keep valuable human capital loyal and productive.

Disney has seen the price of its stock slide in recent years. It faces more competition than ever before in cartoon features for children and from blockbuster children's movies like *Lord of the Rings* and *Harry Potter*. Yet, much of its competition comes from former employees driven away by Chief Executive Officer Michael Eisner's corporate culture. Jeffrey Katzenberg left to start DreamWorks, and Joe Roth left to found Revolution Studios, which provided Sony Pictures Entertainment with high-grossing films. In many industries today, losing the most talented and inspired employees comes at a high cost to a company.

American workers dedicated to technical creativity have grown in number from 42,000 in 1900 to five million in 1999.[4] In 1900, some 25,000 patents were granted in the United States; in 1999, the number was 150,000. Research and development expenditures rose from $5 billion in 1950 to $250 billion in 2000. It is estimated that "creative industry sectors" like research and development, publishing, software, TV and radio, design, music, film, toys and games, advertising, architecture, performing arts, etc., earned $2.24 trillion dollars worldwide in 1999. Those sectors in the United States contributed $960 billion of that total, a significant share of the American gross national product. By 1996, it was estimated that wages for 36 percent of all U.S. employment were paid by the "scientific, professional, and knowledge economy."[5]

A new structure of venture capital flows exploits the achievements of creative people by turning their ideas and innovations into new businesses. Venture capitalists encourage more and more people to seek their fortunes in the creative industries.

The wealth to be made from creative industries depends on recruiting creative people, who have certain special needs. Creative people want to move up based on their abilities and efforts; they are motivated by the respect of their peers. They can move easily from job to job and city to city seeking individuality and self-statement. They will choose a more stimulating environment in which to work over a boring job that pays more. As creative industries become more important to the world's production of goods and services, obtaining reliable creative people becomes more important for corporate profits.

A worker seeking to stay at consulting company Sapient Systems after the dot-com bubble burst stated: "One of the most important things at Sapient is culture and hiring only the best people. Sapient does not pay the best, intentionally, because if you pay top dollar, then you get mercenaries and mercenaries don't help develop culture."[6] Opinion surveys of information technology employees reveal work environment priorities of challenge, flexibility, and stability. They also seek to work where their opinions are valued and they have the respect of their peers.[7]

Decades ago, Chester Bernard, in his radically insightful book of 1938, *Theory and Function of the Executive*, saw the vital importance of employees to the company.[8] After years as a senior manager with AT&T, he sensibly inverted the command and control hierarchy so popular with industrial corporations like General Motors. He pointed to the people on the bottom of the hierarchy as being the most important. They were the ones with autonomy and freedom to implement orders and carry out tasks or not.

From experience in business, Bernard was far from a brutish capitalist. Quite the contrary, he saw the industrial firm as a system of cooperation. If workers refused to cooperate, the firm would grind to a halt. Their cooperation had to be bargained for and obtained through the development of mutual respect and dependence between workers and managers. Such an insight quickly moves our understanding beyond the hunter and his kill metaphors favored by more brutish capitalists. If you figuratively kill your employees, they can't very well contribute to your enterprise.

Inducements, advised Bernard, lead all of us into making contributions toward cooperative endeavors. Thus, engagement of employees on behalf of enterprise goals requires providing them with positive advantages and reducing what they see to be disadvantages. The matter of incentives is complex: there are objective incentives like cash wages and subjective incentives like pride in creation or happiness over official position. And, as Maslow would later note, the evaluation by an employee of both kinds of incentives turns on his or her state of mind, attitudes, beliefs, and perceptions at any given time.

Bernard was convinced that "nonmaterialistic" inducements were of great importance to any successful organization. In fact, he was pointing out in 1938 that organizations do not rest on a simple cash nexus with their workers, or on some adversarial struggle for survival between workers and managers. Bernard was placing some aspect of moral integrity at the heart of functionally successful employer-employee relationships.

<AQ1>: Should th— year be 19— per the en— note?

Interestingly, Bernard shrewdly observed that "the most intangible and subtle of incentives is that which I call the condition of communion." "It is the opportunity for comradeship, for mutual support, in personal attitudes. The need for communion is a basis of informal organization that is essential to the operation of every formal organization."[9]

Bernard looked closely at the phenomenon of authority: just when, exactly, are orders from the top of an organization executed with alacrity and fidelity? Bernard saw that the common notion of power flowing from top to bottom was wrong. In reality, whether an order has authority or not is decided by the person to whom the order is addressed, not by the person "in authority" who issued the order.[10] The dispositive power to take action rests with the subordinate person in the relationship. This necessary attitude of cooperation and mutuality between issuers and receivers of orders and instructions is hard to come by in a world of brute competition for power and victory. Subordinates have great power to sabotage the best-laid plans of senior managers. That is why work flows best if subordinates are brought into a moral relationship with those above them in the hierarchy of command.

Agency law in England and America (before the Common Law absorbed Herbert Spencer's teachings) recognized this upside-down dependency where the bosses must rely on the skill and good faith of the subordinates. Agents were given discretionary power precisely because their principals could not be there on the spot to make those decisions. The distant principals must trust their agents to bring a willing spirit and a skillful mind to the immediate problems at hand and, subsequently, to report the results of their efforts.

The CRT Principles for Business in Section 3, Stakeholder Principles, Employees, set forth guidelines for the development and maintenance of that mutual respect and dependence providing for enterprise success. The Principles regarding employees as stakeholders hold: "We believe in the dignity of every employee and in taking employee interests seriously." Using the language of "dignity" moves the employer-employee relationship sharply away from the cash nexus formula so subject to exploitation.

The CRT Principles continue that businesses "have a responsibility to":

- *Provide jobs and compensation that improve workers' living conditions;*

This responsibility of business is truly fundamental. After satisfaction of consumer needs and desires, providing wealth through wages is the principal social benefit of capitalism.

This responsibility immediately moves moral capitalism away from brutish concerns only for the self. Business can't give away the store to workers as United Airlines may have done in its union contracts; that would bring enterprise to financial failure. (In the case of US Airways in 2003, only bankruptcy brought about cost reductions to keep the company in business—some $1 billion in wages cut and 16,000 employees discharged.) But, business should pay more than a market minimum, very tight-fisted cash nexus price for labor power. Workers should be seen as agents of the business, not beasts of burden hired by the hour. Yet, wise muleteers, for example, kept their animals well watered, rested, and well fed.

Frankly, if the only way to keep the business going, or to go into business, is to pay slave wages or their equivalent, then the business probably has no social justification under the CRT Principles. It is not making a sufficient contribution to society's needs to deserve capital investment.

The CRT's suggested wage standard is enough to "improve" the living conditions of workers. This is a relative standard: lower where living conditions are low and higher where economies are more advanced, productivity levels reflect the past application of capital, and wealth is more generally available.

When Nike and other manufacturers move production to low-wage environments to pay low wages on a global scale, the wages they pay are of still considerable value to workers in the country of production. For all the resentment in affluent economies over their paying only a small proportion of the final price of their product for labor, these companies, nonetheless, bring new employment and thus some new wealth creation to low-income societies. Thus, this use of the global labor market by multinational manufacturers has net advantages for those seeking employment in poor countries, although payment of higher wages by Nike and the others would certainly enhance those net advantages.

The suggested CRT standard for job content cumulatively enhances worker productivity. Jobs should be provided that call on greater application of skill and talent by the workers, so that they can qualify for higher wages as a result of enhanced productivity.

- *Provide working conditions that respect each employee's health and dignity*

Workers are not to be bought, used up, and thrown out as so much coal shoveled into a furnace and then thrown away as ash. Providing for worker health and dignity imposes higher costs on the company than doing otherwise. But the point is not to maximize short-term profits at the expense of workers. As with finding suitable wage levels, the challenge to management in paying for working conditions is to arrive at an equilibrium cost that rightly provides for workers without jeopardizing company sustainability.

- *Be honest in communications with employees and open in sharing information, limited only by legal and competitive constraints*

This recommendation goes to the heart of Bernard's advice: take care of the state of mind, attitude, and beliefs of your employees. Their loyalty and their productivity—critical value drivers for the business—depend on their feelings about the company, its culture, and its prospects. Employees are to be taken into relationship, not held at arm's length.

Gaining authority, the ability to have your instructions welcomed and quickly obeyed, depends on your level of honesty and frankness in communications. Managers need to earn trust, just as political leaders do. Don't deceive your own people; that is the point where you start the process of becoming a good manager.

Once you are trusted, then you will also be trusted to keep some matters confidential. Under those circumstances, secrecy does not become dysfunctional and give rise to divisive office politics.

Managers can build trust in the organization by living out these behaviors: conveying consistent principles, giving plausible explanations for their actions, providing realistic and clear status reports and forecasts—even of bad news, making realistic commitments, showcasing their experience, not bad-mouthing those who are not present, showing compassion, and verifying that they understand the desires and concerns of others.[11]

- *Listen to and, where possible, act on employee suggestions, ideas, requests, and complaints*

This recommendation achieves several objectives. First, it actualizes the principle of looking on employees as trusted agents of the business who constructively bring talent to bear on its challenges and opportunities. The Total Quality Movement proved that workers on the line had better ideas for improvements and for spotting flaws than did white-collar managers working in their glass-windowed offices.

Second, the recommendation obtains valuable innovations and improvements.

Third, listening seriously to employees brings warnings of dangers. If Enron directors had followed the e-mail exchanges on various unofficial employee Internet chat rooms, they would have learned enough to be on guard against the risks that destroyed their company. At WorldCom, a middle manager responsible for internal auditing was on the scent of fraud quite early. Had her concerns been elevated to board attention in time, the company might have been saved from bankruptcy.

- *Engage in good-faith negotiations when conflict arises*

The experience supporting this recommendation recognizes that negotiations with employees are not life and death struggles in which management must win every point or else face business collapse. Although good faith can be a vague standard in contract negotiations or dispute resolutions, bargaining in good faith certainly means recognition of some mutuality to the process, an acknowledgment that both sides should benefit from the proposed relationship. Good-faith negotiation is not a win-lose extraction of maximum benefit for oneself alone, which, in the last analysis, can be successful only through power and intimidation.

- *Avoid discriminatory practices and guarantee equal treatment and opportunity in areas such as gender, age, race, and religion*

This recommendation arises from modern society's sense of justice in affirmation of human dignity. Society demands of business that human dignity be respected. Respecting that dignity in turn demands that features of a person's being or identity such as birth circumstances of gender and race be overlooked as irrelevant to the person's capacity to be an effective agent of the firm.

On becoming an adult citizen, a person's age should not automatically prevent them from qualifying for work. If they can meet the standards, they should be considered on a par with others with similar ability.

- *Promote in the business itself the employment of differently abled people in places of work where they can be genuinely useful*

Like the previous recommendation, this obligation flows from society's concern that human dignity be respected. To the extent a person is able, that person has a claim on work. Tension comes when the cost of providing for different abilities offsets the value such a person brings to the firm; then the differently abled worker cannot really add value to the production process and fully share in the company's responsibility to create wealth for society.

- *Protect employees from avoidable injury and illness in the workplace*

This recommendation finds an analogy with the obligation of a company to show concern for working conditions and the health of workers. To respect a person is to want to prevent harm from coming to him or her.

Because the company is in a better position than the employee to remedy and remove dangers in the workplace, it should do so. The company is in command of the facilities, has financial resources, and can, at little cost, obtain necessary information on sources of potential injury.

Some companies, out of some brute capitalist preference for low costs of production, refuse to be responsible as becomes their station in life. These companies try to impose the costs of injury and illness on their workers. Under these circumstances, the government will step in with regulations, inspections, and fines to take over considerable business decision making, which decisions might be better left with those who know the business.

- *Encourage and assist employees in developing relevant and transferable skills and knowledge*

This requirement, like the first, flows from a company's obligation to create wealth for society. Assisting employees gain in skill permits them to earn higher wages, adding an increment to society's gross domestic product. Further, employees who are at the edge of the learning curve in their specialty or industry help prevent companies from losing out to competition and new advances in the marketplace.

- *Be sensitive to the serious unemployment problems frequently associated with business decisions, and work with governments, employee groups, other agencies, and each other in addressing these dislocations*

The CRT recognizes that change is inevitable in business. New conditions arrive, new technology comes along, new markets open up, customer tastes are fickle. Plants close, companies go out of business, production is moved to communities where wages are lower—jobs are lost. The CRT cannot prescribe permanence for employment, or for any other aspect of capitalism. Companies should not be subsidized and kept alive if they have failed to prove themselves in the markets. That would divert society's wealth away from reinvestment in new wealth and higher living standards, in accordance, no doubt, with non-market forces of political favoritism or the emotional claims of the status quo.

There is risk of failure associated with employment, just as there is with financial investment or any entrepreneurial endeavor. No foreseeable system of moral capitalism can remove risk from the business equation. Nor can moral conduct take the risks out of life. Bad things may happen to good people.

But, the CRT asserts that companies have a responsibility to mitigate the hardships created by their decisions to close down plants or relocate production. In finding a right wage, the company must pay more than it could legally get away with in order to be fair to the needs of its employees who, after all, depend on the company. So too should a company go beyond its minimum legal obligations in deciding on downsizing opportunities. However, the impact of layoffs and plant closings would be less harmful to families, if workers had rainy day savings funds with which to finance their transition to new jobs or to new communities of work and residence.

This recommendation for moral conduct should be analyzed along with the recommendation on providing for upgrades in employee skills and knowledge. Under many circumstances of "self-interest considered upon the whole," the best result for a company many not be plant closure or simple exit from an unprofitable line of business. The better course may well be to reconfigure the business and take advantage of new technology and new opportunities.

For example, as their drive to economic success really got under way in the late 1960s and 1970s, the Japanese did not try to prevent the relocation of textile production from Japan to Taiwan and other rising Asian economic powers. Rather, Japanese companies retrained their workforces, largely female, to manufacture computer chips and components. The women's wages rose dramatically as a result, as did company profits.

Communities, like companies and employees, understand that in life, nothing is certain for long. Communities must prepare for adverse economic changes and assume the risk of not having anything of value to bring to the global table of production and factor inputs. It is the responsibility of communities, not of companies, to amass the social capital that makes successful capitalism possible. It is the responsibility of companies, though, to contribute to that social capital. Cooperation in easing the burdens of economic change is one of those important private sector contributions to resilient social environments that pave the way for future economic growth through new investment.

CONCLUSION

Looking at employees as agents specially qualified for work rather than as units of labor power brings business management into alignment with the tenets of moral capitalism. Chapter 9 looks at the rights of owners and investors under the principles of moral capitalism.

ASSESSING YOUR COMPANY

How well does your company comply with the CRT guidelines for interaction with employees? To make an assessment, score your company on the following criteria:

CRITERION 1.3 (Principle: Beyond Shareholders toward Stakeholders)
How does the company recognize employee interests and take steps to improve employees' lives, individually and collectively?

0   5   10
Lower Quality   Higher Quality   _____

CRITERION 2.3 (Principle: Economic/Social Impact of Business)
How does the company create employment and employability and honor human rights within its operations?

0   5   10
Lower Quality   Higher Quality   _____

CRITERION 3.3 (Principle: Business Behavior)
How does the company elicit employee trust (e.g., through effective communication and dialogue, credible evaluation systems, etc.)?

0   5   10
Lower Quality   Higher Quality   _____

CRITERION 4.3 (Principle: Respect for Rules)
How does the company manage compliance with the letter and spirit of national and international employee-related rules?

0   5   10
Lower Quality   Higher Quality   _____

CRITERION 5.3 (Principle: Support for Multilateral Trade)
How does the company develop its human capital globally while attending to employee needs domestically?

0   5   10
Lower Quality   Higher Quality   _____

CRITERION 6.3 (Principle: Respect for the Environment)

How do employee policies and practices help prevent environmental damage and promote sustainability?

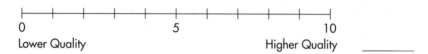

0   5   10
Lower Quality   Higher Quality   _____

CRITERION 7.3 (Principle: Avoidance of Illicit Operations)

How does the company take action to prevent illicit activities by employees (e.g., offering/accepting bribes, violating licensing or copyright restrictions, etc.)?

0   5   10
Lower Quality   Higher Quality   _____

TOTAL SCORE (maximum possible points = 70)   _____

CHAPTER 9

OWNERS AND INVESTORS: EXPLOITERS OR POTENTIAL VICTIMS?

Coat-check girl: "Goodness, what beautiful diamonds!"
Mae West: "Honey, goodness had nothing to do with it."
—from the movie, Night After Night

In making judgments, the Early Kings were perfect, because they made moral principles the starting point of all their undertakings and the root of everything that was beneficial. This Principle, however, is something that persons of mediocre intellect never grasp. Not grasping it, they lack awareness, and lacking awareness, they pursue profit. But while they pursue profit, it is absolutely impossible for them to be certain of attaining it.
—The Annals of Lu Bu Wei, p. 570

IN SECTION 3 OF THE CRT PRINCIPLES FOR BUSINESS, the next stakeholder constituency supporting every business (after consideration of its customers and employees) is its investors—its owners and creditors. If customers provide a moral compass for capitalism, then those who finance private ventures to produce what consumers desire are those who turn value preferences into material achievements, creating wealth in the process.

THE NEED FOR FINANCE

Finance, the providing of money to enterprise—in both legal forms of high-risk equity and lower-risk debt—drives capitalism. Even moral capitalism can't survive without access to money. Owners and investors—the providers of finance capital—are as necessary for business success as are customers and employees.

The CRT Principles for Business contemplate both equity owners and creditors as stakeholders of a business. Creditors would embrace all who extend credit to a business: long-term debt, usually secured by a lien on property, short-term debt, commercial paper, secured and unsecured lines of bank credit, trade credit, payment terms, factoring of receivables, etc. The CRT Principles, by extension, also embrace financing mechanisms with a middle character as well, those standing between equity and debt, such as preferred stock and limited partnership interests, which combine some ownership risk with special priority in receiving a limited share of profits earned.

Equity creates the enterprise. Those who provide it are the owners of the business. They get to pull together, balance, and adjust all the component parts of the business—plant and equipment, raw materials, technology, workers, funded debt, short-term lines of credit, administrative staff, marketing decisions, advertising, sales reps, etc. In most large modern business corporations, however, the owners pass off this very complex task of decision making and decision implementation to others—to a board of directors and subordinate corporate managers.

Ownership has become mostly passive in advanced economies. Corporate owners have the power to elect members of the board to serve as their collective agents. Most corporate laws place the responsibility to manage and direct a corporation exclusively with its board of directors, not with its owners or with its chief executive officer.

Corporate owners, however, retain certain rights to approve major decisions, such as a merger with another corporation, which would impact the value of their stock holdings.

Nonequity investors, on the other hand, buy a ticket to ride along with the business only for a time, until it comes to a certain destination of their liking, when they get off. They don't get to drive. Nonequity investors take the risk that the journey will be safe and that the profit-seeking vehicle will indeed arrive when and where they want. When their loan with all accrued interest is paid off, the lenders have no more to do with the business. They have reached their desired financial destination. Nonetheless, the CRT Principles for Business conclude that nonequity investors also have valuable expectations of profit and advantage that a company should acknowledge and be prepared to serve when necessary.

The impact of creditors on a company's ability to do business can be critical to continued profitability. When the price of its stock dropped as a result of revelations over its accounting practices and its true level of financial liability, Enron's suppliers refused to extend further trade credits to the company. Its banks were afraid to make additional loans, and, within months, the company was out of cash and could not pay its bills.

When a company like Enron, with an excessive debt burden relative to real value, goes bankrupt, its creditors end up in largely in the same position as its equity investors: losing most of their investment owing to bad management. This outside risk born by creditors brings them within the circle of concern over company stewardship that is already so important to equity owners.

THE BUSINESS: MONEY HELD IN TRUST FOR OWNERS AND INVESTORS

The CRT Principles for Business recognize the dependent situation of most equity ownership on the decisions of corporate boards and senior officers and the lesser, but still substantial, dependency of creditors on the company's success. The CRT Principles for Business, therefore, assert that the relationship between the company and its owners and investors is a kind of trusteeship, injecting a moral variable into the business equation.

Owners and investors "trust" their money to the board of directors and the managers of enterprise and expect a profitable return on this "deposit." Owners have one set of expectations as to levels of risk assumed in making the deposit and as to prospects of earning a return on their deposit; creditors have another set.

Under law, corporate directors and officers are explicitly fiduciary agents of the owners, owing them duties of loyalty and due care. Directors are given that status vis-à-vis the owners while corporate officers are given that status vis-à-vis the company that has hired them. The technical status of the directors is that of a fiduciary for the owners; the related legal status of corporate officers is that of agent, which is also a fiduciary position. The owners hire the directors, and the directors (directly or indirectly) hire the employees. Each hiring creates a fiduciary relationship under the law.

Fiduciary law holds that with status and power come responsibilities. Corporate directors have responsibilities to the owners, and corporate employees are responsible for their conduct and their decisions to the directors and, through them, to the owners of the corporation.

The corporation is not a fiduciary for its creditors. Creditors have contract rights only. But, under the CRT Principles, a business may not exploit its creditors as if they were only strangers who must be on their guard against abuse of their contractual expectations regarding corporate performance.

OWNERS AS STAKEHOLDERS

The strongest moral commands in all of business law lie in the fiduciary duties that a board of directors owes to owners and that officers owe to the corporation for which they work. These relationships are based on duty, not commerce.

In bringing specificity to the obligations of a company toward its owners, the CRT Principles for Business state as a general principle: "We believe in honoring the trust our investors place in us."

The CRT Principles then set forth the following business responsibilities. First:

- *Apply professional and diligent management in order to secure a fair and competitive return on our owner's investment*

Note that the CRT requirement is not to serve the profit motive of owners at any cost. Returns on equity need only be within reasonable limits, not phenomenal! Squeezing out the last penny for owners by resorting to violation of other principles is unethical. For example, front-end loading of profits at the cost of long term survival is not permitted. Similarly, temporarily boosting a stock price with aggressive accounting techniques is not fair to equity investors. Such a management policy exposes them to excessive risk of loss of capital when the time comes to pay the piper for past acts of shortsighted, egregious selfishness. And, in business, that day of reckoning always comes, sooner or later. The forgiveness capacity of the markets is small to none at all.

The CRT Principles insist, however, that management not waste the owner's money with earning only low returns or with losses. Returns on investment need to be "competitive." If the business is not creating wealth for society and so earning its way forward, it should go out of business, with its remaining investor equity redeployed to other, more profitable, market opportunities.

Under their obligation to apply professional and diligent management, directors and officers owe their principals a duty of loyalty. They may not serve two masters, even if one such master is their own self-interest. As the CRT Principles put it, directors and officers must "conserve, protect, and increase" the assets given to them by the owners. They can't do this very well if they are trying to exploit corporate opportunities for themselves. The "take-the-money-and-run" acquisitiveness that often motivates brute capitalists has no place within any scheme of fiduciary duty. The door to corporate office is legally barred to any self-interest save only that self-interest "considered upon the whole." The CRT Principles for Business here reflect the dictates of the "moral sense" alluded to by Adam Smith and Mencius.

In the tragic scandal of Enron, the assets of the owners were destroyed by actions of senior officers coupled with supine acquiescence in those actions by members of Enron's board of directors. In addition, senior corporate officers breached their trust. They violated their duty of loyalty by providing for themselves and placing too much risk of failure on the owners. They put themselves in a position to make money from secret special-purpose entities financed by Enron while leaving the owners to carry the can if things went wrong.

Members of the Enron board also breached their duty of loyalty to the company's owners, for the directors put their personal relations with Enron's senior management on a higher plane of self-interest than their responsibility to be good stewards for the stockholders. A conflict between their self-interest and their duty diverted them away from paying skillful attention to the risks being proposed by top management.

When senior corporate officers, many also acting as members of the company's board of directors, provide themselves with golden parachutes and profitable stock options, they may well run afoul of their agency duty to loyally serve the interests of owners above all other interests.

Agents are to be compensated for their efforts, but only for their diligent efforts on behalf of those they serve. There is a calculus of differential benefits at work in determining the right balance between what is good for the agent and what is good for his or her principal. Once the calculus shifts too much toward the agent's interests, imbalance sets in, tilting the course of events toward greater risk of loss for the principal because the agent's judgment is swayed in ways detrimental to the principal's best interests. On the other hand, if the calculus shifts too much toward the principal's interests, agents become underappreciated and underpaid and, therefore, may lose their fervor for service of the principal.

Warren Buffet acknowledged the dangers inherent in agency status when, in his annual letter to the shareholders of Berkshire Hathaway for 2000, written just before the recent wave of ethical scandals hit corporate America, he said that: "Nothing sedates rationality like huge doses of effortless money." By "rationality" he had in mind the standard of "self-interest considered upon the whole," a moral factor in decision making.

Of course, the deeper the moral character of the agent, the greater his or her ability to condition "self-interest" with the teachings of good judgment and of virtues such as integrity and prudence, and the less likely will he or she be to upset the "trust"/dependency equilibrium of an agency-principal relationship.

J.P. Morgan, America's greatest capitalist in the heyday of industrial robber barons, always denied that his more critical decisions were mainly based on considerations of financial reward. In one congressional hearing, the committee's counsel asked Morgan: "Is not commercial credit based primarily upon money or property?"

Morgan replied, "No sir. The first thing is character."

"Before money or property?" the surprised counsel asked.

"Before money or property or anything else," Morgan said. "Money cannot buy it."[1]

Abuse of corporate office for selfish reasons was especially true during the dot.com stock market boom years, when senior officers focused on driving the corporation's stock price higher and higher at almost any cost. To be sure, the higher stock prices were indeed sought by owners and appreciated by them. But such prices came at a cost: they were not sustainable. After the boom collapsed, many equity investors were no better off financially than they had been ten years before, and some, like the owners of Enron, Global Crossing, and World Com, ended up very much worse off. For investors jumping into the global telecommunications bubble, some $1 trillion was invested for no discernable return.

Tyco's free-spending chief executive officer, Dennis Kozlowski, whose stewardship brought the company close to failure, used public perceptions instead of an inner moral compass as his guide to proper business conduct. At first he had no qualms about giving a Tyco director a $20 million finder's fee for the $9 billion purchase of CIT, but in the wake of Enron, Kozlowski changed his mind and demanded that the fee be repaid to Tyco. When asked to explain his change of heart, Kozlowski replied, "Perception, perception, perception. This will go down badly. The world has changed."[2]

Recall the recent failures of these companies: Enron, Tyco, WorldCom, Adephia, Dynegy, Xerox, Sotheby's, Christie's, CSFB, Merrill Lynch, Global Crossing, Qwest, Bristol-Myers, Imclone, Citigroup, Salomon, AOL, ABB in Sweden, Vivendi-Universal in France, Ahold in The Netherlands, and HIH in Australia. They all were under the supervision of boards of directors. What were those boards doing while the risks of eventual loss were accumulating?

The simple answer in many cases was that those boards had been co-opted by senior management. Once each board's check on senior management evaporated, those directors were in derogation of their fiduciary duties to the company's owners.

In a moral warning pointed as much at the undertakings of today's corporate officers as at the kings of ancient Israel, the Old Testament Prophet Ezekiel said: "Woe unto the shepherds of Israel for they have fed themselves and not the flocks."[3]

Directors and corporate officers are hired to be agents not just for their fidelity but also for their skill. Their responsibility is to guard against high risk and imprudent courses of action. As fiduciaries, directors owe to owners duties of due care in the supervision of management and in decision making. They must bring to their stewardship of assets belonging to others the judgment expected of prudent business leaders.

Fiduciaries are not expected to prevail over fate in all circumstances and deliver steady profits come hell or high water. Clairvoyance is not required. But they are expected to be prudent and sensible, to avoid stupidly negligent decisions. Fiduciaries are expected to be alert, to be aware of relevant facts. In particular, directors are expected to question and second-guess management before giving approval to management recommendations. Acceptance of service as a director invites confidence in one's judgment and capacity as a fiduciary. Owners risk their assets in reliance on the quality of that confidence. Accordingly, directors are liable at law for negligence in the discharge of their trust.

The duty to use due care demanded of both directors and senior corporate managers brings home to the corporation its social responsibilities. In using care to promote the best interests of the company for the benefit of stockholders, directors and senior managers should consider prospects for the company "upon the whole." They have a duty to take time future into consideration, to go beyond immediate profit maximization in their calculation of business advantage. When directors and senior managers skillfully act from considerations of due care, they move their business into the zone of overlap between virtue and advantage. Furthermore, the fiduciary duty of due care requires them to weigh the consequences to the company of all the elements of business set forth in the CRT Principles for Business, including showing concern for all the company's stakeholders. The CRT self-assessment matrix briefly noted in Chapter 6 is available to assist directors and senior managers in fulfilling their duty of due consideration of all stakeholders and the seven CRT General Principles.

Directors are to put themselves in the shoes of those for whom they exercise power. Where the interests of stockholders are concerned, directors are to overcome feelings or "otherness" and live by a version of the Golden Rule: doing for others just as they would do for themselves if their own assets were at risk in the enterprise.

In nearly every major American corporation, but not in most British ones, the chief management officer, usually given the title of chief executive officer, or CEO, also serves as chairman of the company's board. As board chair he or she gains the authority to supervise himself or herself as CEO, a rather obvious loophole in the corporate governance system of checks and balances.

And, as both board chair and CEO, the chief executive can easily secure election to the board of friendly faces who will not trouble him or her with unpleasant questions and demands for higher standards and more thoughtful consideration of difficult points. Shareholders have no readily accessible channel for independent nomination of the directors who will serve technically as their fiduciaries. A board committee nominates new board members, and the committee reports to the chair of the board, who is the CEO.

CRT leaders believe that the position of board chair should be separated from the person who serves the corporation as CEO and, second, that directors should be trained and qualified through some professional process. In January 2003 a special commission of The Conference Board based in New York City agreed with the CRT's perspective and recommended that American corporations separate the position of chairman of the board from the position of chief executive officer.

It was thought that insisting on purchase of corporation shares by directors was wise policy. Such stock ownership would better align the interests of the directors with that of their principals, the other share-holders. But the stock option gambits of the 1990s revealed that use of share ownership and options to buy shares and profit from their rising market prices caused many directors to veil their eyes over management tactics and policies if Wall Street applauded and share prices kept rising ever higher.

It is also thought that sheer greed on the part of senior managers for very lucrative compensation packages was responsible for the many recent unwise judgments, manipulations, deceits, and resulting losses. And that may well be true. Yet few ask why boards of directors approved such overly generous, and in some cases, outrageous, compensation packages for CEOs. Directors of these great American corporations created an incentive structure that undermined the sustainability of their corporations, in violation of their duties of care to shareholders.

Many boards of directors in American corporations fall short of proper expectations. They do not present management with constructive analysis and insightful questions to maximize good business judgment. To offset the risk associated with their investment in the company, owners deserve from directors the benefit of good judgment and wise decision making. Anything less leaves the equity investors too exposed to harm.

Directors of American corporations are elected to office without any training or certification. Lawyers, doctors, accountants, engineers, pharmacists, appraisers, surveyors, stockbrokers, acupuncturists, veterinarians, nurses, and others—even taxi drivers in many cities—are not allowed to ply their skills until trained and qualified. Are not corporate directors just as important as these professionals in their power to affect our society and our well-being?

The CRT Principles for Business call for "professional and diligent" management of a business. Should not this requirement for professional competence begin with the board members who hire and supervise the actual managers?

Improving the morality of American capitalism requires corporate boards to assume more responsibility and to hold themselves accountable for higher standards of corporate social responsibility. Their role is to act as the conscience of the corporation, to define its values.

Required director training should focus on the CRT Principles for Business, corporate law, the fiduciary duties of directors, accounting fundamentals, and personal leadership abilities. Such leadership skills are outlined in Chapter 13. The CRT's self-assessment and improvement process, with its comprehensive 49-cell matrix of concerns for business leaders to address, provides a ready and tailor-made framework for the comprehensive training of corporate directors.

It may also be the case that the position of director is no longer suitable for just anyone. Special skills and, more importantly, special traits of character and habits of thinking perhaps should be insisted on in the selection of directors. Not everyone is prepared to be diligent in office.

The diligent management that the CRT Principles for Business require of directors and senior corporate officers is necessary, as the Principles go on to say, to:

- *Conserve, protect, and increase the owners'/investors' assets*

This objective concentrates the judgment and decision making of management and the board in a team effort. Management skill and diligence must be applied collectively to transform capital into profitable enterprise.

Executives, more than managers, need many skills.[4] Technical competence is just the beginning. Good executives should think well: they must have seasoned judgment, be capable of visionary thinking from time to time, possess financial acumen and industry knowledge, and have a global perspective. Good executives should also be managers: shaping strategy, driving execution, fostering open dialogue, and building organizational relationships. Good executives need quality personal skills: a drive for success, mature confidence, adaptability, self-direction, high-impact delivery in interpersonal communications, influencing others. And, good executives need leadership skills: entrepreneurial risk taking, inspiring trust, attracting and development talent, empowering others, negotiating.

Then, the CRT Principles for Business add two more obligations to a company's solicitude toward its owners and investors:

- *Disclose relevant information to owners/investors subject to legal requirements and competitive constraints*
- *Respect owners'/investors' requests, suggestions, complaints, and formal resolutions*

In making disclosures and by respecting the opinions and concerns of owners and investors, businesses contribute to building trust—a key ingredient of every nation's social capital. Making moral capitalism work demands honoring the trust of others. Productive capitalism cannot thrive where the law of the jungle prevails. How much wealth have all the animals created since the dawn of time?

Capitalism grows through creating ever more complex relationships of dependency: people rely on others for salaries, for credit, for supplies, for careful work, for inventions, for accurate communications, for keeping promises. This requirement of capitalism is undermined by mistrust. Where mistrust prevails, people fear entering into dependency relationships. Mistrust always raises the risks of enterprise. Who would invest where risks are excessive and returns uncertain?

Dependency is a special condition of being human. Humans, in general, are more dependent on each other than animals are on the others of their kind; while, high above, the gods of our traditions seem to be more independent of each other than humans are. The human person is born into dependency and grows into adulthood through socialization at the hands of others. To paraphrase the poet John Donne, no person is an island unto himself or herself. Herbert Spencer's analogy of human society to natural selection in the wild was very wrong. People need environments of trust and mutual support in order to live well. With its tendency to ever more divide labor through specialization, market capitalism pushes human societies into greater and greater degrees of dependency and, therefore, into more and more need for trust.

Making material disclosures, rewarding trust, facilitating honor, promoting goodwill—all these are necessary for capitalism. They become obligations that, for reasons of self-preservation, the system demands of those who participate in its activities.

Trust is built, first of all, through disclosure of important, relevant, and, sometimes, confidential information. Secrecy erodes trust as it gives rise to suspicion and fear. Trust leads to a kind of intimacy, a state of no fear and of sharing things in common. A trust relationship is one of mutuality, of dependency and reliance on the reliability, honor, and fidelity of the more powerful side of the relationship.

Disclosure of information serves the needs of lenders as well as owners. Creditors, too, are dependent on corporate success and run risks. True, lending money to a company does not create either a fiduciary or an agency relationship at law. Debtors are not responsible to anyone as to how they manage borrowed funds, only for the payment of principal and interest and the performance of any other tasks that have been mutually agreed on.

The relationship between a company and its creditors is one of contract enforced at law.

Creditors, however, attempt to lower the risks of nonpayment by putting constraints on their borrowers through contract, keeping borrowers from profligate actions. Some contracts for debt go so far as to micromanage the business of the debtor, who must ask for waiver after waiver of the loan provisions in order to do business in a changing world.

The CRT Principles look on a company's relationship with its creditors as a limited form of stewardship. The cash received by the company, after all, still belongs to others in the long run and must be returned to them. The borrower is putting other people's property to use and should be held to moral awareness of the dependency of those owners on the company's success. Where there is dependency on the one hand, there is responsibility to act with care on the other.

Although contracts for loans don't really have a moral dimension other than the keeping of promises, debtor-creditor relations are enhanced by trust, a noncommercial item. On a practical level, creditors want their borrowers to be successful; profitability of the business increases the chance of repayment. Creditors want to be helpful. And, debtors are better off if their lenders show flexibility as times and conditions change. The best debtor-creditor relationship, therefore, goes beyond the terms of a contract to an exchange of information and ideas that builds mutual trust.

In the debtor-creditor relationship, the debtor often possesses the power of valuable information while the creditor holds the whip hand of the law. Each can prosper from forbearance by the other. Maintaining such a mutually advantageous relationship demands disclosure by the corporate debtor.

Providing information to others who may benefit from the knowledge, or who may suffer when left in ignorance of the facts, is part of acting maturely. Such an ethic of disclosure follows upon accepting responsibility for one's decisions and actions.

MONEY: THE BITCH GODDESS

The interest of owners and investors in making money introduces a challenge to moral capitalism. Money is easily idolized, provoking heresy by turning us away from the things of God to the things of Mammon. There are times when we may sell our souls to gain what money promises in the way of power and license. This is especially true in today's culture of consumerism, where we have sanctified appetite over character. Money enables us to do what we want. People seek it; they covet it; they even kill for it. Money provides us with discretionary power, easing our ability to turn people and their needs to our use.

Power, however, tends to corrupt, and absolute power corrupts absolutely. The human soul is not a reliable steward of power. Desires for superiority; to humiliate others; to be seen, noticed, and obeyed; and to supplant parental authorities are cultured in the human soul wherever people are found. These traits are the moral hazards running with ownership or with becoming a creditor.

Money and its power, therefore, expose capitalism to abuse at human hands, bringing on conflict between moral and brutish capitalisms. More than anything else in capitalism, money creates the need for the morality of fiduciary duties.

The American philosopher William James observed during the era of the robber barons that, in America, success was the "bitch" goddess—worshipped and venerated, but who spurned most of her acolytes and left them without self-esteem. James was looking at an America caught up in making great material progress and intellectually in the grip of Spencer's Social Darwinism. Ownership was desired as the benchmark of success in this world.

Much of what James thought of by success can be found in money. Money could easily serve as the measure of success, the source of personal merit, and the justification of a life well lived. Possession of money—a lot of it—could bring the confidence of spiritual superiority, of deserving grace from the goddess of material well-being.

Seeking such worldly grace, and, especially, seeking to possess money as proof of our good fortune, can pervert competition from its higher aspirations of service. It is easy for people to turn after money and the power it brings. They then lose self-restraint and convert competition into a rampage, giving reign to the blood lust, and regressing in the process to more primitive levels of moral engagement. People with character, however—no matter what their position in a corporate hierarchy or the level of their net worth—are more likely to refuse this worship of the Bitch Goddess.

Alexis de Tocqueville observed during his travels in the United States during the 1830s how Americans withstood the temptations associated with money: "Self-interest properly understood cannot make a man virtuous, but its discipline shapes a lot of orderly, temperate, moderate, careful, and self-controlled citizens. If it does not lead the will directly to virtue, it establishes habits which unconsciously turn it that way."[5]

There is a second challenge to moral capitalism arising from the need for money. Money oversimplifies. It leaves out many values that can't be easily reduced to a price internal to a company's calculations of profit and loss. These overlooked values often are externalities, costs born by others outside the enterprise, like the impact of the business on the environment or communities. Money further neglects intangibles like love and honor, respect for wisdom or age. Calculations using money fall short of measuring all that is real and of value. Money, no matter how seductive its promise of power over others may appear, can be an imperfect tool for implementing our highest aspirations within the realm of facticity.

Third, money distorts time, turning our heads away from our self-interest properly "considered upon the whole." Money has its greatest value in the present. We want it now, not next year. We will pay interest over time to get money today, so it is worth less in the future. So in the calculations of capitalism, the worth of things in the future is discounted down to some present value expressed in terms of today's money. Consumption today is thus overvalued compared with the needs of tomorrow.[6]

CONCLUSION

Fiduciary thinking informs the CRT Principles for Business with respect to owners and investors. The fiduciary concept lies at the core of the moral sense, for it attaches responsibility for others to the use of power. In chapter 10 next, we will consider the stakeholder constituency of suppliers.

ASSESSING YOUR COMPANY

How does your company implement the CRT guidelines for meeting its responsibilities to owners and investors? To make an assessment, score your company on the following criteria:

CRITERION 1.4 (Principle: Beyond Shareholders toward Stakeholders)
How does the company's governance structure ensure the health and viability of the business and respond to the concerns of current owners/investors and other stakeholders?

0   5   10
Lower Quality   Higher Quality   _____

CRITERION 2.4 (Principle: Economic/Social Impact of Business)
How does the company use its resources to enhance the economic and social value of its products/services (e.g., through the development of new products/services, new applications for existing products, new production processes, etc.)?

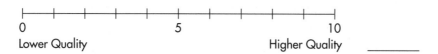

0   5   10
Lower Quality   Higher Quality   _____

CRITERION 3.4 (Principle: Business Behavior)
How does the company elicit the trust of owners/investors (e.g., through responsible disclosures, timely and complete responses to shareholder/investor inquiries, governance policies and practices, etc.)?

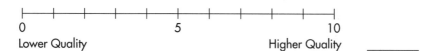

0   5   10
Lower Quality   Higher Quality   _____

CRITERION 4.4 (Principle: Respect for Rules)
How does the company manage compliance with the letter and spirit of national and international owner/investor-related rules?

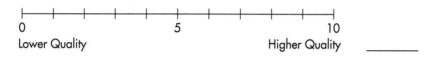

0   5   10
Lower Quality   Higher Quality   _____

CRITERION 5.4 (Principle: Support for Multilateral Trade)
How does the company avail itself of international business opportunities
for the benefit of owners/investors?

0   5   10
Lower Quality   Higher Quality   _____

CRITERION 6.4 (Principle: Respect for the Environment)
How does the company manage environmental issues that impact
owners/investors (e.g., health and safety risks, legacy issues, litigation and
financial risks, etc.)?

0   5   10
Lower Quality   Higher Quality   _____

CRITERION 7.4 (Principle: Avoidance of Illicit Operations)
How does the company take action to prevent such illicit activities as
insider trading and fraudulent reporting?

0   5   10
Lower Quality   Higher Quality   _____

TOTAL SCORE (maximum possible points = 70)   _____

CHAPTER 10

SUPPLIERS: FRIENDS OR FOES?

Haggling over every ounce in purchasing
may not reduce one's cost of capital.

—Ninth Business Principle, Tao Zhu Gong,
Assistant to the Emperor of Yue, 500 B.C.E.

SUPPLIERS ARE A STAKEHOLDER CONSTITUENCY more relevant to the success of manufacturers than other businesses, although all firms rely to some extent on the products and services of other businesses to support their ability to serve their customers. Suppliers intensively support the manufacturing process; their quality shapes the quality of the final product that a business sells to its customers, while suppliers prices impact the cost of manufacturing that product. Yet for all businesses, suppliers of inputs and of services can add to or detract from commercial success. Retail stores, for example, are highly dependent on relationships with the suppliers of the goods they sell. Expensive restaurants rely heavily on quality provisions for customer satisfaction and above-cost pricing.

The company must decide whether to adopt an adversarial or an accommodating stance toward suppliers. The Caux Round Table recommends that the company-supplier relationship be one of mutual dependency, not a series of one-off, buyer-beware transactions. The CRT Principles accordingly advocate that businesses build relations with suppliers out of an awareness of this mutuality. And mutuality, of course, is always a premise for moral conduct.

A company's relationship with suppliers bears some similarity to its relationship with employees. Employees can be easily seen as suppliers of labor, skill, and other human resources. As discussed in Chapter 8 above, quality employees improve a company's profitability. A similar consequence holds true for suppliers as well. Both employees and suppliers must be paid enough to obtain quality inputs for the company but not so much as to waste company assets. Personal qualities in employees and friendship with suppliers have a place in business, but not to the exclusion of price considerations. Seasoned judgment strikes the right balance between cost and overall quality.

Agency concepts give rather comprehensive guidance to a company for successful management of its labor relations. Suppliers, however, are not fiduciaries or agents of the business under any doctrine of law. They have the legal distance from a business similar to that of customers and creditors. Nonetheless, the CRT Principles recommend that a company's "relationship with suppliers and subcontractors must be based on mutual respect."

In this, the Caux Round Table built on the work of W. Edwards Deming. Deming's philosophy of quality management called for a new dedication by a company to improvement of its products and services. Much of that improvement, Deming argued, came from improving relationships with suppliers. From his vision, especially after it was used as an explanation of Japanese excellence in manufacturing, came the Total Quality Movement in the United States, followed by Six Sigma programs, the global ISO standard 9000, and, in the United States, the prestigious Malcolm Baldridge Award for quality.

Deming's philosophy was customer centered. Quality of product and service was sought to sustain customer satisfaction. He connected customer preferences through the manufacturing process to the supply chain supporting that process. He gave suppliers new dignity and importance by connecting them to the central engine of capitalism—customers. For Deming, suppliers became not a cost but a source of value. Proper servicing of suppliers is a value driver for companies.[1]

Deming put the supplier's importance to a business in Figure 10.1: On July 13, 1950, while working for the American occupation administration, Deming presented his ideas on quality control to the twenty-one presidents of Japan's leading industries. He told them, "You can produce quality. You have a method for doing it. ... You must carry out consumer research, look toward the future and produce goods that will have a market years from now and stay in business. You can send quality out and get food back. The city of Chicago does it. The people of Chicago do not produce their own food. They make things and ship them out. Switzerland does not produce all their own food, nor does England." On a blackboard

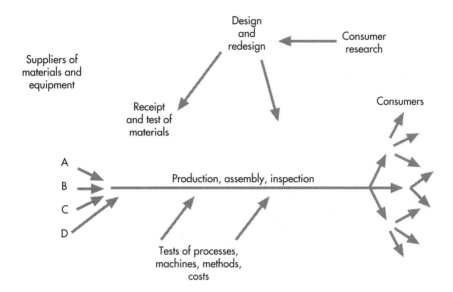

Deming then drew a flowchart that began with suppliers and ended with consumers. "The consumer is the most important part of the production line," he said to his exclusive Japanese audience. How to set up a flow of work that ultimately pleased the consumer became Deming's strategy for success in business. Suppliers were part of that flow.

"I told them they would capture markets the world over within five years," Deming recalled.

The Japanese were faithful learners. So faithful, in fact, that their stunning economic success in manufacturing and export of consumer goods led to jealously and fear in Europe and America and to the foundation of the Caux Round Table in 1986 as a device to ameliorate that commercial rivalry. The Japanese did well for themselves by doing good for the consumers of the world.

As he later developed his philosophy, Deming listed seven deadly diseases that would eat away at the health of a company.

The first business pathology he noted is opportunism—having no constancy of purpose, no long-range plan, no one, big idea for success in the marketplace.

The second disease is emphasis on short-term profits. Just ask the owners of Enron about the correctness of this advice. Enron produced handsome profits in the early years and illusory profits in its last several years before bankruptcy. But those early profits were of no help to its owners when the company filed for bankruptcy protection. Too much emphasis on short-term profits had eaten away the company's long-term viability.

Third is performance evaluation by numbers. This destroys teamwork, nurtures rivalry, builds fear, and leaves employees bitter, despondent, and beaten. Jeffery Skilling, president of Enron, did annual performance reviews based on forced rankings according to income earned for the company and, annually, fired the lowest ranked 20 percent of Enron's employees. Thus, he fostered a culture of "bring in the numbers any way, any how" and, in time, destroyed the company.

Fourth is turnstile managers who are here today but gone tomorrow.

Fifth is running a company on reportable statistics. The most important indicator—a happy customer—is often unknown and unknowable.

Sixth is high medical costs caused by inadequate attention to safety and employee health.

Seventh is excessive product liability costs, paying damages in judgments won by plaintiffs' lawyers.

Deming's recommendations about quality penetrate to the heart of corporate cultures, but the core of his quality movement focused on respectful, long-term relations with suppliers.

Deming recommended that suppliers not be chosen on cost alone. Price, he said, has no meaning without a measure of the quality being purchased. If you buy cheap parts, you get breakdown and failure when you least need it. Lack of quality anywhere in the entire chain of production raises risks and promotes insecurity. Low-quality inputs bring with them delays and frustrations in producing the product, defects in the product, and customer dissatisfaction. Low price may not offer the most cost-effective purchasing option.

Determining the quality of goods and services purchased is an art. Skillful purchasing agents are an asset. But having at hand trustworthy and reliable suppliers who know and care about your business eases the challenges facing your buyers. A buyer will serve his or her company best by developing a long-term relationship of loyalty and trust with a single vendor, Deming recommends.[2]

A supplier assured of long-term contracts is more likely to risk being innovative or to specially modify production processes than is a supplier with a short-term contract, who cannot afford to tailor an input to the very specific needs of a buyer.

Cost-plus purchases should also be avoided. From your supplier's standpoint, they are loss-leaders to get in your door. Once in, prices go up as shortcomings are noticed and changes are requested. Buying mostly on price tag goes better with an adversarial stance toward suppliers.

Company cost-crunchers in finance and accounting like to have several vendors lining up to compete for the company's business. This competition drives down costs, but if engaged in without regard for quality or service warranties and cost-of-change orders, this practice can drive good vendors out of business. If low cost is the only measurement of success for a supplier, survival of the fittest will produce slim pickings on the quality front.

Multiple sourcing also can have its problems for the company seeking sustained success. Multiple sourcing promotes an arm's-length relationship between vendors and buyers, exactly contrary to what is required for obtaining quality inputs. Multiple sourcing tells a vendor "I don't trust you." Treated that way, most vendors will reciprocate and, as the relationship sours, will earn your lack of trust—but much to your sorrow as well.

In multiple sourcing, vendors may not be willing to alter their production processes to meet a firm's revised specifications. The buying firm also loses volume discounts. Inventory costs increase. Confidential information is spread more widely. Setup costs in multiple facilities are required. Increased tooling requirements and variation in incoming quality must be resolved.

After his research into the reasons behind competitive success, Michael Porter concluded, in line with Deming's recommendations, that close working relationships with world-class suppliers help firms innovate. The suppliers provide clues and suggestions as to new methods and opportunities and add to the value chain of competitive advantage with innovations of their own.[3]

In this light, the CRT Principles for Business set as a standard:

- *Long-term stability in the supplier relationship in return for value, quality, competitiveness, and reliability*
- *Sharing of information with suppliers to integrate them into the planning process*

The CRT Principles advise that suppliers be accepted as an extension of the moral community that is the business enterprise "taken upon the whole." The optimal supplier relationship is one of mutual interest and dependability. The CRT Principles demand that companies honor the loyalty implicit in such a relationship. Companies should be fair and truthful with their suppliers.

The CRT Principles hold that companies have a responsibility to:

- *Ensure that business activities are free from coercion and unnecessary litigation*
- *Pay suppliers on time and in accordance with agreed terms of trade*

The CRT Principles would have companies negotiate in good faith with suppliers for quality goods and services and not seek to use market power as a means of squeezing suppliers and subcontractors into operating on very thin and vulnerable profit margins. When any company cuts corners to sell at a lower price, something gives in terms of quality. That loss of quality compromises the entire system and leads to suboptimal results for customers and employees. And, short-term profits made by owners as a result of such trimming cannot outweigh, in the longer term, the losses associated with failure of their companies due to continuing low margins or loss of goodwill. Doing the right thing under the CRT Principles is to do the wise thing, and wisdom most often leads to commercial success. Virtue and interest are not inconsistent. Using market power alone is a tactic of opportunism, not a strategy for prosperous growth.

Companies should ensure that their demands on suppliers are free of coercion, including the coercive use of litigation. In short, companies should not seek to profit from the fear and greed they might induce in suppliers through abusive application of power.

Suppliers should be paid on time and in accordance with agreed-on terms of trade. Suppliers should not be used outside of those normal terms of trade as a source of short-term financing for the enterprise through intentionally delayed payment.

Asking for kickbacks from potential suppliers in return for contracts and other forms of commercial bribery would violate the CRT Principles.

Third, the CRT Principles realize that, in many cases, suppliers and subcontractors become part of a company's identity in the marketplace through their contribution to the product sold under the company's name. Nike lost its reputation when its Korean-owned subcontractors made shoes in Vietnamese factories exploiting their young women workers. Kathy Lee Gifford lost market position when it was reported that products bearing her name were produced in objectionable third-world sweatshops. Ford Motor Company pointed an accusing finger at Firestone, its long-time supplier of tires, when Firestone tires on its Explorer SUVs began exploding and its customers died in resulting accidents.

Therefore, the CRT Principles require companies to:

- *Seek, encourage, and prefer suppliers and subcontractors whose employment practices respect human dignity*

The Caux Round Table would not only have large companies live up to its Principles but would also have its Principles reach down through the supply chain to encompass the broader web of relationships supporting large companies.

This one admonition of the CRT Principles, as well as concerns for employees as stakeholders, can be expanded into operational management goals with the help of another set of corporate responsibility standards, SA 8000. Developed by Social Accountability International in New York City, SA 8000 is a set of requirements for factories. Performance under these requirements can be audited by specialists trained by Social Accountability International. Thus, a company seeking suppliers or using subcontractors can easily write into the purchase contract compliance by the supplier or the subcontractor with the terms of SA 8000, to be verified by outside auditors.

SUPPLIERS OF SERVICES

Although Deming's theories of business success came out of manufacturing, the moral framework for supplier relationships provided by the CRT Principles for Business applies equally to suppliers of services.

Just as agricultural production now employs a small fraction of the workforce in advanced economies, so employment in manufacturing is a declining percentage of the workforce in those economies. Services—the provision of advice, and the facilitation of transactions and the meeting of consumer desires—are a growing contributor to gross domestic product in every country. Lawyers, bankers, accountants, advertising agencies, consultants for public relations and information systems are major suppliers in an era of knowledge-based economies.

A company should seek relationships grounded on integrity and sound judgment with its service professionals. That is the way forward to quality support for the company's needs and interests. Lawyers and accountants should be more than hired guns willing to bend their professional standards just to invoice another billable hour, or two, or three. Enron was not well served by its lawyers in Vincent & Elkins, by its investment bankers in New York, and by its accountants in Arthur Andersen who delivered up without question and for fat fees the "creative" legal arrangements and the corresponding accounting treatments so ardently desired by Enron's top management in its desperate search for "reportable" profits after 1999. Those suppliers of legal, financial, and accounting services made a lot of money for themselves off the company, while leaving their client at great risk. Where was the real quality in their services rendered? If their services had been a manufactured product coming off an asembly line, the defect rate would have been unacceptably high. Poor quality in service support sank the company. Citibank and JP Morgan Chase paid $305 million in fines to the Securities and Exchange Commission for their role in assisting Enron hide the truth about its earnings with "creative" financing packages.

Suppliers of services should be, from the perspective of the Caux Round Table, part of a long-term moral relationship with the company, dedicated to its best interests. Otherwise, the adversarial seeking of short-term advantage between suppliers and companies brings on the circumstances promoted by brute capitalism. A company should discharge any service provider that does not demonstrate a deep sense of responsibility for the company's future.

With regard to licensees and companies that use products or intellectual property of a company, the CRT Principles for Business call for relationships of mutuality. The CRT Principles state that a company has a responsibility to:

- *Seek fairness and truthfulness in all its activities, including pricing, licensing, and rights to sell.*

Here is temptation to leverage market power over licencees, distributors, and franchisees through contractual arrangments that reduce competition and raise benefits to market entry by new firms. A successful company's competitive advantage must be balanced against its moral obligation to contribute generally to the creation of new wealth, even by its competitors or its potential competitors. "Market power should not be used unfairly through contract to restrain wealth creation." The admonition of CRT General Principle 4 on respect for rules that "some behavior, although legal, may still have adverse consequences" aptly applies here.

CONCLUSION

Suppliers and subcontractors should not to be seen as "strangers" to the business. Some balance of interests must be negotiated with them to maximize the company's ability to provide its customers with quality goods and services at an appropriate cost. In chapter 11, the challenge of competition for a moral capitalism is to be considered.

ASSESSING YOUR COMPANY

How well does your company implement the CRT's guidelines for interaction with suppliers? To make an assessment, score your company on the following criteria:

SCORE

CRITERION 1.5 (Principle: Beyond Shareholders toward Stakeholders)
How does the company ensure the practice of honesty and fairness in supplier-partner relationships (e.g., including, but not limited to, issues of pricing, technology licensing, right to sell, etc.)?

```
0                    5                    10
Lower Quality                   Higher Quality        _____
```

CRITERION 2.5 (Principle: Economic/Social Impact of Business)
How does the company ensure stable supplier-partner relationships and the prudent and innovative utilization of resources by supplier-partners?

```
0                    5                    10
Lower Quality                   Higher Quality        _____
```

CRITERION 3.5 (Principle: Business Behavior)
How does the company achieve trust with supplier-partners (e.g., through integrity in the bid evaluation process, protection of proprietary innovations, etc.)?

```
0                    5                    10
Lower Quality                   Higher Quality        _____
```

CRITERION 4.5 (Principle: Respect for Rules)
How does the company manage compliance with the letter and spirit of national and international supplier-partner-related rules?

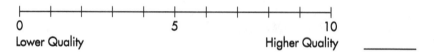

CRITERION 5.5 (Principle: Support for Multilateral Trade)
How does the company seek and utilize international suppliers in both its domestic and nondomestic operations?

CRITERION 6.5 (Principle: Respect for the Environment)
How does the company manage environmental performance standards on a comparable basis throughout its supply chain?

CRITERION 7.5 (Principle: Avoidance of Illicit Operations)
How does the company implement corrective action when it uncovers illicit activities by a supplier-partner?

TOTAL SCORE (maximum possible points = 70)   _____

CHAPTER 11

COMPETITORS: REPEALING THE LAW OF THE JUNGLE

People of the same trade seldom meet together, even for merriment and diversion, but the conversation ends in a conspiracy against the public, or in some contrivance to raise prices.

—*Adam Smith, Wealth of Nations[1]*

CONSUMERS PROVIDE THE COMPASS for capitalism, employees do the work, owners make the arrangements, and suppliers feed the machinery of business, but competition hones business decision making, always driving our attention toward the needs of others. When competitive pressures ease, we can more easily impose our arbitrary will on the markets of capitalism. Competitive markets—for customers, investors, employees, supplies, innovations, reputation, etc.—force accountability on business managers by weeding out poor performance. In this competitive markets perform a moral function; they keep people on their toes and always facing the music.

As argued in Chapter 6 under Caux Round Table General Principle No. 5 on Support for Multilateral Trade, moral capitalism presumes a right of competition. The expression of personhood and personal dignity through use of property permits competitive efforts to better one's condition. Competition opens doors for more robust individuality across society, without regard for restraints imposed by the status quo. Competition cumulates the various impacts people can have on the world around them; it is property in motion changing the way we live.

Mostly, however, business competitors are after money, not the social benefits of market discipline or the moral rights of rival competitors. Competition is often managed only to improve the bottom line with higher margins on sales and lower costs on inputs. Rivals are absorbed, driven out

151

of business or drawn into collusive arrangements; new entrants resisted and undermined; customers ignored; employees and suppliers squeezed and investors are promised as much of the world as they will accept. Financial results correctly measured in money do indeed indicate rather dispositively whether a company is winning or losing. But only the most superficial advocate of capitalism's virtues would agree that fighting over the money gives to capitalism a redeeming purpose.

The money that fuels business endeavors is only a means to an end. Using the analogy of an automobile, we would say that our car's engine works to get us someplace, not just to run on and on, consuming fuel. Similarly, lubricants assist the engine to run smoothly so that it might cause the automobile to reach its destination. In business, therefore, money made is not the end of competition, but only an important combustible giving propulsive force to all the cars in the system so that they may each reach the destination designated by their respective drivers.

Yet, it is true for some competing to win that having the most money at the end of the day does become their end of ends, the highest purpose of their business lives. Money, the very same "bitch goddess" feared by philosopher William James, has the power to distort market competition and turn it against a range of stakeholder interests. Competitive pressures whet the desire to win and to make a lot of money at all costs, unleashing motivations more conducive to brute capitalism than to moral capitalism.

Competitors have a role to perform, an office to undertake. The more wealth they create in office, the more they have met their responsibilities to society. There is more to a moral business than making a profit. How the profit is made becomes the standard of duty.

Accordingly, the CRT Principles for Business assert that businesses have a responsibility to:

- *Foster open markets for trade and investment*
- *Promote competitive behavior that is socially and environmentally beneficial and demonstrates mutual respect among competitors*
- *Refrain from either seeking or participating in questionable payments or favors to secure competitive advantage*
- *Respect both tangible and intellectual property rights*
- *Refuse to acquire commercial information by dishonest or unethical means, such as industrial espionage*

All that is required for the CRT ideal to happen is the exercise of self-restraint, the demonstration of moral character, on the part of business decision makers.

THE SOCIAL ADVANTAGES OF COMPETITION

Adam Smith, the first scholar to effectively describe the inner mechanics of market capitalism, observed that meeting consumer needs keeps the engine of competition running. The machine of capitalism, Smith wrote, arises from "the propensity to truck, barter and exchange one thing for another," in other words, from the propensity to compete for goods and services and, therefore, from the inventiveness to create markets in which to "truck, barter and exchange."[2]

Smith made another observation that has led to no end of controversy. He observed that although people need others to meet their needs and to serve their desires, those others are not particularly motivated toward cooperation by ideals of charity and of benevolence. Few people, for those altruistic reasons alone, will reliably meet our needs or agree to service our desires. As a consequence, Smith advised that to run the machinery of competition, the wiser course would be to appeal to the self-interest of others and not to their benevolence.

Smith wrote that one is "more likely to prevail if he can interest their self-love in his favor, and show then that it is for their own advantage to do for him what he requires of them." For, Smith argued, "It is not from the benevolence of the butcher, the brewer or the baker, that we expect our dinner, but from their regard to their own interest"; "Nobody but a beggar chooses to depend chiefly upon the benevolence of his fellow-citizens."

Actually Smith is not arguing here for immorality, for a brute capitalism. Rather, he is pointing to mutuality as the basis of a more moral capitalism: the bargain and sale that marries together the needs and desires of two independent moral decision makers. The morality of any market exchange is not internal to the buyer or the seller, available for measurement only where their different, possibly selfish motivations can be found. The morality of a commercial transaction, rather, is found at the level of a social process in the reality of reciprocal deference between the buyer and the seller.

Capitalism advances civilization, builds it up, makes more where there was less, and empowers citizens again and again. If market competition were necessarily destructive of civilization, it would not be permitted to survive. But it has survived, even thrived on occasion. From a Darwinian perspective of natural selection, capitalism triumphed over communism because it does not permit competition to go beyond the bounds of its special office, which is to have a positive impact in the creation of wealth. Historical capitalism delivered to a very great extent on its promise of wealth creation for the general good. So, there can be a "right" kind of selfish capitalist competition that furthers the social goal of wealth creation.

That "right" kind of capitalist competition does indeed seek mutual satisfaction, not power or the thrill of "winning." The "right" kind of competition is "other regarding," keeping in mind how we can better meet their needs in the marketplace. This kind of competition arises from our "self-interest considered upon the whole."

Therefore, the foundational duty of a business when it competes is not to cheat or otherwise undermine the positive aspects of competition. Market power should not be sought to abuse rivals, just as it should not be sought to bully consumers, employees, and suppliers. In today's world of specialized undertakings and mutual dependencies, we cannot permit competition to become divisive and destructive of prospects for future exchanges. Competition should promote infinite expansion of opportunities for buying and selling, of growth in markets and of specialization of work and division of labor.

So, regarding competition, the CRT Principles for Business hold that, "We believe that fair economic competition is one of the basic requirements for increasing the wealth of nations and ultimately for making possible the just distribution of goods and services."

THE HUMAN ANIMAL

As Smith looked to a benign common sense within our natures to explain the role of market competition in wealth creation, we can also look at another, darker, aspect of that same human nature. We can easily, and often, observe the propensity of people when they enter into competition with one another to become primitive, even savage. The spirit of rivalry takes over openly, especially for the males of our species. Fair play and moral considerations are left way back in a distant second place. Promotion of this passion for mastery is exactly what brutish capitalism values.

Adam Smith thought that this self-centered drive for power could be contained. In his book *The Theory of Moral Sentiments*, Smith found in human nature a propensity toward sympathy: an innate ability to conceive what other people feel and desire. "How selfish soever man may be supposed, there are evidently some principles in his nature, which interest him in the fortunes of others and rend their happiness necessary to him, though he derives nothing from it except the pleasure of seeing it."[3]

Smith took it as a given that people were more than savages. They lived in society, not in the jungle as beasts. As had Aristotle and Mencius long before him, Smith understood that people coexist with one another. Smith wrote: "It is thus that man, who can subsist only in society, was fitted by nature to that situation for which he was made. All the members of human society stand in need of each other's assistance, and are likewise exposed to mutual injuries. Where the necessary assistance is reciprocally afforded from love, from gratitude, from friendship, and esteem, the society flourishes and is happy. ... Society may subsist among different men, as among different merchants, from a sense of its utility, without any mutual love or affection; and though no man in it should owe any obligation, or be bound in gratitude to any other, it may still be upheld by a mercenary exchange of good offices according to an agreed valuation."[4]

Herbert Spencer missed Smith's point and has been proven wrong for making that mistake. Social Darwinism and the brute capitalism it calls for misunderstand the human condition and human needs and potentials. The evolution of humanity has left us ever more attuned to our social connections, not to our most primitive instincts for violence. Our ancestors who could not survive in social and cultural contexts to prefer living on their own, no doubt died in such isolation, probably young and without leaving behind many heirs to inherit their antisocial dispositions. Those who survived best to have adult offspring demonstrated mastery of social skills, mostly skills of collaboration and successful interrelationships. Humanity's inherited moral orientation can, therefore, encompass the drive of competition within a social framework of mutuality and cooperation. Smith was right.

Smith further esteemed people over beasts by finding in people a capacity for self-control. "The man of real constancy and firmness, the wise and just man, who has been thoroughly bred in the great school of self-command, in the bustle and business of the world, exposed, perhaps to the violence and injustice of faction, and to the hardships and hazards of war, maintains this control of his passive feelings upon all occasions."[5] Such people compete not like savages but with self-imposed restraint giving proportion and moderation to their competitive activities.[6]

The current Dalai Lama echoes Smith's vision, writing: "Now, it could be objected that while we may all share a capacity for loving-kindness, human nature is such that inevitably we tend to reserve it for those closest to us. … This is why, although our nature is basically disposed toward kindness and compassion, we are all capable of cruelty and hatred. It is why we have to struggle to better our conduct."[7]

The Dalai Lama believes that people can develop a faculty of wise discernment, which involves constantly checking our outlook and asking ourselves whether we are being broad-minded or narrow-minded. Mental restraint, he argues, is indispensable because an undisciplined mind is beset by negative and afflictive emotions, which open the door to suffering even in the midst of plenty. In other words, lack of awareness keeps us unhappy unnecessarily because we have a capacity to fill any void of inadequate awareness in our sensibility. If we would but use that capacity for our own benefit, our happiness would flourish without much further ado.

The CRT Principles expect self-restraint in competition. They call on businesses to refrain from either seeking or participating in questionable payments or favors to secure competitive advantage, to respect the property rights of others, and to refuse to acquire commercial information by dishonest or unethical means, such as industrial espionage. And, the CRT Principles expect businesses to compete in open markets, eschewing government favors, special licenses and privileges, or other uses of political power for business advantage.

GAME THEORY

Further evidence that the right kind of competition can bring about social good lies in modern game theory. By assuming a self-interested rationality, game theory and its experiments prove that repeated interactions among the same participants, like the sustained interactions that promote moral capitalism, lead to equilibrium points, or outcomes accepted by the players. Thus, pursuit of individual objectives leads to a common, or social, outcome of value to all.

Years of experiments with the game called prisoner's dilemma demonstrate that people, over time, learn to play by rules that bring them at least some benefit and that reduce their risk of loss. In this game, two prisoners, if given repeated opportunities to play against each other, each learn to arrive at a "win-win" outcome for themselves vis-à-vis the prison wardens. Players learn to abandon more selfish strategies that bring on higher-risk "zero-sum"/"win-lose" outcomes.

THE RIGHT KIND OF COMPETITION

How then can you vigorously compete under the principles of moral capitalism? How can you be self-restrained, as moral capitalism requires, and yet be successful when under pressure from competing businesses? First, and foremost, you can compete through quality and innovation.

Quality provides the highest degree of customer satisfaction. Quality maximizes utility and beauty; it perfects function. It best responds to the moral imperatives of consumers.

Consumers will sacrifice quality for a lower price, depending on their wealth and the value to them of disposable dollars. Even so, they still would rather have the quality that is available at a higher price. Most customers would always prefer to buy a Mercedes over a Yugo if they could have their way. Some people willingly buy beyond their means to acquire expensive goods of high quality, using debt to postpone the time of full payment for the items purchases.

High quality leads to goodwill and favorable reputation. High quality attracts customers and makes a business more valuable. For many years, Ford Motor Company announced that, "Quality is job one." The company borrowed a strategy that seemed to have worked well for its Japanese competitors. Perhaps, too, the company had learned the competitive advantages of quality from its sad experiences in cutting corners on safety with the Pinto. Competing through improved quality enhances the value to society of business enterprise and market interactions. Jack Welsh ended his career at GE as a believer in the Six Sigma program of using quality to attract customers and gain higher profits.

A form of quality enhancement is innovation, which brings about business success fairly and admirably. New goods and services and new ways of making goods with more quality, or of the same quality but for a lower price, bring customers through the door, generate revenues, and improve living standards. Michael Porter concluded from his exhaustive studies of global competition that, "Firms gain competitive advantage from conceiving of new ways to conduct activities, employing new procedures, new technologies or different inputs."[8]

In this intellectually creative process, firms perceive or discover new and better ways to compete and bring the results of those "innovations" to market. Possibilities for new and better ways of competing grow out of new technologies, new or shifting buyer preferences, emergence of a new industry segment, shifting input costs or availability, and changes in regulation.[9] Porter advises firms to avoid seeking the benefits of lower-order competitive advantages such as low labor costs or cheap raw materials and rather to invest in acquiring lasting advantages that differentiate the firm's products or services.

The CRT Principles hold in General Principle No. 2 that, "Businesses should contribute to the economic and social development not only in the countries in which they operate, but also in the world community at large, through effective and prudent use of resources, free and fair competition, and emphasis upon innovation in technology, production methods, marketing and communications."

Adam Smith understood that innovation was the best method for business success under capitalism. The wealth of nations was founded on innovation, not on beggar-thy-neighbor dumping of tired old goods at distressed prices. Innovation looks into the future and seeks reciprocity between sellers and buyers at a higher standard of living for both.

Smith was captivated by the effect of innovation on the division of labor. New machines, new materials, and new ways of organizing production created new tasks, dividing the work in new ways, and produced new value. His famous example was pin making. The old way was to have one person in the shop make each pin from start to finish. But with a few machines introduced, each worker would be responsible for one part of the pin-making process, with each pin passing in stages through the hands of several workers in eighteen distinct operations. With the new method, the quality of the pins increased and the cost of production per pin dropped. Innovation created wealth for the owner (higher output), for the workers (higher productivity per person), and for the consumers (lower costs for a better quality of pin). Innovation, changing the competitive posture of the firm, enhanced its prospects. During the nineteenth century as industrialization came into its own in Europe, prices were falling. Prosperity was nonetheless brought about through competition in quality and brand reputation and in the provision of good service.[10] W. Edwards Deming picked up where Adam Smith left off. Deming's management philosophy of putting quality at the core of a business starts with continuous improvement of product and service.

Quality and innovation require well-trained, loyal, and motivated employees. Managers must discover and remove the barriers that prevent workers from taking pride in what they do. Workers need to be trained. And, they need to be consulted as to how best to improve quality and innovate production methods or service delivery. How companies should treat their employees according to the CRT Principles for Business (see Chapter 8) creates the very corporate culture required if the company is to compete successfully through quality and innovation.

In today's conditions, much innovation requires substantial capital expenditure, which becomes sunk costs demanding offset from pricing goods above the marginal cost of production. Professor William J. Baumol from Princeton has noted that these conditions tend to produce concentrations of producers, or oligopolies, in many contemporary industries.[11] Yet, Baumol establishes that even under such conditions of innovation, there are winners and losers within concentrated industries to keep the innovation machine running smoothly.

COMPETITION THROUGH PRICE

Price does make a difference. Customers have demand curves and will buy more of an item if it is cheap than if it is expensive. But competing on price alone is not recommended. If we buy cheap, it is to sell our output at a better profit in the future; if we cut our prices, it is also done to please potential customers. But wise judgment will recognize that to sustain our ability to create new wealth, there are downside limits on how cheaply we should buy and how cheaply we should sell.

First, the temptation to lower prices to the point where goods can be moved or services provided may not produce sufficient revenue to sustain the enterprise. Businesses have a responsibility to be profitable.

Second, the pressure of markets is to move prices down to where they provide only a very low profit margin. For the same good, market transactions grind away until all sellers come down to the lowest possible price consistent with production costs. The good becomes a commodity and is mass produced under industrywide standards of quality where one company's product is just as good as another's. This saves money for consumers and makes for an efficient use of resources, but profits will be driven out of that line of enterprise.

Under these competitive conditions, returns can still be earned (1) through innovation that reduces production costs still further, (2) through production to scale where large volume on small margins justifies continued operation of the business, and (3) through branding where goodwill or special reputation is attached in consumers' minds to the product as made by one producer (General Mills' Cheerios oat cereal still sells in competition with cheaper generic alternatives).

However, as Baumol has pointed out, where there is production to scale, prices equal to marginal cost cannot bring the firm sufficient revenue to cover its total costs.[12] Competition through price alone, therefore, will not lead to sustained business success.

The inexorable pressure of markets to move toward commodity pricing is a much resented feature of capitalism. The downward movement of prices brings about competitive obsolescence, threatening workers with loss of employment and stodgy owners with loss of investment. Companies that can't innovate to lower prices or improve quality to justify maintaining a noncommodity price will go out of business. Their employees will lose their jobs, their stockholders will have little to show for their investment, and their host communities will lose tax revenues and purchasing power. Companies in the industry will merge and consolidate to reduce labor costs and increase use of existing plants and machinery, sustaining profitability while producing at lower costs.

Another response to market fundamentalism drives production from high-cost countries to low-cost environments overseas as managers seek ever lower costs of production in an effort to sustain profit margins as market prices drop. This cost-driven movement of production has been a powerful incentive for globalization. Companies move production from Japan, Europe, and the United States to poor and developing countries to maintain quality but at a lower cost. Textiles, consumer goods, computers, and VCRs are made from Mexico to Bangladesh, from Shenzen to San Salvador, taking jobs from wealthy countries and improving wages and living standards in poor countries.

American labor unions protest free trade to stop this movement of manufacturing jobs. Protestors rail against the World Trade Organization, smashing windows in Seattle and Genoa. To prevent job transfers to poor countries, pressure is brought on them to raise their labor costs by introducing unions and forcing employer payment of social security taxes, unemployment stipends, and workers' compensation premiums.

The CRT supports free trade and the global movement of capital and employment. But it values competition through quality and innovation, which would provide new skills and jobs for workers in higher-cost economies as they face the business failure inherent in maintaining the status quo. Their old tasks may go abroad for others to perform at lower cost, but they don't have to lose employment if their companies are commercially nimble and strategically innovative. The Japanese demonstrated how employment can be reconfigured to manufacture new products when Japan's textile industry collapsed under competition from lower-cost producers in other Asian countries.

MERGERS AND MONOPOLIES AND OTHER ANTITRUST PRACTICES

Merging firms and seeking monopoly power is another way some businesses seek to compete. Obtaining monopoly power is the key to making money in systems of crony capitalism, for example. Having structural market power through the elimination or the co-option of rivals avoids the downward slide toward commodity pricing. The monopolist can sell at a price far above cost and sustain the enterprise, not with fair competition but through the elimination of competition. Such practices are inconsistent with the obligation of a business to serve customers with fidelity.

Monopolies and cartels on the selling side of markets, and similar concentrations on the buying side (called "monopsonies" by economists), repress competition. They are a way of cheating on market discipline. And the duties of office placed on the competitive business require that it refrain from cheating. A business must learn to succeed under competitive pressures, not by acquiring power that distorts market fundamentals, as Microsoft did when it used its market dominance, arising from the success of its Windows program, to force computer producers to embed only Microsoft's Internet browser into the computers they sold.

Cheating by accumulating structural market power resistant to the forces of competition is flatly contradictory to the CRT Principles, profitable though it may be. CRT General Principle No. 4 states, "To avoid trade frictions and to promote freer trade, equal conditions for competition, and fair and equitable treatment for all participants, businesses should respect international and domestic rules. In addition, they should recognize that some behavior, although legal, may still have adverse consequences."

Most advanced countries have laws to ferret out instances of monopoly power and break up those combinations to restore genuine competition. These legal restraints are fully embraced by the requirement of General Principle No. 4 on respect for rules. Similarly, agreements in restraint of trade, retail price manipulations, and other selling schemes do not comply with the CRT Principles for Business and are against the law in many countries as well.

DANCING WITH FINANCIERS: COMPETING FOR INVESTMENT

Should a company receive investment because it is creating new wealth through the sale of goods and services or merely because some investors are willing to gamble that it might make money some day? Persuading investors to provide financial support for enterprise can set companies on the road to profit, but if the focus of the business for its senior managers remains on securing recurring infusions of investment cash and not on creation of real wealth, then the company is headed for trouble.

In the last analysis, Enron failed because it didn't earn enough money from the sale of goods and services. In fact, offshore commodity "deals" (called "prepays") arranged by banks—Citibank and JP Morgan Chase—provided virtually all of Enron's net cash flow from operating activities in 1999 and 32 percent of its net operating cash flow in 2002. The high-flying dot.com companies of the 1990s went down primarily for the same reason—lack of real earnings. Few of them made real profits, but for a time they were the darlings of investment bankers, with their loyal in-house analysts urging profit-minded customers to buy, buy, buy.

When word of Enron's true earnings came out, the market promptly put a realistic value on the company—it was bankrupt, owing more debt than could be serviced by its earnings. And, over time, the dot.coms produced no earnings with which to justify the price of their shares, until, finally, their share price dropped to realistic levels. Competition from companies that were earning money and could pay dividends to their investors justly played a role in driving the dot.com stocks out of the financial markets.

In 2003 even giant Microsoft finally had to pay cash dividends, as an inducement to support its stock price when the equity markets were not recovering from their collapse two years earlier. With the prices of high-teck stocks no longer rising from hour to hour, Micorsoft owners demanded an alternative way to profit from their investment. They wanted a company to make money for them one way or another. The stock market may fund much of capitalism, but it is not the essence of moral capitalism.

Enron and the dot.coms, like the conglomerates and the real estate investment trusts of the 1970s and the junk bonds of the 1980s, did not really compete fully on the basis of quality and innovation in the market-place of goods and services. Many of these companies were formed expressly as investment vehicles to meet investor greed. But, sadly, it was a greed focused too narrowly on the selling price of securities. Those flash-in-the-pan investment vehicles lived—but only for a short while—off speculative bubbles, where early investors made a lot of money and later investors lost money after the bubbles burst.

Again and again, history has seen financial markets run to excess before collapsing into recessions and depressions. First, at the very beginning of cap-italism, there was the tulip mania in Holland. Then, there was the South Sea Bubble in London in the early 1700s and the Mississippi Company bubble in France a few years later. The nineteenth century in America seesawed between booms and busts, ending with the great stock market bubble of the 1920s crashing into the Great Depression. Even after reforms of banking and the sale of securities were put in place by Franklin Roosevelt to prevent future depressions, the United States experienced the savings and loan/junk bond/real estate boom-bust cycle in the 1980s and the dot.com/telecom/and Enron investment illusions in the 1990s. In Japan, impressively successful eco-nomic growth in the 1970s and the 1980s fueled massive lending against real estate. When real estate prices collapsed after 1989, the Japanese economy went into doldrums from which it has not yet recovered.

Financial markets seek to win your heart with promises of effortless and riskless reward financed with easy credit. But, as more and more investors chase the promised pot of gold, passion for the bitch goddess takes over otherwise rational minds so that prices for the offered securities, land, etc. spin out of control. The big winners at the gaming tables of financial investment often are those who quickly take their winnings out in cash—securing their rewards before the bubble bursts.

Certainly, the imprudence of investors created these many bubbles and brought about the ensuing losses, but the companies involved contributed to the dysfunctional process by competing in surreal ways of hype and unjustified optimism. Companies living off financial bubbles devise business plans to fit investor preconceptions. They provide rosy projections of future earnings and may even use contrived accounting methods to boost reported income. For a while, running like lemmings in a pack, investors believe in the proffered appearances, buy the touted stocks or invest in the hyped certificates, debentures, or bonds.

After the collapse of the dot.com and telecom bubbles, some companies seemed to have grown wiser about how to manage capitalism better. AT&T, McDonald's, Coca-Cola, and Gillette announced that they would henceforth not offer guidance to investors and stock analysts regarding future quarterly and full-year earnings. Josef Ackermann of Deutsche Bank and John Thain of Goldman Sachs called on investors, analysts, and investment bankers and the media to avoid short-term assessment of business prospects. Ackermann concluded that "short-termism" was one of the causes of corporate misbehavior. Fixation on the short-term is a peculiar phenomenon of financial markets where traders keep the markets going with hour-to-hour decision making. Markets focus on what is brought before them, on the immediate spot preference of buyers and sellers. If the prices brought to markets do not reflect long term prospects and concerns, markets will easily breed dysfunctional episodes of illusion and excess consumption and investment. A moral capitalism needs to counter this short term feature of freely competitive financial markets with wisdom regarding economic fundamentals, sound business principles, and pricing mechanisms reflecting "self-interest considered upon the whole."

CONCLUSION

Market competition can provide moral capitalism with discipline and rigor, forcing hard decisions on owners, investors, employees, customers, and community alike without giving rise to destruction of wealth and investment prospects. In Chapter 12 next we consider the impact of business on the community.

ASSESSING YOUR COMPANY

How does your company compete? To make an assessment of its use of the CRT guidelines for competition, score your company on the following criteria:

SCORE

CRITERION 1.6 (Principle: Beyond Shareholders toward Stakeholders)
How does the company ensure honesty and fairness in its relationships with competitors?

0   5   10
Lower Quality   Higher Quality   _____

CRITERION 2.6 (Principle: Economic/Social Impact of Business)
How does the company promote free and fair competition in its home market and in other countries in which it operates?

0   5   10
Lower Quality   Higher Quality   _____

CRITERION 3.6 (Principle: Business Behavior)
How does the company achieve trust with competitors (e.g., by demonstrating respect for confidential competitor information, preventing the acquisition of commercial information by unethical means, etc.)?

0   5   10
Lower Quality   Higher Quality   _____

CRITERION 4.6 (Principle: Respect for Rules)
How does the company manage compliance with the letter and spirit of national and international competitor-related rules?

0   5   10
Lower Quality   Higher Quality   _____

CRITERION 5.6 (Principle: Support for Multilateral Trade)
How does the company take action to generally promote the opening of
new markets to free and fair trade?

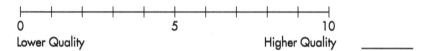

0   5   10
Lower Quality   Higher Quality   _____

CRITERION 6.6 (Principle: Respect for the Environment)
How does the company participate in the development of industrywide
standards for environmental management, promoting performance measurement and compliance?

0   5   10
Lower Quality   Higher Quality   _____

CRITERION 7.6 (Principle: Avoidance of Illicit Operations)
How does the company take action to prevent illicit competitive activities
(e.g., illegal payments to secure a competitive advantage, collusion with
competitors, etc.)?

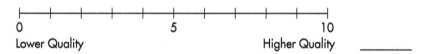

0   5   10
Lower Quality   Higher Quality   _____

TOTAL SCORE (maximum possible points = 70)   _____

CHAPTER 12

COMMUNITY: ENHANCING SOCIAL CAPITAL

As for those that have faith and do good works, God will bestow on them their rewards and enrich them from his own abundance.

—The Holy Koran, Surah Women at 4:173

... there is no truth more thoroughly established than that there exists in the economy and course of nature an indissoluble union between virtue and happiness; between duty and advantage; ...

—G. Washington, April 30, 1789

TO ARGUE THAT COMMUNITY IS A STAKEHOLDER for a business is to reject out of hand the selfish temptations of brute capitalism. The Caux Round Table presumes that business lives within a civic order, not in a jungle where competition must be vicious, where its results may well prove to be "solitary, poor, nasty, brutish, and short," and where the "cash nexus" stands in for fiduciary responsibilities.

Immutable relationships of mutual dependency and advantage bind business and society together. Business serves society with wealth creation, and society advances business by enhancing social capital.

Business has power in society; its decisions affect the lives of many. Power necessitates accountability, for without concern for consequences, bad masters will easily put power to bad uses. Power abused calls forth mistrust and raises fears over dependency status. Power abused undermines civil order. As long as capital is powerful, therefore, the moral sense of humanity requires that business be accountable for the ways in which it creates wealth.

The autonomy of the individual owner and the "privacy" of his or her property are consistent with duties to society, if life is to be lived in a moral community. Each individual has autonomy and, in addition, property ownership with which to express that autonomy. Use of that property in self-expression requires avoidance of injury to others through the timely application of foresight and prudence. The free will of the human individual is not a license for the heedless disregard of others. The free will of anyone is to be constrained by his or her moral sense, for free will is not an ultimate good, only an instrument with which to serve higher values.

A business corporation can ask for no more undisciplined power than civilization grants to individuals, because it is created subordinate to individual dignity. In meeting its responsibilities to society, business can readily follow the CRT Principles for Business, which assert that, essentially, a business has fiduciary-like obligations to its stakeholders to act with a view to corporate self-interest "considered upon the whole."

THE OFFICE OF BUSINESS

Each business has an office to perform for society. It exists to create wealth that will flow in many directions. Business must, therefore, lower its risks and watch wisely over its responsibilities. That is the command of duty. Various efforts are now under way around the world to impose the duties of office on business corporations. The failures of Enron, WorldCom, and Arthur Andersen are just the spark setting off a prairie fire of calls for reform and for more regulation of corporate decision making. The dry grass of mistrust has been all around us for some time.

First, there is the movement for corporate social responsibility. Simply put, corporate social responsibility is a concept whereby companies are asked to integrate social and environmental concerns in their business operations and in their interaction with stakeholders. Companies are now asked to go beyond minimalist compliance with laws and regulations to invest "more" in human capital, the environment, and relations with stakeholders. The United Nations has issued a Global Compact by which a corporation can agree to hold itself to certain international standards for human rights, protection of the environment, and labor relations. The Commission of the European Communities issued a Green Paper in 2001 to promote a European framework for corporate social responsibility. In the United Kingdom, Tony Blair's government created a Minister of State for corporate social responsibility.[1] In the that country as well, financial regulators demanded that certain retirement investment trusts disclose what they have done to invest in socially responsible companies. In 2001, more extensive legislation to the same effect appeared out of nowhere in the Australian Parliament and rather sailed through adoption and ratification by both houses.

Second, the investment community is taking at new look at measures of corporate performance. Dow Jones has launched a sustainability index of companies given high marks for environmental sustainability. In the United Kingdom, there is the FTSE for Good, an index of socially responsible companies. Standard & Poor's is providing for the first time ratings of the quality of a corporation's governance.[2]

Third, there is the debate over globalization. The protestors in Seattle, Genoa, and Davos of 2000 and 2001 hark back to the chants of the early utopian socialists: abolish private property and show compassion for the poor. In current demands to burden international trade with requirements to raise wages, form unions, protect the environment, change conditions for women, and overthrow abusive regimes, we hear the echo of Proudhon and other anarchists of the 1840s.

The opposition to globalization is a rejection of capitalism, asserting against it the competing interests of communities. Nongovernmental organizations, "NGOs" for short, demand that multinational corporations produce specific outcomes for consumers, workers, the environment, indigenous peoples, and endangered species. Having lost faith in the ability of government to deliver these outcomes through legislation and regulation, social justice activists in these NGOs seek to transform business corporations into instruments of public purpose. They want to give business a political office to perform.[3]

There is power to back up these demands. Woe to the corporation that survives on brand reputation but that runs afoul of powerful NGO constituencies. Companies totally reliant on consumers, such as Shell and Nike, learned of NGO power when they stumbled in regard to protecting the environment, communities in Nigeria, and working conditions in Vietnamese factories.

Fourth, NGOs press competing codes and standards on business to define social responsibilities for corporations. The first set of standards for business ethics or corporate social responsibility was the1994 CRT Principles for Business. But now, Kofi Annan has his Global Compact of nine points, while the UN Commission on Human Rights, ignoring the secretary general's Global Compact, has drafted its own code of corporate behavior. The International Standards Organization, or ISO, has begun a process that will most likely lead to the promulgation of an ISO standard for corporate social responsibility similar in nature to the existing ISO standards for quality (ISO 9000) and environmental sustainability (ISO 14000). The Organisation for Economic Co-operation and Development has issued its core principles for good corporate governance. The environmental advocacy organization CERES (Coalition for Environmentally Responsible Economies) promotes a set of environmental standards for companies to follow. Social Accountability International has developed SA 8000, an ISO-like set of standards for factories, primarily in developing countries. Other apparel and shoe manufacturers that do not welcome the rigor of SA 8000, especially its terms on wages and unionization, follow their own code of fair labor practices. The U.S. State Department took the lead in developing a set of human rights standards for private companies, mostly in extractive industries, which hire their own security forces in developing nations.

Fifth, companies are asked to report publicly on all their activities so that their decisions can be monitored and second-guessed by activist NGOs. So-called triple bottom line reporting provides information on social and environmental impacts of business in addition to financial results. Shell was an early convert to this public accountability. Ford, CONOCO, and Westpac Bank in Sydney, Australia, now publish triple bottom line reports. In a major effort, funded with millions of foundation dollars, the Global Reporting Initiative, or GRI, was launched by CERES to develop an accounting format by which corporations can report the results of their activities from the perspective of social and cultural concerns as well as from a financial perspective. By December 2002, it was estimated that some 2,500 companies around the world published social and environmental reports on their operations, including nearly half of the Global Fortune 250.[4] In February 2003, the French government issued Decree No. 2002-221 requiring that, from 2003 onwards, all French listed companies issuing annual reports must publish information on social and environmental effects of business practices.

WHY THIS DEMAND ON CORPORATIONS FOR MORE SOCIAL RESPONSIBILITY?

Globalization is driving a reconceptualization of capitalism. With the collapse of communism, the suggestion that government ownership and planning could match capitalism in wealth creation and improve on the results of capitalism by reaching higher levels of social justice lost all credible support. Markets, not socialist ideals, now rule the world. Not everyone is happy with this turn of events. Though faith in socialism has died, the romantic impulse behind utopian thinking survives. Those ill at ease with global capitalist reality now seek to use business as an instrument of social justice in lieu of government. Whoever holds power—and business has much power—is called upon to change the world for the better.

We are back in the intellectual arena of the 1840s, when nascent capitalism so offended Charles Dickens, Proudhon, and Friedrich Engels. Karl Marx and Engels then took us on a detour via their disastrous labor theory of value, class oppression, and the virtue of the proletariat as a utopian force for good. With the collapse of the Marxist project, capitalism is back, all alone on center stage.[5] Many, however, still doubt that capitalism can effectively serve community stakeholders, or its workers, investors, and consumers. Capitalism eats its children just as any leftist revolution does. Where are the buggy makers of yesteryear? Where are the once mighty Xerox and Polaroid? Or AT&T for that matter. Or Enron, Arthur Andersen, Global Crossing, K-Mart, and WorldCom? Joseph Schumpeter noted that the dynamic of capitalism, its heart and soul, is creative destruction.[6] New products and services created by the market replace part of the status quo; market rejection of the ill-fitting enterprise or the unwanted skill set opens doors for new business opportunities.

For all their creation of new jobs and new wealth—of better health, longer lives, and empowerment of consumers—markets destroy that which no longer serves their demands. This destruction without remorse or second thought creates unemployment, changes cultures, upsets gender role models and family patterns, puts companies out of business, and renders communities obsolete. In the words of the Tao Te Ching, markets are like nature itself—they treat all things like straw dogs. They are a force of nature, bending and flowing wherever the dynamic of profit and loss drives them just as flowing water seeks the lowest level. Markets have no moral sense, only people do. Markets are manipulated by cold calculation of monetary price, creating and destroying business value without judging whether the creation and destruction serves any higher good than keeping the market moving forward.

Creative destruction—the essence of market capitalism—creates anxiety, which in turn precipitates a call for control of the system. Today that call goes by the name of corporate social responsibility. Defining an office for business through standards of social responsibility tries to provide not control of markets (communism failed when it sought to implement that approach) but confidence that the creative-destructive process of capitalism will, over time, provide better outcomes for all. The market system—to work its will and achieve its ambitions—cannot and should not be controlled by the state. But capitalism still needs to secure public confidence in its procedures. Raw, Darwinian capitalism is not sustainable in human community; too many people will get hurt without recourse. The current movement promoting standards, principles, new metrics, and benchmarks all under the slogan of business ethics and corporate social responsibility provides an opportunity to improve on classical capitalist theory.

But the current movement asking for corporate social responsibility needs cohesion, congruence, and convergence if it is to be of significant help to business owners and managers. If the thinking and demands of the movement remain scattered and at cross-purposes, the effort will be an irritant, not a welcome enlargement of our understanding of capitalism.

THE SPECIFIC DUTIES OF CORPORATE OFFICE

First, as global corporate citizens, businesses can contribute to reform and human rights in the communities in which they operate. Businesses, therefore, have a responsibility in those communities to:

- *Respect human rights and democratic institutions, and promote them wherever practicable*

This requirement of a moral capitalism recognizes the close affinity between capitalism and democracy. Both systems seek respect for human dignity. Therefore, both systems emphasize the open architecture of procedure so that individuals have opportunity to assert their values. Moral capitalism and democracy leave people with free will, moral choice, and the possibility of doing wrong.

Human rights and democratic institutions presume that a nation respects the rule of law and permits private property to receive protection from the state. Those are two structural conditions necessary for the social capital incubating capitalist wealth creation.

Second, under the CRT Principles for Business, business leaders should:

■ *Recognize government's legitimate obligation to the society at large and support public policies and practices that promote human development through harmonious relations between business and other segments of society*

Business should not demand total license to do as owners of enterprise may please. Since business serves social ends as well, it must not seek excessive power over workers, intellectuals, farmers, unions, political parties, housewives, and other social segments. Too much power for business and too little power for the state do not promote the success of capitalism. In fact, such conditions rather contribute to the rise of crony capitalism as the enforcement mechanisms behind law, contracts, and private property atrophy. Business will then suffer as cronyism and mafialike enforcement organizations emerge. For example, after the collapse of the Soviet dictatorship, Russia, under Boris Yeltsin, was a weak state. With the attendant corruption, favoritism, insider trading, coercive shakedowns, and non-market ways to get rich, capitalism did not grow there as many had fondly hoped it would. Capital, in fact, fled Russia, depressing its rate of economic growth. The breakdown of government in Iraq right after the American war to eliminate Saddam Hussein's Ba'athist regime from power did not permit Iraq's economy to revive on its own.

One of the offices of business is to sustain the social conditions—such as the rule of law—that permit business to thrive in the first place. Business needs to live in a culture that rewards trust and risk taking. Since robust respect for human rights and effective democracy are likely to foster required cultural conditions, they deserve the care and concern of business. In addition, it is the proper role of government to create conditions under which the wealth produced by the private sector is of growing benefit to all in society.

Another aspect of social capital to which business must thoughtfully attend is the quality of the workforce. Standards of education, health, and morality suitable for sustained productivity enhancement should be in place. Such standards are often set by government. Since business will benefit from always having higher and higher standards of human capital in place, it is an easy office to support such efforts by government and other activists in civil society.

Third, according to the CRT Principles for Business, business should:

- *Collaborate with those forces in the community dedicated to raising standards of health, education, workplace safety, and economic well-being*

Here, the Caux Round Table recommends directly that business assume the duty of providing assistance for the cultivation of rich resources in available human capital. Business statesmanship can make a difference in the setting of social norms in these areas of developing social capital. Therefore, a presumption arises that business should exercise that leadership with a view toward the well-being of all who constitute that improved social capital.

Fourth in this list of obligations, business should:

- *Promote and stimulate sustainable development and play a leading role in preserving and enhancing the physical environment and conserving the earth's resources*

Under communism and capitalism, industrialization has degraded the earth and its environment. Of that there is no doubt. However, human ingenuity and technical innovation have successfully remediated much of that degradation in air and water quality. Nonetheless, the productive side of capitalism consumes natural resources and introduces pollutants into the natural environment, even though there seems to be no requirement that it do so.

Another office of business, therefore, looks to modification of technologies and support for innovation to arrive at methods of sustainable production and deployment of labor-saving devices such as automobiles so that humanity can live well without degrading our natural environment.

Where aspects of market capitalism such as private ownership of rights can improve the environment or mitigate its degradation, business has an obligation to advocate that governments adopt such mechanisms of private ownership. Achieving a common good with less use of regulatory power enhances the dignity of individuals.

Fifth, business should:

- *Support peace, security, diversity, and social integration*

This recommendation asks that business contribute to the formation of social capital. Wealth for an entire society cannot be created under conditions of war and insecurity. In war, property is destroyed, taxes deplete profits and financial reserves, and few are willing to invest in new plants and equipment. When society is insecure, people live in fear and don't trust institutions. Money is kept in gold, in jewelry, and under mattresses, not in banks and stock markets. Fewer loans are made. Interest rates rise, deterring equity investments.

A society at peace, where people are politically, economically, and psychologically secure, and where no one suffers from being "different," is most likely to enjoy high levels of trust and to possess other important components of desirable social capital.

Sixth, business should:

- *Respect the integrity of local cultures*

This recommendation tracks concerns over globalization. The culture that follows upon successful economic growth is a global one, rooted in American consumerism and the free identity formation habits of teenagers. It is a shallow culture of self-indulgence that subverts traditional elites and values. The devaluation of local cultures in a world of air-conditioned shopping malls, McDonald's eateries, and Britney Spears advertisements is a threat to important human values.

Global business is the carrier of this culture, responding to consumer demands. It is legitimate for business to deliver what people want, but at the same time business should take care that local cultures are not permanently asphyxiated under the new shallowness.

The special case of extractive industries in energy and mining deserves attention. These global businesses penetrate into very traditional rural communities, seeking nature's bounty. The higher wages paid by the foreign multinationals, the intrusion of new work opportunities and roads into local social arrangements, and the disturbance of the local ecology can easily harm preliterate and barely literate peasant communities. In the deployment of its power, business has a responsibility to moderate its impact on those communities, which can hardly protect themselves against the intrusions.

The CRT Principles recognize diversity and the moral integrity of local cultures. Not every society and culture will validate the norms and recommendations of some human rights activists living in the wealthy subculture of postmodern psycho-social license. Local desires may be more tolerant of local political leaders than are far-away activists. A company doing business abroad needs to weigh the preferences of local leaders as part of its obligation to play the citizen's part in that community.

An example of successful application of this approach was the response to apartheid in South Africa. Many foreign companies did not disinvest to bring pressure for political change through economic boycott, though some did, but rather took steps within the political context permitted in South Africa to question and modify apartheid norms and practices. The end result was a peaceful transfer of citizenship power from the Afrikaans minority to all the inhabitants of the country.

Seventh, business should:

- *Be a good corporate citizen through charitable donations, educational and cultural contributions, and employee participation in community and civic affairs*

Here, the CRT Principles advocate a general principle that business pay back to the community some share of financial wealth created by business in order to increase the community's stock of human and social capital.

By allowing its employees to participate in community and civic affairs, business contributes expert human capital to civil society, thereby enhancing the community's social capital.

WHO SHOULD PAY FOR SOCIAL CAPITAL?

It is self-evident that society will benefit if business fulfills the duties of its office. But what of the owners, who stand to gain more in residual profits if the costs to their companies do not include service to community? Honoring their dignity as investors and giving them the power to express themselves through their ownership of property requires, does it not, channeling back to them maximum returns from business operations?

With corporations in particular, it is not a proper goal of business managers to use shareholder equity to express the values and desires of management. The corporation, therefore, it is argued, should seek to maximize shareholder return and pay out cash dividends so that the shareholders can build society's capital directly on their own.[7] This view asserts that the business is not needed to act on its own for the accumulation of the necessary social capital supporting capitalism.

The argument for limiting the duties of a business to society has a practical side as well. Businesses will be more successful in creating wealth if they are not distracted from that undertaking. Seeking too many objectives at once, many of which will be in conflict with one another, frequently causes decision makers either to muddle through attempting to please too many different interests and points of view or to make no decision at all, as their resolve withers in the face of conflict and opposition. In either case, action is postponed or its impact is diffused.

Recall Figure 1.1 (in Chapter 1), which illustrates the flow of a successful business, left to right, from inputs of capital to sustainable profit. One element of success, however, is the return flow, right to left, of profits back to capital. To attract capital, business must pay a return for its use. The principle applies with no less force to social capital as well. If no return is paid for social capital by the businesses in a society, social capital will diminish. The CRT Principles for Business, as they note the obligations of business to community, indicate what form that repayment of social capital should take.

In poor countries without sufficient social capital, for example, there is a serious chicken-and-egg problem of promoting economic growth. There is no business sector sufficiently dynamic and so well-to-do that it can stimulate on its own the accumulation of social capital, and there is insufficient social capital to stimulate the growth of a strong private business sector. Where, therefore, should one start the process of social improvement: by building social capital or by investing in whatever businesses are at hand?

The important point to be made by this reference to societies stuck in poverty is that, in every circumstance, business has an interest in the accumulation of social capital. Better social capital will encourage more investment, the growth of companies, and the emergence of more reliable market opportunities. Enhancing social capital is the rising tide of history that lifts all boats.

Pragmatically, business needs to invest in social capital. As George Washington believed, there is advantage in doing one's duty.

THE OFFICE OF BUSINESS: CITIZEN

Businesses, especially corporations, cannot thrive without law; sophisticated markets cannot survive without enforceable property rights, trust in the fairness of competition, and protection of one person's reliance on others. Those conditions are found only in a civic order. Social capital is civic in origin.

Those who participate in a civic order are citizens, a status provided with rights of enjoyment but also one encumbered with responsibilities. All the recommendations of the CRT Principles for Business regarding community as a stakeholder constituency derive from the obligation of business to play the citizen's part in support of the civic order.

The noncitizen is just a consumer, a taker and a user, a stranger, or a guest, here today and gone tomorrow. The noncitizen's presence is felt mostly through the "cash nexus," in one-time transactions or short-term relations. Noncitizens are not expected to know a community's language or its customs or to meet its expectations. Their concern for its future is theoretic and attenuated—a matter of curiosity rather than commitment. The noncitizen is the egotistical individual, motivated by wants only, in whom greed and license and dutilessness are not necessary moral faults. The noncitizen is rootless and wary, living outside society, closer to where a primitive law of the jungle is more likely to prevail. Noncitizens populate the world of brute capitalism.

Where civic order breaks down, during times of war or in the urban jungles fostered by crime and dominated by gangs, the status of noncitizen prevails over the civilized state. Under such conditions, greed and fear drive us all to insecurity. Power rules supreme; nihilism prevails in culture. Just as individuals can reject citizenship, so can businesses. Businesses can place themselves in a normative wilderness, where everything is permitted and nothing is required.

But no business, save an extortionate one imposed through force, could survive a breakdown of civic order. Sustainable business and civic order are two parts of a single social condition. Business, therefore, acting to preserve the social state—which is the condition of morality—has an obligation to assume the status of citizen.

The ability of individuals to have the material means to carry out the duties of their office of citizen must be assisted by business. Business should raise standards of health, education, workplace safety, and economic well-being; preserve and enhance the physical environment and conserve resources; and make charitable donations to educational and cultural institutions that prepare, guide, and give moral uplift to citizens. The moral autonomy of free and responsible citizens must be honored by companies. Companies should respect diversity, honor the integrity of local cultures, and maintain harmonious relations with other segments of society. All of this is provided for in the CRT principles.

Corporate citizenship, simply put, is a norm for that capitalism which is conducted under conditions of moral capacity.

The obligation for business to accept the office of citizen in part rests on small and medium enterprises as well as on great corporations. In the case of corporations, those who manage and direct the business of the corporation as fiduciaries of the owners stand in the citizenship shoes of the owners. Directors, therefore, are constrained to act as citizens when they make decisions for their corporations. In other words, owners cannot avoid the responsibilities of citizenship by hiring others to manage their business affairs by a set of lower standards. Just so, one who hires another to commit a crime is still bound by the law and cannot escape punishment for that crime.

THE CITIZENSHIP RESPONSIBILITIES OF BUSINESS: AVOIDING THE TANGLE OF CORRUPTION

As citizens, businesses are jointly responsible for the quality of the political order. Businesses can and should contribute to politicians and political campaigns. They should speak out on political issues. Many, however, fear the influence of money politics for good reason. Bribery and corruption, either to secure unfair advantage through government interference in the market or to gain some personal preference, are not permitted of citizens. These favors lead not to moral, but to crony, capitalism. Bribery and corruption infect the civic order with abuse of power when citizens rather should be responsible for maintaining its moral health.

In democracies, society's wealthy interests, including profitable businesses and great corporations, can spend their money openly and honestly to influence the outcome of elections. They can favor one party with disproportionate access to advertising and paid workers. The first requirement of any business expenditure in politics must be its full and immediate disclosure to the voting public. Businesses are accountable as citizens, not for their views, but for their tactics in expressing their views. Accountability can only come with exposure. Jurisdictions may want to limit business participation in campaigns or the amount companies can spend on candidates as a precaution against the indirect use of bribery or the emergence of crony capitalism. Such steps are well within the responsibility of a government to take to nourish a healthy and vital civic order.

THE CITIZENSHIP RESPONSIBILITIES OF BUSINESS: PROTECTING CULTURE

In thinking of its responsibilities to community, business should not shrink from charitable contributions to the arts and culture. From the perspective of promoting all facets of human dignity, better business as a patron of culture than government. Culture promotes, deepens, and enlivens the   Au: ?? bond between citizens and the civic order.[8] Isolated egoism, if left untreated, corrodes citizenship. Culture creates citizens out of noncitizens. In all this, culture encourages the formation of social capital and undermines Social Darwinism

Aesthetics—the love of beauty—has always seemed to stimulate civic orders and social participation. The perfect proportions of the Parthenon, the compelling statutes of Michelangelo (*David* and *Pieta*, not to mention his Sistine Chapel frescos), the intensity of Van Gogh's presentations, and more, bring us closer to an appreciation of that which is outside ourselves, that which has order and balance and gives us a sense of place. Patronage of art is living for eternity and invokes ideals of excellence and transcendence. These perceptions make any community's life that much more worth living.

Decision makers in business need not follow politically correct conventions; they are private actors able to give voice to a range of values and beliefs. In particular, business should ensure the survival of traditional forms of expression, forms that have shaped the capacity for civic virtue over the generations. These forms give weight to more fundamental relationships among citizens and should not, therefore, be slighted in favor of fads and trends. The duty of a citizen is not to ensure the cultural triumph of the avant garde, for the avant garde too frequently disrespects citizenship and settles into the passions of egotistical individualism.

THE CITIZENSHIP RESPONSIBILITIES OF BUSINESS: PROMOTING EDUCATION

From the perspective of civic order, business charity has particular relevance in support of education. Citizens are made, not born. Self-mastery, the ability to earn a living, a sense of history, knowledge of others, insight into current affairs, an understanding of economics, and appreciation of art and music make the citizen.

Respect for human dignity, again, argues for pluralism in education rather than politically correct teaching at the hand of government. With financial resources from the private sector, business can direct philanthropic support to a range of educational institutions and initiatives. The criteria for support of educational initiatives should not be a fascination with trendy ideas of the moment but rather a passion for that which is sound and fundamental. As with markets, however, some experimentation with new educational products is desirable to sort out through experience that which actually enhances social capital.

Education that contributes to the disaggregation of the civil order, to aimless normlessness, has a very low claim to society's solicitude. Education that predisposes people to desire dutilessness actually destroys social capital and should not be encouraged.

AVOIDING WASTE OF SOCIAL CAPITAL

The resources accumulated by the civic order—its social capital—can be wasted and degraded. This often happens in war and under political regimes of tyranny and brigandage. Civic orders are not stones; rather, they are living organisms, with soft tissues needing constant nourishment. Citizens must act to prevent waste of social capital. A citizen, therefore, also has duties to self to maintain his or her capacity for citizen action. Without self-respect and some concern for self-interest, a citizen will become unable to contribute to the civic order.

Fittingly, the CRT Principles require that companies preserve their economic health and viability. This limits the extent to which they can and should assume public responsibilities. Companies are not charities; they must earn a reasonable profit. Companies are not governments; they need not pay for public education, security, and other public goods. Neither it is the responsibility of companies to provide a society with protection for human rights. When governments fail, it is not the role of companies to pick up the tasks of public management.

Many advocates of human rights, for example, demanded that Shell Oil Company take over from the government of Nigeria responsibility for conditions in the Ogoni region of Nigeria, where Shell made money by exploiting oil reserves and the central Nigerian government was cruelly abusive of the local people. Similar demands were made on ExxonMobil in Aceh in Indonesia and UNOCAL in Burma. Given the necessity for good government to play its part in nourishing the civic order, companies should not step in where governments fails to do their duty. The bad government should be changed instead. Democracy, free markets, and peace are public goods in that an effective state is needed to establish each of them.[9] Business should not get in the way of improving the quality of public governance.

There is something to the argument that companies doing business in a foreign country should act as good citizens of that country. The CRT Principles so require this in Principle No. 2, which states: "Businesses should contribute to human rights, education, welfare, and vitalization of the countries in which they operate." But, that obligation is constrained by a prior obligation to maintain the economic health and viability of the business. If the two obligations come into grave conflict in the circumstances of some developing nation, then the company should end its activities there.

When social capital is missing, many must invest in its creation. Social capital and civic order are premarket institutions. Businesses and corporations can contribute to the formation of social capital; indeed, they have a duty to do so. But they should never seek to shoulder the burden of civilization alone.

CONCLUSION

In creating wealth, business uses power and creates power. For civilization, but not in nature, power is held morally accountable; it is burdened with responsibilities; it is elected to office. Every office—including the office of capitalist business—has its own set of beneficiaries. The beneficiaries of private enterprise are its stakeholders. The community from which it obtains social capital is a very important stakeholder, deserving of special consideration. In the concluding chapter next, we return to the initial theme of moral character as necessary for moral capitalism.

ASSESSING YOUR COMPANY

How does your company build social capital? To make an assessment, score your company on the following criteria drawn from the CRT Principles for Business:

SCORE

CRITERION 1.7 (Principle: Beyond Shareholders toward Stakeholders)
How does the company demonstrate respect for the integrity of local cultures and for democratic institutions?

0   5   10
Lower Quality   Higher Quality   _____

CRITERION 2.7 (Principle: Economic/Social Impact of Business)
How does the company contribute to the social and economic advancement of the communities in which it operates (e.g., promoting human rights, employability, the community's economic vitalization, etc.)?

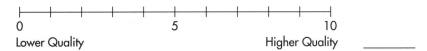

0   5   10
Lower Quality   Higher Quality   _____

CRITERION 3.7 (Principle: Business Behavior)
How does the company identify important constituencies within its communities, eliciting trust from them (e.g., through effective dialogue, responsible disclosures, etc.)?

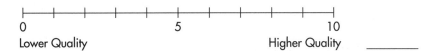

0   5   10
Lower Quality   Higher Quality   _____

CRITERION 4.7 (Principle: Respect for Rules)
How does the company manage compliance with the letter and spirit of national and international community-related rules (e.g., the Worker Adjustment and Retraining Notification Act, affirmative action requirements, etc.)?

0   5   10
Lower Quality   Higher Quality   _____

CRITERION 5.7 (Principle: Support for Multilateral Trade)
How does the company manage the impact of international trade on its communities (e.g., issues related to increased or decreased employment levels, capital mobility and labor immobility, etc.)?

0   5   10
Lower Quality   Higher Quality   _____

CRITERION 6.7 (Principle: Respect for the Environment)
How does the company manage community-related environmental impacts (e.g., land management, water contamination, air pollution, noise pollution, etc.)?

0   5   10
Lower Quality   Higher Quality   _____

CRITERION 7.7 (Principle: Avoidance of Illicit Operations)
How does the company take action to prevent such illicit activities as illegal campaign contributions and the avoidance of legitimate taxation?

0   5   10
Lower Quality   Higher Quality   _____

TOTAL SCORE (maximum possible points=70)   _____

PRINCIPLED BUSINESS LEADERSHIP: STEPPING UP TO THE CHALLENGE OF MORAL CAPITALISM

To see what is right and not do it is want of courage.
—Confucius, The Analects, Bk. II, Chap. XXIV, 2

The difficult we do at once; the impossible takes a little longer.
—U.S. Seabees, Pacific Theater, 1942–1945

Things fall apart; the center cannot hold;
Mere anarchy is loosed upon the world,
The blood dimmed tide is loosed, and everywhere
The ceremony of innocence is drowned;
The best lack all conviction, while the worst
Are full of passionate intensity.

...

And what rough beast, its hour come round at last,
Slouches towards Bethlehem to be born?
—W. B. Yeats, The Second Coming

We have met the enemy and he is us.

—Pogo

THE PROBLEMS MANY PEOPLE ASSOCIATE with capitalism are not really caused by market rationality; rather, the systems' shortcomings arise from how markets are used, or more precisely, how market power is abused.

185

Whether brute capitalism or moral capitalism prevails turns on decisions made by people in business: which values will they live by?

WITHOUT PERSONAL LEADERSHIP, MORAL CAPITALISM IS ONLY RHETORIC

Principles and dreams share a common impotence—neither has power on its own to alter reality. It takes people to put principles to work. Putting ideals and values into action is the task of leadership, regardless of the position one holds in a business hierarchy. Without principled business leadership, therefore, moral capitalism will be benched for the duration of history.

Contemporary culture conspires against principled leadership. We are told by Hollywood and politically correct opinion-shapers that character no longer counts, that it has become social and cultural repression of individual freedom. We are told by multiculturalists that character is the basis for injustice and the cultural hegemony of old ruling elites, mostly white males. Modern culture has turned us towards a realm of relativity where razzle-dazzle is all you need for success. In Cole Porter's words, "anything goes." There are no firm standards and no conviction that truth exists. If there is no truth any more, and reality is whatever you can get someone to accept it to be, why not present your company's financial condition as you would prefer others to see it?

Make your case and see if you can sell it—that became the code by which many American companies were managed in the boom years of the late 1990s. And, well-paid professionals in accounting and law firms were ready at hand to spiff up and add credibility to these stories of coming corporate triumphs.

One solution to this widespread ethical collapse is to ask for moral character once again. Ethics is the work of leadership, and character gives leadership its course headings and its determination.

Leadership brings quality to organizational life—for good or bad depending on the character of the person asserting power. Leadership works through values; values, ideals, and vision create the leader's "charisma," which attracts others into cohesive cooperation. Leadership acts as a field of energy, aligning individuals with purpose by providing them with clarity through messages explicit and implicit. The leader, it is often said, has inner authority, an authentic passion for results, integrity of values and actions, and a kind of "charisma"—all due to an ability to invoke more transcendent perspectives on truth and virtue and the natural order.

THE NEED FOR CHARACTER

Capitalism creates power—private power. Since abuse occurs whenever people get close to power, capitalism expands society's potential for making mistakes. Further, capitalism works through competition. At times, competition checks and balances the self-seeking actions of buyers and sellers, and frustrates their temptation to abuse power by forcing them to equilibriums of mutual satisfaction. But, at other times, competition is unrestrained and competitors do whatever it takes to win. Capitalism by itself cannot eliminate abuse of power. As long as people will want to work the system for their own reasons and for their own values, the potential for abuse will survive.

Abuse of power within capitalism can be corrected, to be sure, by laws and regulations, and by the clever design of market incentives to maximize socially responsible wealth creation. But laws and market mechanisms can always be outmaneuvered by more clever competitors playing on the innate greed and fear of others.

A necessary part of the solution addressing the increased risks brought about by capitalism, therefore, must be people of character. Self-restraint counteracts, and can even overcome, self-indulgence. A capacity for dignity and rectitude permits assumption of stewardship and fiduciary responsibilities, even toward total strangers.

Character triggers awareness of "self-interest considered upon the whole." Character opens the mind up to contemplation of consequences, to possession of the "awareness" recommended by the Dalai Lama. Through character we extend our time horizon out from the present far into the future, and through character we extend our sense of self out to include the perceptions and feelings of others.

The Koran teaches that we need only "have faith and do good works" to be of good character. Confucius explained that with control of the self we can immediately attain active "reciprocity." All Buddhists seek to overcome the passions that only serve to delude the self into false consciousness. The Apostle Paul warned that the love of money was the root of all evil—abuse is not in the coins and the notes, only in our selfish emotional attachment to them.

Fear often drives people away from assuming the responsibilities of leadership. Out of fear, people adopt values and goals that are inconsistent with their more genuine leadership instincts. Moral courage is needed to rise above fear. Character provides a basis for courage. Greed, interestingly, can be a device to deal with fear when we lack character. Obtaining money presumably brings us power with which we can suppress that which makes us fearful.

Yet, in contemporary capitalism, in public schools, in programs of business education, and in the hiring of senior managers and members of boards of directors, we do not train for character, we do not select for character, and we do not reward character.

Bernard trenchantly defined "moral character" as a personal force that tends to inhibit, control, or modify immediate specific desires, impulses, or interests that are inconsistent with the moral sense within the person and to intensify those that are consistent with such moral sense. This personal force is a matter of sentiment, feeling, emotion, and internal compulsion, rather than one of rational process or deliberation.[1]

Similarly, Thomas Reid defended the existence of "self-evident" intuitive judgments such as the proposition that "all men are created equal and are endowed by their creator with certain unalienable rights." The grounds on which moral character rest require no searching for evidence, wrote Reid; no weighing of arguments; the propositions upholding the principles of our character are not deduced or inferred from others; they have the light of truth in themselves and have no occasion to borrow explanations from another source.[2]

Reid called the human capability of detecting first principles of conduct "common sense," as it was a part of reason. He asserted that, "It is this degree of reason, and this only, that makes a man capable of managing his own affairs, and answerable for his conduct towards others."[3]

Asking for moral character is not an imposition on anyone; each of us within the bounds of cognitive and emotional normality has a capacity for common sense, and from that level of awareness, each of us can establish a moral sense to guide our conduct.

We can learn management skills more easily than we can acquire the courage of leadership. Leaders arise out of their capacity to act on their ethical convictions. They have character.

The Great Learning, a text of the Confucian tradition, teaches us:

Wishing to order well their states, the ancients first regulated their families.

Wishing to regulate their families, they first cultivated their persons.

Wishing to cultivate their persons, they first rectified their hearts.

Wishing to rectify their hearts, they first sought to be sincere in their thoughts.

Wishing to be sincere in their thoughts, they first extended to the utmost their knowledge.[4]

LEADERSHIP'S CENTER OF GRAVITY

The animating soul of leadership requires living in community through values. Consider first that leadership always occurs in relationship. Without followers, there are no leaders. Leaders are called forth in community—large or small; they cannot lead in isolation.

The leadership relation is one of reciprocity. Fundamentally, it is a status of fiduciary obligation where power is conjoined with responsibility. Leadership is an office. It can come with position, a formal office, or it can flow out from the character of one who has no such position but, because of charisma, is recognized by others as an authority, as were Jesus Christ, Confucius, and the Gautama Buddha in their day.

Principled leadership as defined by the Caux Round Table is different from being a "boss." It is also far from schemes of intrigue seeking promotion into positions of power and material influence. In principled leadership there must be a holdback of certain self-centered drives. In this regard, we can learn from the Chinese Taoists, who taught that in nonassertion of self can be found the most profound leadership. Consider these passages:

To win the world, one must renounce all.

If one still has private ends to serve,

One will never be able to win the world.

—No. 48

Therefore, the Sage reigns over the people

by humbling himself in speech;

And leads the people

By putting himself behind.

—No. 66

The way of Heaven has no private affections,

But always accords with the good.

—No. 79

The Way of Heaven is to benefit, not to harm.

The way of the Sage is to do his duty,

not to strive with anyone.

—No. 81

Chester Bernard held that the business executive has the responsibility to create morals for others.[5] This secures, creates, and inspires organizational "morale," mobilizing a set of cooperating persons. It requires inculcating points of view, fundamental attitudes, and loyalties that will result in subordinating individual interest and the minor dictates of personal moral codes to the good of the cooperating whole. Whereas cooperation is the process leading to success, personal leadership is the fulminator of its forces, Bernard said.

Leadership in anyone, regardless of position, implies vision and articulation of values. Leaders have a capacity to cause others to suspend their own powers of judgment and adopt instead the leader's point of view. Business consultant Peter Senge would burden leaders with the task of promoting a shared vision for those who are asked to cooperate in a venture. Visions, Senge tells us, are exhilarating, creating the spark and the excitement that lifts an organization out of the mundane. Moving to a shared vision creates common identity and relationships and removes mistrust. Building the shared vision is creating a moral order. It is necessary for organizational success, and it is the work of leadership.[6]

Former Medtronic CEO William George holds that "the best path to long-term growth in shareholder value comes from having a well-activated mission that inspires employee commitment."[7]

As presented in this book, leadership works from the top of a value pyramid down through standards and benchmarks towards action implementation. A leader starts with principles and ends with results.

Bernard further advised that organizations endure in proportion to the breadth of the morality by which they are governed: "Long purposes and high ideals," not calculations of short-term interests, are the basis for the persistence of cooperation in organizations. "Thus," Bernard wrote, "the endurance of organizations depends upon the quality of leadership; and that quality derives from the breadth of the morality upon which it rests.... A low morality will not sustain leadership long, its influence quickly vanishes, it cannot produce its own succession."[8]

The cogency of Chester Bernard's advice has been demonstrated in the research of Jim Collins, the author of the well-received business books *Built to Last* and *Good to Great*. In his examination of successful companies, Collins saw a similarity among the chief executive officers of outstanding corporate performers. He called the personal quality that fostered success "Level 5 Leadership." Those very successful chief executive officers had a personal capacity (the character we might say) to channel their ego needs away from themselves and into the larger goal of building a great company.[9] These senior officers blended "extreme personal humility with intense professional will."[10] Collins' level 5 leaders had an incurable need to produce results; they had a calling; their work was about building, creating, and contributing.

The contrasting group of chief executive officers, men like Lee Iacocca, talented but egocentric, could produce a leap in company performance, but the gains were ephemeral. For these executives, work was more about what they could get for themselves—fame, fortune, adulation, power, etc.

Peter Senge is a best-selling modern commentator on business leadership. His widely read book is *The Fifth Discipline*. He offers various "learning disciplines" to help business executives. He grounds his advice on the common sense tradition also advocated by Chester Bernard that leadership rests on an ability to form judgments that determine decisions. In particular, Senge advocates what he calls the "fifth discipline" of systems thinking, a shift of mind from seeing parts to seeing wholes.[11] Seeing the whole is an integrative process of open awareness and induction. It employs the dynamics of the common sense, looking for first principles more than for rational intellectualism.

To develop our leadership capacity, we begin with awareness, developed by practices that sensitize our mental faculties. (Recall Figure 1.2 in Chapter 1) Then, out of our awareness, we usually settle on some understanding of truth and goodness, which for most people constitutes their religion. Religious teachings promote virtues and encourage us to bring these virtues into our conduct and our living. Possessing virtues shapes our character, and our character sets forth our goals in life. To realize our goals, we learn skills and competencies and put them to work in earning a living and acting the citizen's part in our communities. Our leadership comes from the integrity, authenticity, and fidelity through which we incorporate our awareness with our religion, our virtues, our goals, our competencies, and our actions. Spiritual freedom, which is the operative essence of the ethical life, vitalizes our faculty of conscience and, hence, our sense of responsibility.

Leadership has been called the "power of individuals to inspire cooperative personal decision by creating faith: faith in common understanding, faith in the probability of success, faith in the ultimate satisfaction of personal motives, faith in the integrity of objective authority, faith in the superiority of common purpose as a personal aim of those who partake in it."[12] Faith, argued experienced businessman Chester Bernard, is the catalyst by which human efforts are sustained.[13]

PRINCIPLED BUSINESS LEADERSHIP

The Caux Round Table proposes Principled Business Leadership as a road map for the improvement of capitalism. The core competencies of principled business leaders are 1) moral courage to take the road less traveled, 2) a sense of personal responsibility leading to decisive commitment, 3) analytical skills to define relevant decisions, and 4) interpersonal skills to bring people together for action.

Principled business leadership demands thoughtful responses to three challenges:

First, such leaders must be alert to ethical norms, to principles, and to what is expected of a good person. They must have an affinity for virtue, a sense of calling or vocation in their work. They should spontaneously acknowledge that work is more than instrumental and prudent conduct; that it is connective with goals and ends bringing meaning to a group or a community; that it extends us into a moral universe of purpose on a scale larger than our own ends. The root of principled business leadership grows out of this moral sensitivity, itself rooted in religious reflection.

Second, the principled business leader must have the skills to apply principles to specific situations in a process of analysis, synthesis, and interpretation. This process works best through use of inductive thought, the seemingly effortless and often intuitive perception of "fit" between principles and their applications in a business setting. Creativity is required, for leadership must confront new situations and challenges where no one has gone before and there are no templates or "how-to" manuals. Reflection can make a difference as, under its gentle guidance, simple solutions, fears, and emotional attachments are put aside for the moment in order for the decision maker to draw on a range of thoughts and considerations. One often applies principles by thinking from analogies.

In May 2002, *Fortune* magazine made a list of the "Ten Big Mistakes" famous companies had made.[14] Nine of the mistakes were failures of leadership in the application of principles to the facts. The tenth mistake—death spiral—applied only to Enron and Arthur Andersen. The nine other big mistakes were being a slave to Wall Street (short-termism), seeing no evil, overdosing on risk, having a dysfunctional board, being softened by success, adopting a strategy du jour, acquisition lust, fearing the boss, and having a dangerous culture. All of these mistakes would have been avoided by principled business leaders.

Third, the principled business leader needs to know the business from both a practical and a theoretical perspective. A sound program of business education will provide much of the necessary understanding.

Success in these three areas is achieved by developing deeply held and clearly perceived values and beliefs. Since leaders are those who set direction, they must know where they want to lead others and why. The principled business leader is an "inner-directed" person, in the understanding of American sociologist David Riesman.[15] "Other-directed" people lack convictions and certainties of their own and, accordingly, find it very difficult to step to the fore before others are willing and eager to move ahead.

The writings of Ralph Waldo Emerson on self-reliance add richness and enthusiasm to Riesman's observations.[16] "Trust thyself," Emerson wrote, "every heart vibrates to that iron string."[17] "A man should learn to detect and watch that gleam of light which flashes across his mind from within…" "Nothing is at last sacred but the integrity of your own mind." "Society everywhere is in conspiracy against the manhood of every one of its members. Society is a joint-stock company, in which the members agree, for the better securing of his bread to each shareholder, to surrender the liberty and culture of the eater."[18]

Being inner directed—guided by one's moral sense and having confidence in its power of truth—is a subtle cast of personality. It is an individual distinction in determination, persistence, endurance, and courage that determines the quality of our actions.[19]

PRINCIPLED BUSINESS LEADERSHIP APPLIED: GOOD JUDGMENT IN MAKING CHOICES

Leadership is always an applied skill; it is contextual, not theoretical. It is living in the substance of decisions, not in back and forth consideration of possibilities or else in "other-directed" concern for the unceasing approbation of our "teammates" when we can only act on the value choices made by others. In making decisions, leaders should begin with first principles, as discovered and affirmed by their moral sense. The task of leadership is then to impose those first principles on reality. Our best leaders form a bridge from our mundane concerns to the eternal and the divine.

How are first principles applied in decision making?

The brilliant and astute judge Benjamin Cardozo sought to give us guidance in the art of decision making whenever principles are invoked. In 1921 he gave a set of lectures at Yale Law School on the ways of the judicial process at the common law. Like Adam Smith and Thomas Reid before him, Cardozo presumed that, "There is in each of us a stream of tendency, whether you choose to call it philosophy or not, which give coherence and direction to thought and action."[20] This tendency is our personal response to the "total push and pressure of the cosmos." It is our moral core of intuitive common sense, our first principles.

From his experience, Cardozo asserted that when common law judges decided given cases consisting of very, very specific sets of facts, "some principle, however unavowed and inarticulate and subconscious, has regulated the infusion [of different ingredients]."[21] Judicial decision making begins with the application of principle. Business leaders can therefore learn from judges about decision making.

When different interests conflict and hard choices must be made, the business leader, like the judge, must fit the decision to some end. In law, one such end, a fundamental social interest, is that the law be uniform and impartial, with no savor of prejudice, favor, arbitrary whim, or fitfulness. In business, the principal end is the making of sustainable profits. The creative moral function exercised in the application of principle to the present facts is the unique competency of leadership.

Corporate officers who lack an ability to analyze the decision-making environment with a view to a more accurate determination of the strategic factors at play in the situation will fail. Bernard even calls this business acumen a "judicial process."[22]

The "invention" of justifications that preserve morale within the business is the creative function of the executive, just as giving written opinions to justify legal decisions is the special function of the judge. Providing justification in either case is a moral undertaking. Few business leaders can carry out this function of preserving morale for long except on the basis of inner direction—of genuine personal conviction—"not conviction that they are obligated as officials to do it, but conviction that what they do for the good of the organization they personally believe to be right."[23]

FINDING VIRTUE

Not every conviction is a wise one, and not every corporate culture reflects the teachings of moral capitalism. In today's moral milieu of relativism with its deficit of moral courage and where the center cannot hold, ersatz leadership is commonplace. Leadership said to be "politically correct" often goes by the name of sincerity or authenticity. Any passion, if sincerely valued, counts in the minds of some as deserving deference. In giving way to the demands of that sincere person, we suspend our own beliefs in public to accept their value leadership. Even greed can meet the requirement of sincerity. Many sincerely want to be rich and famous, seeking to lead us from the standpoint of those values.

Emerson saw the problem with trying to lead from personal sincerity alone in his essay on self-reliance: "What have I to do with the sacredness of tradition, if I live wholly from within? My friend suggested—'But these impulses may be from below, not from above.' I replied, 'They do not seem to be to be such; but if I am the Devil's child, I will live then from the Devil.'"[24] If Emerson was willing to live from the Devil, where, then, shall we find virtue?

Not strictly from ourselves. The Koran records the admonition of Allah thusly: "Woe betide those that write the scriptures with their own hands and then declare 'This is from god," in order to gain some paltry end. Woeful shall be their fate, because of what their hands have written, because of what they did."[25] Not every self-disclosed virtue found within us should be given a right to elevate us in leadership over others. Some values are better than others. The problem of moral relativity, which is idolatry of the self, cannot be ignored if there is to be a moral capitalism within the confines of human civilization. Markets will serve moral relativism just as well as moral goodness for market machinery looks upon all things of human value as "straw dogs." Brute capitalism would be quite content with moral relativity.

The best teaching is for us to listen, not to what we would tell ourselves, but to something deeper, something which, at first, is hidden from our senses, but which, by and by, reveals itself to break through our more petty fixations and concerns. Only then, does this profoundness enter into our more conscious awareness of life. Listening is an underused, action-oriented discipline; it is a hidden treasure in finding life's meaning for you and your unique contribution to building a better world. Listening well will quickly open the door to enhanced leadership capacity.

Emerson asked us to listen to what he called the "oversoul." Christians improve themselves through prayer; Buddhists and Taoists find the right way forward through meditation and silence. Native Americans of the Dakota tribes have "vision quests." The Tao Te Ching is to the same effect:

"He who knows men is clever;

He who knows himself has insight.

He who conquers has force;

He who conquers himself is truly strong.

He who knows when he has enough is rich,

And he who adheres assiduously to the path of Tao

Is a man of steady purpose.

He who stays where he has found his true home

Endures long."

—No. 33

There are many ways to virtue, but they all share the same requirement that we first go within in order to find the highest in the "without." When we find principled moral values that are very comfortable living deep within our innermost nature, we are ready to lead and, by leading, to impress those values on our surroundings.

The purpose of invoking our moral sense is not to find satisfaction with ourselves but to venture beyond our little precinct into the world at large. Emerson recommended seeking for understanding where our deepest instincts lead: "In that deep force, the last fact behind which analysis cannot go, all things find their common origin. For the sense of being which in calm hours rises, we know not how, in the soul, is not diverse from things, from space, from light, from time, from man, but one with them and proceeds obviously from the same source whence their life and being also proceed."[26] Mentor and personal coach to many senior executives, Kevin Cashman, too, writes that leadership comes from somewhere inside us. "Leadership," he says after working one-on-one with hundreds of senior corporate executives, "is a process, an intimate expression of who we are. It is our being in action."[27]

KEEPING VIRTUE

Finding virtue is one task; keeping constant to its commands is another. Since moral capitalism thrives in the intersection of virtue and self-interest, good people in business will always be caught between the demands of virtue and the entanglements of self-interest. Keeping our judgments in touch with virtue is the great civilizing work of social capital.

Moral capitalism cannot take it for granted that principled business leadership will prevail. Environments that encourage and facilitate the adoption of principled business leadership skills and that preserve habits of mind and heart happily conversant with virtue need constant cultivation. Character, which keeps virtue active in our lives, needs daily sustenance and reassurance.

Workshops and sessions for reflection and deepening of purpose and awareness need to be conceived and organized. At times, only with second or third thoughts does the shape of our self-interest considered upon the whole become clear in our minds. Mentors should be found and encouraged to take younger business executives under their wings. Writings to provoke reflection and inspiration need to be published. Finally, the effort at cultivation of leadership insights should be opened to young, aspiring business executives now in business schools throughout the world.

For people in business, a regimen of personal practice to enhance the capacity for ethics would promote more ethical decision making. This requires integration of one's faith, core values, and spiritual life into one's work life. The leadership proposition is that one's life in business must reflect integrity and wholeness. Failing to do this leads to fragmentation, broken relationships, and missed opportunities to make a difference. But insisting on deep integrity measured by the greatest and highest values acknowledges accountability to one's conscience, inner voice, or Creator as well as to all other moral objects in this world. Alignment of the person with principles that run deeply through life brings about effectiveness for that person as well as a pleasing sense of vocation. That alignment permits one to hold an office such as management of a business with grace and commitment.

CONCLUSION

A true Social Darwinist dreaming of success in the zero-sum game of brute capitalism finds it hard to be a leader. The Social Darwinist has little need for moral character or virtue, or any inner journey of faith.

Raising up principled business leaders involves nurturing the development of mature, inner-directed, courageous, and selfless people who will be effective in bringing needed moral responsibility into the world.

The Caux Round Table vision implies that people can have a vocation in business, to be creators of hope in a world plagued by cynicism, fear, dishonesty, and abuse of power.

How will you help bring that hope into being?

THE CAUX ROUND TABLE PRINCIPLES FOR BUSINESS
Published in 1994

INTRODUCTION

The Caux Round Table believes that the world business community should play an important role in improving economic and social conditions. As a statement of aspirations, this document aims to express a world standard against which business behavior can be measured. We seek to begin a process that identifies shared values, reconciles differing values, and thereby develops a shared perspective on business behavior acceptable to and honored by all.

These principles are rooted in two basic ethical ideals: kyosei and human dignity. The Japanese concept of kyosei means living and working together for the common good, enabling cooperation and mutual prosperity to coexist with healthy and fair competition. "Human dignity" refers to the sacredness or value of each person as an end, not simply as a mean to the fulfillment of others' purposes or even majority prescription.

The General Principles in Section 2 seek to clarify the spirit of kyosei and "human dignity," while the specific Stakeholder Principles in Section 3 are concerned with their practical application.

In its language and form, the document owes a substantial debt to The Minnesota Principles, a statement of business behavior developed by the Minnesota Center for Corporate Responsibility. The Center hosted and chaired the drafting committee, which included Japanese, European, and United States representatives.

Business behavior can affect relationships among nations and the prosperity and well-being of us all. Business is often the first contact between nations. As a cause of social and economic changes, business has a significant impact on the level of fear or confidence felt by people world-wide. Members of the Caux Round Table emphasize putting one's own house in order and seeking to establish *what* is right rather than *who* is right.

SECTION 1. PREAMBLE

The mobility of employment, capital, products, and technology is making business increasingly global in its transactions and its effects.

Law and market forces are necessary but insufficient guides for conduct.

Responsibility for the policies and actions of business and respect for the dignity and interests of its stakeholders are fundamental.

Shared values, including a commitment to shared prosperity, are as important for a global community as for communities of smaller scale.

For these reasons, and because business can be a powerful agent of positive social change, we offer the following principles as a foundation for dialogue and action by business leaders in search of business responsibility. In so doing, we affirm the necessity for moral values in business decision making. Without them, stable business relationships and a sustainable world community are impossible.

SECTION 2. GENERAL PRINCIPLES

Principle 1. The Responsibilities Of Businesses: *Beyond Shareholders Toward Stakeholders*

The value of a business to society is the wealth and employment it creates and the marketable products and services it provides to consumers at a reasonable price commensurate with quality. To create such value, a business must maintain its own economic health and viability, but survival is not a sufficient goal.

Businesses have a role to play in improving the lives of all their customers, employees, and shareholders by sharing with them the wealth they have created. Suppliers and competitors as well should expect businesses to honor their obligations in a spirit of honesty and fairness. As responsible citizens of the local, national, regional, and global communities in which they operate, businesses share a part in shaping the future of those communities.

Principle 2. The Economic and Social Impact of Business: *Toward Innovation, Justice, and World Community*

Businesses established in foreign countries to develop, produce, or sell should also contribute to the social advancement of those countries by creating productive employment and helping to raise the purchasing power of their citizens. Businesses also should contribute to human rights, education, welfare, and vitalization of the countries in which they operate.

Businesses should contribute to economic and social development not only in the countries in which they operate, but also in the world community at large, through effective and prudent use of resources, free and fair competition, and emphasis upon innovation in technology, production methods, marketing, and communications.

Principle 3. Business Behavior: *Beyond the Letter of Law Toward a Spirit of Trust*

While accepting the legitimacy of trade secrets, businesses should recognize that sincerity, candor, truthfulness, the keeping of promises, and transparency contribute not only to their own credibility and stability but also to the smoothness and efficiency of business transactions, particularly on the international level.

Principle 4. Respect for Rules

To avoid trade frictions and to promote freer trade, equal conditions for competition, and fair and equitable treatment for all participants, businesses should respect international and domestic rules. In addition, they should recognize that some behavior, although legal, may still have adverse consequences.

Principle 5. Support for Multilateral Trade

Businesses should support the multilateral trade systems of the GATT/ World Trade Organization and similar international agreements. They should cooperate in efforts to promote the progressive and judicious liberalization of trade and to relax those domestic measures that unreasonably hinder global commerce, while giving due respect to national policy objectives.

Principle 6. Respect for the Environment

A business should protect and, where possible, improve the environment, promote sustainable development, and prevent the wasteful use of natural resources.

Principle 7. Avoidance of Illicit Operations

A business should not participate in or condone bribery, money laundering, or other corrupt practices: indeed, it should seek cooperation with others to eliminate such practices. It should not trade in arms or other materials used for terrorist activities, drug traffic, or other organized crime.

SECTION 3. STAKEHOLDER PRINCIPLES

Customers

We believe in treating all customers with dignity, irrespective of whether they purchase our products and services directly from us or otherwise acquire them in the market. We therefore have a responsibility to:

- provide our customers with the highest quality products and services consistent with their requirements;
- treat our customers fairly in all aspects of our business transactions, including a high level of service and remedies for their dissatisfaction;
- make every effort to ensure that the health and safety of our customers, as well as the quality of their environment, will be sustained or enhanced by our products and services;
- assure respect for human dignity in products offered, marketing, and advertising; and respect the integrity of the culture of our customers.

Employees

We believe in the dignity of every employee and in taking employee interests seriously. We therefore have a responsibility to:

- provide jobs and compensation that improve workers' living conditions;

- provide working conditions that respect each employee's health and dignity;

- be honest in communications with employees and open in sharing information, limited only by legal and competitive constraints;

- listen to and, where possible, act on employee suggestions, ideas, requests, and complaints;

- engage in good faith negotiations when conflict arises;

- avoid discriminatory practices and guarantee equal treatment and opportunity in areas such as gender, age, race, and religion;

- promote in the business itself the employment of differently abled people in places of work where they can be genuinely useful;

- protect employees from avoidable injury and illness in the workplace;

- encourage and assist employees in developing relevant and transferable skills and knowledge; and

- be sensitive to the serious unemployment problems frequently associated with business decisions, and work with governments, employee groups, other agencies, and each other in addressing these dislocations.

Owners/Investors

We believe in honoring the trust our investors place in us. We therefore have a responsibility to:

- apply professional and diligent management in order to secure a fair and competitive return on our owners' investment;

- disclose relevant information to owners/investors subject to legal requirements and competitive constraints;

- conserve, protect, and increase the owners/investors' assets; and

- respect owners/investors' requests, suggestions, complaints, and formal resolutions.

Suppliers

Our relationship with suppliers and subcontractors must be based on mutual respect. We therefore have a responsibility to:

- seek fairness and truthfulness in all our activities, including pricing, licensing, and rights to sell;
- ensure that our business activities are free from coercion and unnecessary litigation;
- foster long-term stability in the supplier relationship in return for value, quality, competitiveness, and reliability;
- share information with suppliers and integrate them into our planning processes;
- pay suppliers on time and in accordance with agreed terms of trade; and
- seek, encourage, and prefer suppliers and subcontractors whose employment practices respect human dignity.

Competitors

We believe that fair economic competition is one of the basic requirements for increasing the wealth of nations and ultimately for making possible the just distribution of goods and services. We therefore have a responsibility to:

- foster open markets for trade and investment;
- promote competitive behavior that is socially and environmentally beneficial and demonstrates mutual respect among competitors;
- refrain from either seeking or participating in questionable payments or favors to secure competitive advantages;
- respect both tangible and intellectual property rights; and
- refuse to acquire commercial information by dishonest or unethical means, such as industrial espionage.

Communities

We believe that as global corporate citizens we can contribute to reform and human rights in the communities in which we operate. We therefore have a responsibility in those communities to:

- respect human rights and democratic institutions, and promote them wherever practicable;

- recognize government's legitimate obligation to the society at large and support public policies and practices that promote human development through harmonious relations between business and other segments of society;

- collaborate with those forces in the community dedicated to raising standards of health, education, workplace safety, and economic well-being;

- promote and stimulate sustainable development and play a leading role in preserving and enhancing the physical environment and conserving the earth's resources;

- support peace, security, diversity, and social integration;

- respect the integrity of local cultures; and

- be a good corporate citizen through charitable donations, educational and cultural contributions, and employee participation in community and civic affairs.

CAUX ROUND TABLE PRINCIPLES FOR GOVERNMENTS

FUNDAMENTAL PRINCIPLE

1. Public power is held in trust for the community.

Power brings responsibility; power is a necessary moral circumstance in that it binds the actions of one to the welfare of others.

Therefore, the power given by public office is held in trust for the benefit of the community and its citizens. Officials are custodians only of the powers they hold; they have no personal entitlement to office or the prerogatives thereof.

Holders of public office are accountable for their conduct while in office; they are subject to removal for malfeasance, misfeasance, or abuse of office. The burden of proof that no malfeasance, misfeasance, or abuse of office has occurred lies with the office holder.

The state is the servant and agent of higher ends; it is subordinate to society. Public power is to be exercised within a framework of moral responsibility for the welfare of others. Governments that abuse their trust shall lose their authority and may be removed from office.

GENERAL PRINCIPLES FOR GOVERNMENTS

1. Discourse ethics should guide application of public power.

Public power, however allocated by constitutions, referendums, or laws, shall rest its legitimacy in processes of communication and discourse among autonomous moral agents who constitute the community to be served by the government. Free and open discourse, embracing independent media, shall not be curtailed except to protect legitimate expectations of personal privacy, sustain the confidentiality needed for the proper separation of powers, or for the most dire of reasons relating to national security.

2. The Civic Order shall serve all those who accept the responsibilities of citizenship.

Public power constitutes a civic order for the safety and common good of its members. The civic order, as a moral order, protects and promotes the integrity, dignity, and self-respect of its members in their capacity as citizens and, therefore, avoids all measures, oppressive and other, whose tendency is to transform the citizen into a subject. The state shall protect, give legitimacy to, or restore all those principles and institutions which sustain the moral integrity, self-respect, and civic identity of the individual citizen, and which also serve to inhibit processes of civic estrangement, dissolution of the civic bond, and civic disaggregation. This effort by the civic order itself protects the citizen's capacity to contribute to the well-being of the civic order.

3. Public Servants shall refrain from abuse of office and corruption, and shall demonstrate high levels of personal integrity.

Public office is not to be used for personal advantage, financial gain, or as a prerogative manipulated by arbitrary personal desire. Corruption— financial, political and moral—is inconsistent with stewardship of public interests. Only the Rule of Law is consistent with a principled approach to use of public power.

4. Security of persons, individual liberty, and ownership of property are the foundation for individual justice.

The civic order, through its instrumentalities, shall provide for the security of life, liberty, and property for its citizens in order to insure domestic tranquility.

The civic order shall defend its sovereign integrity, its territory, and its capacity to pursue its own ends to the maximum degree of its own choice and discretion, within the framework of international law and principles of natural justice.

5. Justice shall be provided.

The civic order and its instrumentalities shall be impartial among citizens without regard to condition, origin, sex, or other fundamental, inherent attributes. Yet the civic order shall distinguish among citizens according to merit and desert where rights, benefits, or privileges are best allocated according to effort and achievement, rather than as birthrights.

The civic order shall provide speedy, impartial, and fair redress of grievances against the state, its instruments, other citizens, and aliens.

The Rule of Law shall be honored and sustained, supported by honest and impartial tribunals and legislative checks and balances.

6. General welfare contemplates improving the well-being of individual citizens.

The state shall nurture and support all those social institutions most conducive to the free self-development and self-regard of the individual citizen. Public authority shall seek to avoid, or to ameliorate, conditions of life and work which deprive the individual citizen of dignity and self-regard or which permit powerful citizens to exploit the weak.

The state has a custodial responsibility to manage and conserve the material and other resources that sustain the present and future well-being of the community.

7. Transparency of government ensures accountability.

The civic order shall not act with excessive secrecy or provide its citizens with inadequate information as to the acts and intentions of the civic order and its instruments. Secrecy or withholding information would prevent citizens from participating in the discourse that provides the civic order with its legitimate authority.

8. Global cooperation advances national welfare.

Governments should establish both domestic and international conditions under which justice and respect for the obligations arising from treaties and other sources of international law can be maintained; live together in peace as good neighbors; and employ international machinery and systems for the promotion of economic and social advancement.

IMPLEMENTATION FRAMEWORK

note1: Please check editing of this paragraph. riginal text as awkward nd a run-on. <zaq1>The CRT recommends that governments implement these Principles for Globalization. To that end, the CRT further recommends adoption of a "Declaration of Intent" and the 12 core "Best Practice Standards for National Fiscal and Economic Management," monitored by eStandards Forum. A form for such a declaration is suggested as follows:

AFFIRMATION OF INTENT BY RESPONSIBLE GOVERNMENTS:

The following Declaration of Intent is suggested for Heads of Governments as a statement of their intent to pursue these Principles of Globalization:

"The government of _____ declares that improving the prosperity and welfare of our citizens in peaceful conditions is a matter of highest national priority.

This government embraces the opportunities and responsibilities of participation in the global economic and financial system and believes that such participation is indispensable to the promotion of sustainable development in _____.

We believe that an open international trading system, a market economy, and responsible private domestic and foreign equity investment in income and employment-generating activities are the only realistic, effective paths to achieve stable growth. We wish all friends of _____ to know that this government and its loyal opposition are committed to observing the Caux Round Table Principles for Globalization, including especially the Principles for Governments, sound general policies, best international practices, and a moral/ethical climate to facilitate higher standards of living and better lives for the people of _____.

We urge those who would invest in _____ to be guided by the Caux Round Table Principles of Globalization, including especially the Principles for Business, and other, similar standards and principles. This government will do its utmost to assure a positive experience for investors who respect these values in the conduct of their affairs in our country."

CHAPTER 1

1. Michael Porter, *The Competitive Advantage of Nations* (New York: Free Press, 1990), 42.
2. James Collins, *Built to Last,* with Jerry I. Porras (New York: HarperCollins, 2002); *Good to Great* (New York: HarperCollins, 2001).
3. John P. Kotter and James L. Heskett, *Corporate Culture and Performance* (New York: Free Press, 1992).
4. Simon Webley and Elise More, *Does Business Ethics Pay? Ethics and Financial Performance* (London: Institute for Business Ethics, 2003).
5. John Dalla Costa, *The Ethical Imperative* (Toronto: HarperCollins, 1998).
6. Thomas Reid, *Essays on the Intellectual Powers of Man* (Cambridge: MIT Press, 1969); *Essays on the Active Powers of the Human Mind* (Cambridge: MIT Press, 1969).
7. Who would not want to experience a satisfaction from work that lay

   "In some deep sense of giving and sharing, far below any surface pleasure of work well done, but rooted in the relief of escaping the loneliness and boredom of oneself, and the unreality of personal ambition. The satisfaction derived from sinking individual effort into the community itself, the common goal and the common end. This is no escape from self; it is the realization of self."

   This is the way Francis Biddle described his work for President Franklin Roosevelt in the opening months of the New Deal as Roosevelt's team strove to keep the banks open, raise prices for farmers, and boost employment for factory workers. Arthur M. Schlesinger, Jr., *The Coming of the New Deal* (Cambridge: Houghton Mifflin, 1959), 19.
8. Margaret J. Wheatley, *Leadership and the New Physics* (San Francisco: Berrett-Koehler, 1999), 35.
9. Ibid., 35–36.
10. Matt. 4:4.
11. Jurgen Habermas, *Between Fact and Norm,* trans. William Rehg (Cambridge: MIT Press, 1996); *A Theory of Communicative Action,* trans. Thomas McCarthy (Boston: Beacon Press, 1984–1987).
12. "Analects," Bk. IV, Chap. V, 3, in *The Chinese Classics,* trans. James Legge (Hong Kong: Hong Kong University Press, 1960).
13. Ibid., Bk. VII, Chap. XXIX.
14. Wee chou Hou, *The Inspirations of Tao Zhu Gong* (Singapore: Prentice Hall, 2001). After a career in politics, Tao Zhu Gong went into business, we are told, and became very rich. By following his principles, he encountered no resistance

to success and had no difficulty in dealing with people and gaining their trust. Mr. Tao's principles are:

1. Knowing the character of people will ensure the soundness of your accounts.
2. Treating people with respect will gain one wide acceptance and improve the business.
3. Forgoing the old for the new is the curse of many businesses.
4. When products are well displayed, they will attract the attention of many people.
5. Hesitation and indecisiveness will end in nothing.
6. Diligence and prudence will gain a lot more for the company.
7. Choosing the right person for the right job will ensure than he can be trusted and depended upon.
8. Eloquence can be a way of gaining fortune and enlightening people.
9. Haggling over every ounce in purchasing may not reduce one's cost of capital.
10. Shrewd business practices require the ability to sell and store at the right time.
11. Comradeship and trust will emerge naturally when discipline and high standards are enforced.
12. When to go for more and when to tighten or loosen depend on the situation.

15. Margaret J. Wheatley, *Leadership and the New Physics* (San Francisco: Berrett-Koehler, 1999), 13.
16. The Gospel According to Thomas, A. Guillaumont, et al. trans. (E.J. Brill/ Harper Brothers; New York, NY, 1959) on line 116 at page 57. See also Luke 17:20 and Mark 12:34.
17. Sigmund Freud, *Civilization and Its Discontents* (New York: W. W. Norton, 1962).
18. Abraham H. Maslow, *Toward a Psychology of Being*, 3d ed. (New York: John Wiley & Sons, 1999); see also, Abraham H. Maslow, *Motivation and Personality* (New York: Harper & Row, 1970). See also Harry Stack Sullivan, *The Interpersonal Theory of Behavior* (New York: W. W. Norton, 1953).
19. Lawrence Kohlberg, *Essays on Moral Development* (San Francisco: Harper & Row, 1981).
20. Robert Spitzer, *The Spirit of Leadership* (Provo, Utah: Executive Excellence Publishing, 2000).
21. Abraham H. Maslow, *Toward a Psychology of Being*, 3d ed. (New York: John Wiley & Sons, 1999), 93–94.
22. Ibid., 173.
23. Thomas Hobbes, "Leviathan," in *The English Philosophers from Bacon to Mill*, Edwin A. Burtt, Ed. (New York, NY; The Modern Library, 1939) p. 161.
24. Abraham H. Maslow, *Toward a Psychology of Being*, 3d ed. (New York: John Wiley & Sons, 1999), 93–94.
25. Ibid., 173.

26. Dalai Lama, *Ethics for the New Millenium* (New York: Riverhead Books, Penguin Putnam, 1999). The Dalai Lama warns us of "afflicting emotions" that arise within our feelings and distract us from higher purposes, leading to unhappiness and unnecessarily selfish behaviors.

27. Daniel Bell, *The Cultural Contradictions of Capitalism* (New York: Basic Books, 1978); Joseph Lasch, *The Culture of Narcissism* (New York: W. W. Norton, 1978); Robert Bork, *Slouching Towards Gomorrah* (New York: Regan Books, 1996).

CHAPTER 2

1. Michael Porter, *The Competitive Advantage of Nations* (New York: Free Press, 1990), 109.

2. Ibid.

3. "The Doctrine of the Mean," in *The Chinese Classics,* trans. James Legge (Hong Kong: Hong Kong University Press, 1960).

4. Y. P. Mei, *The Ethical and Political Works of Motse* (London: Arthur Probsthain, 1929), 55–56; see also, Richard Solomon, *Mao's Revolution and the Chinese Political Culture* (Berkeley: University of California Press, 1971).

5. "The Tiananmen Papers," *Foreign Affairs,* January/February 2001, 32.

6. See J. J. L. Duyvendak, *The Book of Lord Shang* (London: Arthur Probstain, 1928); W. K. Liao, *The Works of Han Fei Tzu* (London: Arthur Probstain, 1959); Homer H. Dubs, *The Works of Hsun Tze* (London: Arthur Probstain, 1928); W. Allyn Rickett, *The Quan Zi* (Princeton: Princeton University Press, 1985).

7. Takeo Doi, *The Anatomy of Dependence* (Tokyo: Kodansha International, 1973); Ruth Benedict, *The Chrysanthemum and the Sword* (Cambridge: The Riverside Press, 1946).

8. Benedict, *Chrysanthemum and the Sword*; Takeo Doi, *Anatomy of Dependence*; James C. Abegglen and George Stalk, Jr., *Kaisha The Japanese Corporation* (Tokyo: Charles Tuttle, 1987).

9. Margaret J. Wheatley, *Leadership and the New Physics* (San Francisco: Berrett-Koehler, 1999), 54–55.

CHAPTER 3

1. Gaius Suetonius Tranquillus, *The Twelve Caesars,* trans. Robert Graves (New York: Penguin Books, 1957), 30.

2. Adam Smith, *The Theory of Moral Sentiments* (Indianapolis: Liberty Classics, 1982).

3. In 1861, Sir Henry Maine published his *Ancient Law,* a study of the evolution of law from primitive societies to modern nation states. In line with Herbert Spencer's advocacy of individual autonomy, Maine famously said that "the movement of the progressive societies has hitherto been a movement from *status* to *contract.*" Henry Sumner Maine, *Ancient Law* (London: John Murray, 1906), 174.

4. *Business Week*, 10 March, 2003.
5. Andrew Carnegie, *Triumphant Democracy* (New York: Charles Scribers & Sons, 1888), 365.
6. Andrew Carnegie, *Problems of Today* (New York: Doubleday, Doran & Co., 1908, 1933), 124–125.
7. Father Charles Coughlin, quoted in Arthur Schlesinger, Jr., *The Politics of Upheaval* (Boston: Houghton Mifflin 1960), 18–19.
8. Robert Green, *The 48 Laws of Power* (New York: Penguin Books, 1998).

CHAPTER 4

1. Adam Smith, *An Inquiry into the Nature and Causes of the Wealth of Nations* (New York: Random House, The Modern Library, 1937, 1965), 423.
2. G. W. F. Hegel, *Philosophy of Right* (Oxford: The Clarendon Press, 1942).
3. Hernando de Soto, *The Mystery of Capital* (New York: Basic Books, 2000).
4. Timothy Fry, OSB, Ed., *RB 1980: The Rule of St. Benedict*, (Collegeville, Minnesota: The Liturgical Press, 1981).
5. William Bradford, *Bradford's History of Plymouth Plantation 1606–1646*, William T. Davis, Ed. (New York: Charles Scribner & Son, 1908), 146–147.
6. Thomas Reid, *Essays on the Active Powers of Man*, Cambridge: M.I.T. Press.
7. "Analects," in *The Chinese Classics*, trans. James Legge (Hong Kong: Hong Kong University Press, 1960).
8. United States v. Holmes, 1 Wall Jr. 1, Circuit Ct. E.D. Penn, April 22, 1842.
9. Heaven v. Pender, 11 Q.B.D. 503, 509 (1883).
10. Dohonue v. Stevenson, A.C. 562, 580 (1932).
11. Analects, Bk. I, Chap. III, in *The Chinese Classics*, trans. James Legge (Hong Kong: Hong Kong University Press, 1960).
12. Ibid., Bk. II, Chap. X.
13. Dalai Lama, *Ethics for the New Millenium* (New York: Riverhead Books, Penguin Putnam, 1999), 47.
14. Ezek. 34.
15. Pope John Paul II, *Centisimus Annus* (1991), 86.
16. Dalai Lama, *Ethics for the New Millenium* (New York: Riverhead Books, Penguin Putnam, 1999), 61.

CHAPTER 5

1. John Micklethwait and Adrian Wooldridge, *A Future Perfect* (New York: Crown, 2000).
2. David Landes, *The Wealth and Poverty of Nations* (New York: W. W. Norton, 1998).
3. Sam Beard, *100 Million Millionaires* (Oakland, Calif: Institute for Contemporary Studies, 1995); Sam Beard, *Restoring Hope in America: The Social Security Solution* (Oakland, Calif: Institute for Contemporary Studies, 1996).
4. William Easterly, *The Elusive Quest for Growth* (Cambridge: MIT Press, 2001).

5. Milliman USA, *Financial Times*, 17 April 2003. As of December 2002, Caterpillar's estimated underfunding of its pension plan soared 180% to $2.8 billion needed to make up the shortfall. Caterpillar decided to cut some retiree benefits and impose a spartan plan on all hires after January 1, 2003. General Motors' pension plan was $19.3 billion underfunded, forcing GM to divert $4 billion each year for two years into its pension plan. Northwest Airlines, short $223 million in payments due, asked the Internal Revenue Service for more time to pay and the Labor Department for permission to contribute to the plan not cash, but shares of a planned spin-off company. Companies with traditional forms of pension plans were losing their welcome with Wall Street investors because of concerns over future obligations for pension expenditures.

   In addition to the drain of earnings into its pension plan, in 2003 GM faced a $500 million increase in the health care expenses it pays for its retirees, for a total expenditure of $4.4 billion for retiree health care that year. In March 2003, Ford's worldwide pension liabilities were underfunded by $15.6 billion, and its health care costs for pensioners were underfunded by $27 billion. That year, Ford's cash flow from the sale of automobiles was only $200 million. And in the United Kingdom, BT Group had to pay an additional $1.5 billion into its pension fund. Morgan Stanley identified a nearly $100 billion deficit in the pension accounts of the one hundred largest companies in the United Kingdom. Credit rating agencies such as Moody's Investors and Standard & Poors warned at the time that such deficits in pension funds would lead to lower credit ratings for companies, a move that would make it harder for them to borrow money.

6. William Easterly, The Elusive Quest for Growth (M.I.T. Press; Cambridge, Mass 2001) p. 43.

CHAPTER 6

1. Douglas Johnson and Cynthia Sampson, eds., *Religion, the Missing Dimension in Statecraft* (New York: Oxford University Press, 1994).

CHAPTER 7

1. Michael Porter, *The Competitive Advantage of Nations* (New York: Free Press, 1990), 89.
2. Erich Jantsch, *The Self-Organizing Universe* (Oxford: Pergamon Press, 1980), 10.
3. "Mencius," Bk. III, Pt. I, Chap. IV, 3, in *The Chinese Classics*, trans. James Legge (Hong Kong: Hong Kong University, 1960).
4. "Analects, Bk." XV, Chap. XXIII, in *The Chinese Classics*, trans. James Legge (Hong Kong: Hong Kong University Press, 1960).

CHAPTER 8

1. Henry Sumner Maine, *Ancient Law* (London: John Murray, 1906), 174.
2. Lochner v. New York, 198 U.S. 45, 75 (U.S. Supreme Court April 17, 1905).

3. Howard S. Gitlow and Shelly J. Gitlow, *The Deming Guide to Quality and Competitive Position* (Englewood Cliffs, NJ: Prentice-Hall, 1987), 208.
4. Richard Florida, *The Rise of the Creative Class* (New York: Basic Books, 2002), 45 passim.
5. Ibid., 72.
6. Ibid., 87.
7. Ibid., 90–91.
8. Chester Bernard, *Theory and Function of the Executive* (Cambridge: Harvard University Press, 1968).
9. Ibid., 148.
10. Ibid., 163.
11. David Peterson and Mary Dee Hicks, *Leader as Coach* (Minneapolis: Personnel Decisions International, 1997).

CHAPTER 9

1. F. L. Allen, *The Lords of Creation* (New York: Random House, 1935; Random House trade paperback, 1975, ASIN 0812960335), 184.
2. *The New Yorker*, 17 and 24 Feb. 2003, 144.
3. Ezek. 34.
4. Susan H. Gebelein, David G. Lee, Elaine B. Sloan, *The Executive Handbook* (Minneapolis: Personnel Decisions International, 1998).
5. Ibid.
6. Bernard Lietaer, *The Future of Money* (London: Century, 2001).

CHAPTER 10

1. Samuel A. DiPiazza, Jr., and Robert G. Eccles, *Building Public Trust* (New York: John Wiley & Sons, 2002).
2. Mary Walton, *The Deming Management Method* (New York: Perigee Books, 1986), 62; W. Edwards Deming, *Quality, Productivity and Competitive Position* (Cambridge: MIT Center for Advanced Engineering Study, 1982), 23.
3. Michael Porter, *The Competitive Advantage of Nations* (New York: Free Press, 1990), 103.

CHAPTER 11

1. Adam Smith, *An Inquiry into the Nature and Causes of the Wealth of Nations* (New York: Random House, The Modern Library, 1937, 1965), 128.
2. Ibid., 13.
3. Adam Smith, *The Theory of Moral Sentiments* (Indianapolis: Liberty Classics, 1982).
4. Ibid., 86.
5. Ibid., 146.
6. "Analects," Bk. III, Chap. VII, in *The Chinese Classics*, trans. James Legge (Hong Kong: Hong Kong University Press, 1960). Living long before Smith in a very different, but still humanly evolved, culture, Confucius understood the possibility

of personal self-mastery: "The student of virtue does not contend. But if it be pointed out that he can't avoid competition, is it not in archery? But, consider: he bows complaisantly to his competitors; with this mind he ascends the pitch, descends, and exacts the honor of a drink. In his contention, he is still a gentleman."

7. Dalai Lama, *Ethics for the New Millenium* (New York: Riverhead Books, Penguin Putnam, 1999), 70.

8. Michael Porter, *The Competitive Advantage of Nations* (New York: Free Press, 1990), 41.

9. Ibid., 45–46.

10. "When Growth Is Not an Option," *The Economist,* 7 Dec. 2002.

11. William J. Baumol, *The Free Market Innovation Machine* (Princeton: Princeton University Press, 2002), 162.

12. Ibid., 166.

CHAPTER 12

1. The Copenhagen Center, a unit of the Danish Ministry of Social Welfare, promotes private-public partnerships between socially responsible companies and public bodies as an exciting new means of resolving social problems and promoting better outcomes culturally and environmentally.

2. In 2001, Steve Dillenburg, a member of the Caux Round Table, launched a mutual fund based on eighty criteria drawn from the CRTs Principles for Business to invest in the S&P 500 companies in proportion to their conformity to the CRT Principles. The Dillenburg criteria exposed weaknesses at Enron, K-Mart, and General Electric before these companies ran into financial difficulty.

3. Amnesty International is considering adding the goals of the Covenant on Economic and Social Rights to the basket of core human rights demands. Since most of the goals can be achieved only by the private sector, this step would transform most corporations into public agencies subject to audit for failure to raise living standards or provide education or bring about equality for women. In Canada, the Canadian Democracy and Corporate Accountability Commission—after holding focus groups with hundreds of Canadians—recommended that Canadian corporations be ordered by law to serve all their stakeholder groups.

4. Alison Maitland, "Social Reporting," *Financial Times,* December 2002,

5. Francis Fukuyama, *The End of History and the Last Man* (Boston: Free Press, 1992).

6. Joseph Schumpeter, *Capitalism, Socialism and Democracy* (New York: HarperCollins, 1984).

7. Milton Friedman and Rose Friedman, *Capitalism and Freedom* (Chicago: University of Chicago Press, 2002).

8. David Selbourne, *The Principle of Duty* (Notre Dame, Ind.: University of Notre Dame Press, 2001).

9. Michael Mandelbaum, *The Ideas That Conquered the World: Peace, Democracy, and Free Markets in the Twenty-first Century* (New York: PublicAffairs, 2002).

CHAPTER 13

1. Chester Bernard, *Theory and Function of the Executive* (Cambridge: Harvard University Press, 1986), 261.
2. Thomas Reid, *Essay on the Intellectual Powers of Man* (Cambridge: M.I.T. Press, 1969), 593.
3. Ibid., 567.
4. "The Great Learning," in *The Chinese Classics,* trans. James Legge (Hong Kong: Hong Kong University Press, 1960).
5. Chester Bernard, *Theory and Function of the Executive* (Cambridge: Harvard University Press, 1968), 270. See also: William George, *Authentic Leadership* (San Fransisco: Jossey Boss, 2003), 198. George, successful CEO of Medtronic, believes that "As a leader you have the tasks of engaging the hearts of those you serve and aligning their interests with the interests of the organization you lead. Engaging the hearts of others requires a sense of purpose and an understanding of where you're going."
6. Peter Senge, *The Fifth Discipline* (New York: Currency Doubleday, 1990), 69.
7. William George, *Authentic Leadership* (San Fransisco: Jossey Boss, 2003), 62.
8. Chester Bernard, *Theory and Function of the Executive* (Cambridge: Harvard University Press, 1986), 282–283.
9. James Collins, *Good to Great* (New York: HarperCollins, 2001), 21.
10. Ibid.
11. Peter Senge, *The Fifth Discipline* (New York: Currency Doubleday, 1990), 69.
12. Chester Bernard, *Theory and Function of the Executive* (Cambridge: Harvard University Press, 1968), 259.
13. Ibid.
14. "Why Companies Fail: Ten Big Mistakes," *Fortune,* 27 May 2002, 54.
15. David Riesman, *The Lonely Crowd* (New Haven: Yale University Press, 1961).
16. Ralph Waldo Emerson, "Self-reliance," in *The Portable Emerson,* ed. Carl Bode (New York: Penguin Books, 1946, 1981).
17. Ibid., 139.
18. Ibid., 141.
19. Ibid., 260.
20. Benjamin Cardozo, *Selected Writings of Benjamin Cardozo* (Albany: Mathew Bender, 1947), 109.
21. Ibid, 109.
22. Ibid., 280.
23. Ibid., 281.
24. Ralph Waldo Emerson, "Self-reliance," in *The Portable Emerson,* ed. Carl Bode (New York: Penguin Books, 1946, 1981), 141.
25. *The Koran,* trans. N. J. Dawood (London: Penguin Books, 1999).
26. Ralph Waldo Emerson, "Self-reliance," in *The Portable Emerson,* ed. Carl Bode (New York: Penguin Books, 1946, 1981), 149.
27. Kevin Cashman, *Leadership from the Inside Out* (Provo, Utah: Executive Excellence Publishing, 2001), 18.

Stephen B. Young has been Global Executive Director of the Caux Round Table since 2000. Educated at Harvard College and with a law degree from the Harvard University Law School, Young has taught and practiced law, writing in the area of fiduciary duties and agency relationships. His scholarly examination of accountability has ranged from the law of war to the special status of native tribal communities in the United States as "domestic dependent nations." Young has examined in nineteenth century common law court decisions how moral notions of stewardship accountability gave rise to modern standards of accountable business behavior in negligence and other tort liability.

He was an Assistant Dean at the Harvard Law School, and Dean of the Hamline University School of Law. He has taught at the University of Minnesota and Minnesota State University, Mankato.

Young attended high school in Bangkok, Thailand where he learned to speak Thai; later, he also learned Tzotzil Maya and Vietnamese. In 1966 Young discovered the bronze-age culture of Ban Chiang, Thailand, now a UNESCO World Heritage Site. He worked in rural and economic development for the United States Agency for International Development in the Republic of Vietnam from 1968 through 1971. In 1975 Young initiated efforts to bring refugees from South Vietnam to the United States and in 1989 proposed the initiative of a United Nations interim stewardship administration as a formula for bringing peace to Cambodia.

At the Harvard Law School East Asian Studies Program, Young assisted with the translation and analysis of the *Quoc Trieu Hinh Luat*, the Vietnamese national law code of 1433, and, with Prof. Nguyen Ngoc Huy, wrote on human rights values in China and Vietnam—*The Tradition of Human Rights in China and Vietnam* (published by Yale Southeast Asian Studies). Young has written on Chinese moral and political philosophy and has published on the psycho-cultural dynamics of politics in Vietnam and Thailand as well. In 1976 he co-authored a monograph, *Thailand: Domino by Default*, which led to significant political reform in Thailand. As Dean of the Hamline University School of Law, Young initiated the *Journal of Law and Religion*.

As a commentator on public affairs, Young has been published in the *Wall Street Journal*, *The New York Times* and *the Washington Post*. He has been a commentator on television and public radio. His essays are published monthly on www.fifthcolumnmag.com.

Berrett–Koehler
Publishers

Connecting people and ideas
to create a world that works for all

Dear Reader,

Thank you for picking up this book and joining our worldwide community
of Berrett-Koehler readers. We share ideas that bring positive change into
people's lives, organizations, and society.

To welcome you, we'd like to offer you a free e-book. You can pick from
among twelve of our bestselling books by entering the promotional code
BKP92E here: http://www.bkconnection.com/welcome.

When you claim your free e-book, we'll also send you a copy of our e-news-
letter, the *BK Communiqué*. Although you're free to unsubscribe, there are
many benefits to sticking around. In every issue of our newsletter you'll find

- A free e-book
- Tips from famous authors
- Discounts on spotlight titles
- Hilarious insider publishing news
- A chance to win a prize for answering a riddle

Best of all, our readers tell us, "Your newsletter is the only one I actually
read." So claim your gift today, and please stay in touch!

Sincerely,

Charlotte Ashlock
Steward of the BK Website

Questions? Comments? Contact me at bkcommunity@bkpub.com.

Certified

Corporation
bcorporation.net